REASONABLE CARE

Reasonable Care

Legal Perspectives on the Doctor–Patient Relationship

HARVEY TEFF

CLARENDON PRESS · OXFORD
1994

Oxford University Press, Walton Street, Oxford OX2 6DP
Oxford New York
Athens Auckland Bangkok Bombay
Calcutta Cape Town Dar es Salaam Delhi
Florence Hong Kong Istanbul Karachi
Kuala Lumpur Madras Madrid Melbourne
Mexico City Nairobi Paris Singapore
Taipei Tokyo Toronto
and associated companies in
Berlin Ibadan

Oxford is a trade mark of Oxford University Press

Published in the United States
by Oxford University Press Inc., New York

British Library Cataloguing in Publication Data
Data available

Library of Congress Cataloging in Publication Data
Teff, Harvey.
Reasonable care: legal perspectives on the doctor–patient
relationship/Harvey Teff.
p. cm.
Includes bibliographical references and index.
1. Medical care—Law and legislation—Great Britain. 2. Patients—
Legal status, laws, etc.—Great Britain. 3. Physician and patient—
Great Britain. I. Title.
KD2945.T44 1994   344.73'041—dc20
[347.30441] 94–29497
ISBN 0–19–825578–0

1 3 5 7 9 10 8 6 4 2

Typeset by Cambrian Typesetters Frimley, Surrey
Printed in Great Britain
on acid-free paper by
Bookcraft Ltd, Midsomer Norton, Avon

To
Martin and Helen

Acknowledgements

I am particularly indebted to Bob Sullivan for reading the entire text and making many valuable suggestions. Thanks are also due to Colin Warbrick for helping to clarify a number of issues. I am indebted to Francis Pritchard and Robin Widdison for their invaluable instruction in the art of word-processing. It is also a pleasure to record my gratitude to Alison Hunt for her skilled assistance with the manuscript in the final stages of preparation.

I am pleased to acknowledge an initial research award from the University of Durham in support of this project. Finally, my thanks are due to the publishers, and in particular to Richard Hart, for consistent help and encouragement.

Contents

Table of Cases

Table of Legislation

Introduction

Current developments in health care provision prompt a number of questions about the nature of medical relationships and the legal principles which govern them. Until recent times, there was relatively little opposition to the traditional medical view of patients as the passive recipients of medical care. It was widely accepted that doctors might decide unilaterally what treatment should be provided and presume how much a patient wanted or needed to know. Such paternalistic attitudes and practices were entrenched features of medicine, conventionally justified as serving the interests of patient welfare. In the Hippocratic tradition, failure to involve patients in their treatment was proclaimed a virtue. Expressly encouraged in the exhortation to doctors to conceal most things from patients lest they take a turn for the worse,[1] it was also implicit in a principle of beneficence that allowed the doctor to decide what 'beneficence' entailed in the particular case.

English law has endorsed this approach to a much greater extent than other comparable systems.[2] Our courts have readily acquiesced in the historically dominant medical tradition, when articulating the legal principles to be applied in medical litigation. In matters of civil liability, they are still broadly willing to let doctors set their own standards. Though doctors tend to see the law as unduly intrusive, it is rather the lack of judicial engagement with medicine which is striking. As Lord Scarman observed not long ago, 'the law so far as it concerns the doctor–patient relationship has been, at any rate within the United Kingdom, static for a number of years, indeed for a number of generations'.[3]

---

[1] 'Decorum', XVI, in W. Jones (trans.), *Hippocrates*, 4 vols. (Cambridge, Mass.: Harvard University Press, 1923–31), ii. 297–9.

[2] Giesen goes as far as to say that 'American (and to some extent, Canadian) courts . . . are almost light years ahead of the English position': D. Giesen, *International Medical Malpractice Law* (Tübingen: J. C. B. Mohr; Dordrecht: Martinus Nijhoff Publishers, 1988) xi.

[3] Lord Scarman, 'Law and Medical Practice' in P. Byrne (ed.), *Medicine in Contemporary Society* (London: King Edward's Hospital Fund for London, 1987), 131.

In recent times we have witnessed rapid advances in medicine, major structural change in health care delivery and calls for new ways of conceptualizing medical relationships. We have also seen substantial growth in medical litigation. But though more medical cases go to appeal, there is little concrete evidence of legal principles being adapted to accommodate changing social expectations of the doctor–patient relationship. The courts are generally disinclined to explore such matters. True to its reputation for 'marching with medicine but in the rear and limping a little',[4] the law has, if anything, remained more sympathetic to a doctor-centred approach than the profession itself.

The mounting criticism of this approach over the last thirty or forty years has taken a variety of forms, but a central theme has been concern that the patient's voice is insufficiently heard. The impetus for much of the criticism, and still a driving force, has been disquiet about denial of patients' rights. The assertion of 'patients' rights' is presented as a natural antithesis to medical paternalism, proclaiming the moral agency of the individual and the intrinsic value of respect for the patient as person. The concern is political as well as moral. At the level of individual medical relationships, suppression of the patient's voice is considered incompatible with legitimate expectations about individual choice and freedom to decide what is done to one's body. These expectations, in turn, argue a right to the kind of disclosure and dialogue that will permit informed decision-making. Clearly such issues have important legal ramifications, and when one does encounter judicial misgivings about paternalistic medical practice, insufficient concern for patients' rights has been the main theme, a theme rather more vigorously pursued in modern scholarly legal writing on medical law.[5]

A conception of medical practice centred on patients' rights is also proclaimed in the 'rights' and standards of the Patient's Charter (an offshoot of the Citizen's Charter) and is said to be a central feature of the recent National Health Service reforms. Associated Government White Papers boasting titles such as

---

[4] *Mount Isa Mines* v. *Pusey* (1970) 125 CLR 383, 395 *per* Windeyer J.

[5] e.g. I. Kennedy, 'Patients, Doctors and Human Rights' in *Human Rights for the 1990s* R. Blackburn and J. Taylor (eds.) (London: Mansell, 1991), Ch. 9; S. McLean, *A Patient's Right to Know* (Aldershot: Dartmouth, 1989).

Working for Patients and *Caring for People* freely invoke expressions such as 'consumer/customer sovereignty' and 'patient choice'. The commercial values which underlie the restructuring of health care and the language of the market place which pervades the legislation challenge conventional assumptions about the provision of medical services. In so far as they subordinate professional norms to a conception of medicine as trade, they imply greater readiness to view doctors' duties in terms of patients' rights and represent a pronounced threat to the dominant tradition.[6]

These rights-based criticisms have originated mainly, although not exclusively, from outside the world of medicine. Inside it, though they have made some impact, patient welfare as traditionally conceived continues to take pride of place. The nature of medical practice may have changed considerably in recent times, but the hospital setting—our main focus of concern and the source of most medical litigation—still bears the stamp of the Hippocratic tradition. By comparison with trends in general practice,[7] the typically more impersonal, and hierarchical, hospital regime still in many ways reflects a time-honoured ethos which remains a potent force in medical schools. There are signs that its hold is weakening, in the face of new managerial policies and financial constraints dictated by the governmental drive for cost containment and greater accountability. But such developments do not argue a professional conversion to the primacy of patient choice and patients' rights.

If the dominant tradition in medical practice has come under attack for neglecting the rights of patients, much less has been heard about its potentially adverse effects on their health. This is partly because concern for patient well-being is itself a defining feature of medical paternalism. However, an important therapeutic dimension has fortified the rights-based critiques of the dominant model, challenging it on its own ground. It has begun to permeate medical theory, building on evidence from clinical and empirical studies which show how failure to involve patients can

---

[6] See D. Partlett, 'Professional Negligence in America' in P. Finn (ed.), *Essays on Torts* (Sydney: The Law Book Co., 1989), 104.

[7] See e.g. C. Williamson, *Whose Standards?* (Buckingham: Open University Press, 1992), 119.

lead to error in diagnosis and treatment, delay recovery, and adversely affect long-term outcomes. By the same token, it is apparent that to experience a measure of control over one's illness can itself be therapeutic and reduce levels of anxiety and depression. The importance of communication, dialogue, and the participation of patients in decision-making has become a common theme in official documents[8] and in the publications of professional medical bodies—so much so that the opening sentence of the BMA's most recent work on practical medical ethics reads as follows: 'The relationship between doctor and patient *is* based on the concept of partnership and collaborative effort.'[9] This holds promise. How far it reflects the reality of doctor–patient relationships or even contemporary medical training is open to question.

So far we have touched on several different conceptions of medical relationships, which vie with one another to modify, if not replace, the traditional approach.[10] Though it is not, of course, suggested that doctors never vary their approach to match their assessment of a patient's needs, or that any of these models exists in a pure form in medical practice, they can be loosely classified as patient autonomy, medicine as trade, and 'therapeutic alliance' (the collaborative model). The debate over their respective merits is directly relevant to legal liability.[11] Our conception of the doctor–patient relationship and the language we use to describe it are pointers to the appropriateness of particular legal regimes and concepts and to the likely outcome of litigation. To the extent that paternalistic attitudes persist, their endorsement in the legal principles relevant to medical negligence reduces a plaintiff's prospects of success. Conversely, greater legal commitment to

---

[8] See e.g. the NHS Management Executive, *A Guide to Consent for Examination or Treatment*, HC (90) (22) (London: Department of Health, 1990).

[9] British Medical Association, *Medical Ethics Today* (London: BMJ Publishing Group, 1993), 1. Emphasis added.

[10] See e.g. J. Childress, 'Metaphors and Models of Medical Relationships' (1982) 8 *Social Responsibility* 47; D. Ozar, 'Patients' Autonomy: Three Models of the Professional–Lay Relationship in Medicine' (1984) 5 *Theoretical Medicine* 61.

[11] Cf. 'Presuppositions about professions deeply influenced liability rules. But the presuppositions no longer adhere as medicine, and other professions, adopt methods, norms, mores, and attitudes more akin to business or industry. Tort rules fashioned to impose liability on industry are then easily applied with full force to the professions. At the same time, tort rules built upon those presuppositions now lack foundation': Partlett, n. 6 above, 98–9.

patient autonomy would, on the face of it, enhance such prospects. A legal analysis which stressed the commercial attributes of medical transactions would facilitate the use of contractual principles; one which acknowledged that it was appropriate for the relationship to be based on 'partnership and collaborative effort' could provide a broader basis for liability in negligence and, in emphasizing honesty, trust, and good faith, permit more scope for fiduciary concepts.

Among those who consider that medical relationships tend to be too doctor-centred, views differ on whether more attention should be paid to the *rights* of patients or to their *welfare*. Should the emphasis be on the accountability of doctors or on their responsiveness, on the legal entitlements of the 'purchaser' of health care, or on the therapeutic benefits of being involved in one's treatment? It is perhaps inevitable that the critical focus has centred on patients' rights. They are, after all, more overtly subordinated by paternalistic practice than is patient welfare, its proclaimed *raison d'être*. Moreover, as far as legal analysis is concerned the language of 'rights' would seem to be the natural mode of critical discourse.

First and foremost, however, patients want to 'get better'. Though patients' rights deserve respect, and exercising decisional autonomy can itself contribute to their health and well-being, they rarely wish to exercise it to the extent of excluding or dictating to the doctor. 'The primary principles in medical ethics are the special needs of the patient and the commitment physicians have to the patient's well-being.'[12] Typically, greater autonomy is seen as both a desired outcome and a part of the process whereby a dependent person's health is improved or restored. But in that process patients are more likely to seek co-determination than self-determination, and genuine communication rather than contractualism.[13] That the doctor and the patient may perceive the patient's condition differently need not preclude their working towards a shared understanding of it and of how most appropriately to treat it. In the overwhelming majority of cases, what is primarily

---

[12] T. Brennan, *Just Doctoring: Medical Ethics in the Liberal State* (Berkeley: University of California Press, 1991), 80.

[13] Cf. 'Men's capacity to become joint adventurers in a common cause makes possible a consent to enter the relation of patient to physician . . . This means that

at stake is the recovery or improvement in health of patients, and they are more likely to be assisted in this process by a broadly collaborative effort than by a potentially contentious insistence on rights. It will be argued that in the search for appropriate conceptions of the doctor–patient relationship, the interest of patients in their well-being should not be reduced to such interest as they may have in the assertion of rights.

It is submitted that otherwise cogent criticism of legal acquiescence in medical paternalism has overstated the case for viewing the law as a vehicle for asserting patients' rights. In so doing, it has tended to neglect the law's potential for promoting patient welfare, both substantively and in a symbolic way, through the standards which it lays down. Medical litigation is admittedly, by definition, concerned with the resolution of disputes, and it is thus the court's function to pronounce on the rights and duties of the parties. Implicit in the legally condoned model of paternalism is the subordination of patients' rights. To redress any resultant imbalance, the tort of trespass and the law of contract may seem the appropriate legal categories. They are, as it were, the legal analogues of patient autonomy and medicine as trade. It will be argued, however, that (under English law) neither has proved to be a particularly appropriate or effective mechanism for protecting the rights of patients, the assertion of which may in any event not be conducive to the maximization of welfare.

By contrast, the key legal category of negligence could accommodate a medical model of 'therapeutic alliance', an approach rooted in the doctor's responsibility for patient welfare which at the same time affords due respect for patients' rights. In negligence, what is primarily in issue is whether the doctor has fallen below the requisite level of care. The individual rights of

partnership is a better term than contract in conceptualizing the relation'. P. Ramsey, *The Patient as Person* (New Haven, Conn.: Yale University Press, 1970), 6. Somerville notes that ' *"participation* in decision-making" is a value in itself, and a different value from self-determination if it envisages shared, rather than sole decision-making authority regarding oneself'. M. Somerville, *Consent to Medical Care* (Ottawa: Law Reform Commission of Canada, 1980), 8. See also Campbell: 'the autonomous individual is a mere philosopher's abstraction . . . Thus a stress on autonomy is . . . the *minor* key in medical ethics—the major key should be to discover how to foster appropriate and nurturing dependency': A. Campbell, 'Dependency Revisited: The Limits of Autonomy in Medical Ethics' in *Protecting the Vulnerable* M. Brazier and M. Lobjoit (eds.) (London: Routledge, 1991), 105.

patients are not addressed, except in a derivative sense. Liability for negligence is essentially a form of public ordering, a standardized mechanism for regulating doctors' conduct. In Kennedy's words: 'If there is a unifying premiss which informs the law, it is to be found . . . in the concept of duty.'[14] Doctors are required to have the skill appropriate to their work and are under an obligation to exercise due care in undertaking it. The implicit aim of their calling, as endorsed by the law, is to ensure or promote the well-being of patients—their welfare rather than their rights as such.

Much then hinges on what constitutes due care. We have said that negligence 'could' accommodate a medical model of 'therapeutic alliance' because the prevailing view of the English courts is that, in the medical context, the criterion of due care is satisfied by the relatively undemanding requirements of the *Bolam* test'.[15] Lord Scarman has said that:

The *Bolam* principle may be formulated as a rule that a doctor is not negligent if he acts in accordance with a practice accepted at the time as proper by a responsible body of medical opinion even though other doctors adopt a different practice. In short, the law imposes the duty of care: but the standard of care is a matter of medical judgment.[16]

In effect this means that customary or accepted professional practice, as vouched for by expert medical evidence, is regarded as all but dispositive. It will be argued that this acceptance, or perhaps overly narrow reading, of the *Bolam* test[17] is both doctrinally and historically unsound; that the correct test of medical negligence, like that of negligence generally, is failure to attain a standard of care which is reasonable in the circumstances; and that this entails consideration of the individual patient's circumstances. In particular, given the way that the case law has developed, the patient's interest in the doctor disclosing the risks of proposed treatment and discussing alternatives to it can be adequately protected only within a negligence framework. Consequently, though in law, as in moral and political discourse, one's natural impulse is to analyse this interest in terms of the 'right to

---

[14] I. Kennedy, *Treat Me Right* (Oxford: Oxford University Press, 1988), 318.

[15] *Bolam v. Friern Hospital Management Committee* [1957] 1 WLR 582.

[16] *Sidaway v. Board of Governors of the Bethlem Royal Hospital and the Maudsley Hospital* [1985] 1 AC 871, 881.   [17] See further, Ch. 5.

know', it, too, is more accurately expressed for legal purposes as a welfare interest shaping the standard of care which the doctor is obliged to attain.

It is in the realms of decision-making and consent to proposed medical procedures that the most obvious legal application of a collaborative approach arises. Yet even those common law jurisdictions most sympathetic to the 'informed consent' doctrine[18] have so minimized subjective considerations in determining whether the patient can establish liability for inadequate disclosure that the courts have ended up addressing the hypothetical concerns of an average patient rather than the actual claims of the individual plaintiff. The effect is virtually to negate the principle of self-determination on which the informed consent doctrine purportedly rests. It will be apparent that, in our view, what is to be regretted in all of this is not the negation of self-determination as such, but the failure to recognize that the negligence framework admits of an analysis which is conducive to the maximization of patient welfare at the same time as affording due respect for patients' rights.

A model of 'collaborative autonomy'[19] offers what most patients critical of traditional medical practice would prefer, in that it is premised on notions of genuine involvement and deepening medical relationships. It may be thought that the scope for 'deepening medical relationships' will inevitably diminish with the advent of more episodic treatment and increasingly automated health care.[20] But should these developments occur on a significant scale, it will make all the more salient an emphasis on the quality of doctor–patient interaction which collaborative autonomy can offer. In different ways, the other approaches to which we have alluded run the risk of minimizing patient involvement and thereby reducing patient welfare. Moreover, the therapeutic case for a collaborative approach, being medically inspired, rooted in

---

[18] Typically defined as consent to treatment on the basis of disclosure by the doctor of such information as would be deemed material by a reasonable person in the patient's position. This approach has been adopted in a number of United States jurisdictions, in Canada, and in Australia. See further, Ch. 6.

[19] See M. Simpson *et al.*, 'Doctor–Patient Communication: The Toronto Consensus Statement' *British Medical Journal* 303 (1991), 1385.

[20] See 'The Future of Medicine', *The Economist*, 19 Mar. 1994; National Association of Health Authorities and Trusts, *Reinventing Healthcare* (Birmingham: NAHAT, 1993).

patient welfare, and non-confrontational in nature, is far more likely than an appeal to 'patients' rights' to elicit the sympathy and co-operation of the medical profession, a key practical consideration which is too often neglected. The law obviously cannot determine the nature of medical relationships, but it could have a positive influence on them by proclaiming more responsive standards as norms for medical practice.

PART ONE

The Emergence of Medical Law

1

Involving the Law

SOURCES OF MEDICAL UNEASE ABOUT THE LAW

A few years ago, in a much-publicized case,[1] the House of Lords
authorized the sterilization of a mentally retarded 17-year-old girl.
Condemning the judgment, a leading academic physician declared
that 'the law is becoming an insatiable cormorant in matters of
medicine'.[2] Though the specific issue was emotive, such a
forthright general charge of legal overreach is unsustainable. The
view that the courts are meddlesome intruders in medical affairs
may be popular among doctors, but it is very much at odds with
judicial attitudes towards the medical profession and with the
principles which govern the legal liability of its members.

Admittedly the law has increasingly been invoked to determine
the decision-making powers of doctors, sometimes in highly
dramatic circumstances. In 1992, over a period of no more than
five weeks, courts authorized the performance of a caesarian
operation contrary to religious objections[3] and the withdrawal of
artificial feeding from a patient in a persistent vegetative state
(PVS),[4] while a jury convicted of attempted murder a doctor who
took active steps to relieve the agony of a dying patient.[5] There
has also in recent years been a marked upsurge in medical
negligence litigation, as well as occasional comments by judges
which could herald a more interventionist stance. But whatever

---

[1] *Re B (A Minor)(Wardship: Sterilization)* [1988] AC 199.
[2] P. Rhodes, *The Times*, 12 May 1987, correspondence col. Cf. in the American
context, L. Rosenberg, 'Merely mentioning the phrase "medical malpractice" in
the company of practising physicians is like tossing a match into a container of
gasoline': 'Medicine under Siege' in *Law and Medicine in Confrontation: A Deans'
Dialogue*, Yale Law School Program in Civil Liability: Working Paper No. 45
(1986), 6.
[3] *Re S (Adult: Refusal of Treatment)* [1992] 3 WLR 806.
[4] *Airedale NHS Trust* v. *Bland* [1993] AC 789.
[5] *R.* v. *Cox* (1992) unreported. See (1993) 1 *Medical Law Review* 232.

the depths of medical unease, English courts in particular have typically been more than content to let medical perceptions of patient welfare prevail.

Though one might question how far the law can impinge on medical practice, or really seeks to do so, many doctors undoubtedly perceive it as seriously intrusive and threatening. Members of a highly respected profession, accustomed to assuming responsibility and making their own judgements, they do not take kindly to externally imposed constraints. As Zussman has put it, the law constitutes 'a symbolic representation of the limits of medicine's authority' and doctors, commonly armed with only a hazy understanding of medical law, are 'fighting a battle of symbols . . . to defend their jurisdiction'.[6] It will however become apparent that, more often than not, they have been defending it against a phantom enemy.

The generally negative attitude of doctors towards the law is the more regrettable if legal involvement in medicine, whatever its precise impact, is destined to grow. There are good reasons for believing this to be the case. The increasing tendency to litigate in standard areas of medical treatment is likely to be reinforced by the prevailing emphasis on consumerism in health care provision. Novel legal problems are constantly arising, whether as a result of major advances in reproductive technology or such malign developments as the spread of AIDS. In familiar but unresolved areas of controversy, such as the selective treatment of neonates and euthanasia, there are persistent demands for more clearly-defined legal boundaries. Meanwhile establishing the limits of experimental research becomes an ever more pressing concern. At the close of 1993, there were numerous accounts in the media of mixed-race egg donations and of post-menopausal women becoming pregnant after fertility treatment, as well as speculation about the possible future use of eggs taken from aborted foetuses for embryo research and assisted conception.[7] The Human Genome Project to unravel all human DNA and map the estimated 100,000 genes that program human growth and development portends a host of legal dilemmas, covering issues as diverse

[6] R. Zussman, *Intensive Care* (Chicago: University of Chicago Press, 1992), 183, 185, respectively.

[7] See the Human Fertilisation and Embryology Authority, *Donated Ovarian Tissue in Embryo Research and Assisted Conception* (London: HFEA, 1994).

as confidentiality about genetic information, the concept of criminal culpability, patents and intellectual property, and the spectre of employers and insurance companies engaging in discriminatory practices.[8] The need for mutual understanding between the legal and medical communities on such matters is self-evident, and though obviously only part of the story, doctors' misgivings and misconceptions about the law remain a serious obstacle to constructive dialogue.

The attitude of doctors towards the law's role in medicine is to some extent shaped by the educational priorities and traditional ethos of the medical school. Often in this setting a fragmentary and unfavourable view is conveyed. Once acquired, it is unlikely to be altered, either by subsequent exposure to legal processes or by the coverage of medico-legal issues in 'trade' journals and the media. Formal legal instruction for medical students—a poor antidote to colourful accounts of disastrous encounters with the law—has been minimal. It is still mainly devoted to the more routine aspects of forensic medicine such as death certification and coroners' practice. Even in this restricted form, the subject is in decline, almost obliterated by the vast and growing body of detailed medical material which students are required to master. As for the broader legal responsibilities of doctors: 'consent, professional confidence, drug legislation, failure to communicate and the whole expanding field of negligence and malpractice form a minefield into which many new graduates now seem to wander unprotected by little if any knowledge, or even awareness of the problem.'[9]

The strong emphasis on forensic medicine reflects its dominant role in the history of medico-legal scholarship. Its capacity to improve the quality of evidence underpinning medical knowledge served to enhance the scientific and social standing of medicine itself. 'The administration of justice might be peripheral to the concerns of medicine, but it was an area in which the power and

---

[8] See The Hon. Justice M. Kirby, 'Legal Problems: Human Genome Project' (1993) 67 *Australian Law Journal* 894.

[9] B. Knight and I. McKim Thompson, 'The Teaching of Legal Medicine in British Medical Schools', *Medical Education*, 20 (1986), 246, 247; Cf. N. Jones, Chairman, Committee on the Legal Aspects of Medicine, Royal College of Physicians, *The Times*, 10 Feb. 1992, correspondence col.

excitement of scientific medicine could be unambiguously demonstrated.'[10] Thus, in the early nineteenth century, 'trial reports,
articles, notes, and long expository reviews on medico-legal
matters appeared frequently in the leading medical journals',[11]
where legal procedures and rules of evidence were favourably
contrasted for their perceived rigour and objectivity with the
unsubstantiated theories and hearsay which passed for medicine in
an age when charlatanism was rife.[12] The manifest concern of
medical reformers to give such prominence to forensic medicine as
a field of study was the more marked because they were acutely
aware of its unique and highly public visibility. The performance
of medical witnesses in coroners' courts and malpractice suits was
widely reported and inevitably affected the reputation of the
profession as a whole.

Until recently, medico-legal scholarship was often virtually
equated with forensic medicine. Forensic aspects of pathology and
toxicology remain the central focus of the principal medico-legal
societies and their journals,[13] even though such a narrow conception of the field is hard to reconcile with the terminology used to
describe it. Expressions such as 'medical jurisprudence', 'legal
medicine', and 'medico-legal' itself more naturally suggest a
broadly-based discipline concerned with legal aspects of medical
issues in general. Yet several texts which employ these terms are
essentially manuals on medical matters of evidential significance in
court proceedings.

The apparent incongruity between title and content is most
glaring in the continued use of the term 'medical jurisprudence' to
describe works wholly or predominantly devoted to forensic
medicine. Jurists have long protested at this rather grandiose
usage. In the words of Holland: 'Perhaps the least pardonable
application of the term [jurisprudence] takes place when a treatise
upon such medical facts as may incidentally become important in

---

[10] C. Crawford, 'A scientific profession: medical reform and forensic medicine
in British periodicals of the early nineteenth century' in (eds.) R. French and
A. Wear, *British Medicine in an Age of Reform* (London: Routledge, 1991), 210.
[11] Ibid. 204.   [12] Ibid. ch. 9, especially at 207.
[13] Notably the British Academy of Forensic Sciences and the Medico-Legal
Society, which publish *Medicine, Science, and the Law* and the *Medico-Legal
Journal* respectively.

legal proceedings is described as a book upon "Medical Jurisprudence".[14]

Medico-legal texts with a broader coverage have also often been
conceived as practical, if somewhat eclectic, guides for doctors.
Various aspects of medicine with some legal application to
litigation or medical practice are presented, accompanied by a
brief sketch of the legal system and the disciplinary jurisdiction of
the General Medical Council (GMC). The impression of eclectic-
ism is apt to be reinforced by the inclusion of assorted legal
decisions on particular injuries and illnesses. Several works of this
kind first appeared before the study of law in general had achieved
a secure academic foothold. The current thematic and analytical
approach to medical law is a very recent phenomenon, its growing
significance as a systematic area of study underlined by the
emergence of two series of law reports[15] and two academic
journals devoted entirely to the subject,[16] as well as by an
increasing number of scholarly works and university courses.

Irrespective of their merits as practical guides, and whether
strictly forensic or broader in scope, one thing is clear about the
more traditional texts. They are essentially *medical* in orientation.
That is, they aim to provide a basic exposition of legal principles
for medical students and practitioners rather than to pursue
complexities of legal analysis or consider why and to what extent
the law should be involved in medical matters. They are functional
in the narrowest sense and, as such, have helped to create in the
minds of doctors a 'trade school' image of medical law. In much
the same way as 'medical ethics' are prone to be equated by
doctors with standards of competence and professional codes of
conduct,[17] such texts have conveyed the impression that medico-
legal discourse is the preserve of doctors and is to be defined by
their practical concerns.

[14] T. Holland, *Jurisprudence* (13th edn.) (Oxford: Oxford University Press,
1924), 4–5, n. 4. And see W. Curran, 'The Confusion of Titles in the Medicolegal
Field: An Historical Analysis and a Proposal for Reform' (1975) 15 *Medicine,
Science, and the Law* 270.

[15] The Medical Law Reports (1989–) and Butterworths Medico-Legal Reports
(1992–).

[16] The *Medical Law Review* (1993–) and *Medical Law International* (1993–).

[17] See C. Chapman, *Physicians, Law and Ethics* (New York: New York
University Press, 1984), 66. Cf. Institute of Medical Ethics, *Report of a Working
Party on the Teaching of Medical Ethics* (The 'Pond Report') (London: IME
Publications, 1987), ch. 1.

Prominent among those concerns is the prospect of being involved in litigation, whether by providing a routine medical report, acting as an expert witness, or appearing in the role of defendant. The fact that adversarial proceedings are a major point of contact between doctors and lawyers is highly significant. It goes a long way towards explaining the aversion for the law felt by many doctors, despite its substantial acquiescence in professional medical standards and broad judicial empathy for the medical profession.

At the simplest level, any required participation in legal processes may be resented by doctors as a distraction from their 'real' work. Ideally, perhaps, helping to clarify a patient's legal position would be seen as wholly appropriate for members of a caring profession. Understandably, busy practitioners often see things differently. However, such routine contacts with legal processes are scarcely a major source of disenchantment. This is more likely to set in when doctors assume the role of expert witness and seek to reconcile the demands of scientific detachment with the adversarial nature of court proceedings.[18] The medico-legal expert of today is unlikely to endorse the legal procedural model of truth-finding to the same extent as did medical reformers in the early nineteenth century.[19]

Unless they are regular forensic practitioners, doctors giving expert evidence must adjust to unfamiliar and disconcerting surroundings and to an alien set of ground rules which, to the lawyers who cross-examine them, are as familiar as the forum itself. 'The physician, normally masterful and self-confident in the setting of medicine, becomes infantilized in the setting of adversarial litigation'.[20] The tension between the duty to provide independent, objective expertise and the reality of being in some sense partisan is immediately apparent, and more problematic than is often admitted. Experts acting 'for' one side against another are hard put to it not to compromise their professionalism.

The assertion that expert evidence should be 'the independent

---

[18] See generally, C. Jones, *Expert Witnesses* (Oxford: Clarendon Press, 1993).
[19] Though they did recognize that medical testimony was in practice often distorted in cross-examination and that ill-informed juries would commonly give short shrift to medical opinion: Crawford, n. 10 above, 213–16.
[20] B. Dickens, 'The Effects of Legal Liability on Physicians' Services' (1991) 41 *University of Toronto Law Journal* 168, 180.

product of the expert, uninfluenced as to form or content by the exigencies of litigation'[21] is a counsel of perfection.[22] It sits uneasily with the not uncommon complaint of experts that their opinions are distorted by legal advisers modifying, one hesitates to say 'doctoring,' their reports and that they are manipulated by techniques of advocacy which discourage qualified responses and over-simplify complex causal issues.[23] For example, medical evidence suggests that cerebral palsy in newborn infants is much more often the result of antenatal developmental defects than negligent delivery.[24] According to Havard, commenting recently on the increased incidence of successful negligence claims in such cases, 'It is likely that our courts have been seriously misled about the importance of electronic fetal heart monitoring in preventing this condition as a result of the adversarial and confrontational procedures through which they obtain expert evidence.'[25] Such misgivings about the threat thus posed to the objectivity and overall quality of expert evidence have not been lost on the courts themselves.[26]

Disputes between patients and doctors, or patients and hospitals, are unavoidable. But even if one cannot simply wish away the elements of conflict which may exist, there is much to be said for investigating matters in a way which is likely to reveal what happened and to do so with minimum confrontation. Doctors are

[21] *Whitehouse* v. *Jordan* [1981] 1 WLR 246, 256, *per* Lord Wilberforce.

[22] See A. Bartlett, 'The Preparation of Experts' Reports', *Counsel*, Oct. 1993, 21; Nov./Dec. 1993, 23.

[23] See J. Spencer, 'The Neutral Expert: An Implausible Bogey' [1991] *Criminal Law Review* 106; R. Lee, 'Vaccine Damage: Adjudicating Scientific Dispute' in G. Howells, ed., *Product Liability, Insurance and the Pharmaceutical Industry: An Anglo-American Comparison* (Manchester: Manchester University Press, 1991).

[24] D. Acheson, 'Are Obstetrics and Midwifery Doomed?': William Power Memorial Lecture to the Royal College of Midwives (1990), *Midwives Chronicle* (1991) 104; cf. A. Campbell, 'The Paediatrician and Medical Negligence' in M. Powers and N. Harris (eds.) *Medical Negligence* (London: Butterworths, 1990), 460.

[25] J. Havard, ' "No Fault" Compensation for Medical Accidents' (1992) 32 *Medicine, Science, and the Law* 187, 189. In Virginia and Florida, claims of birth-related neurological injury are now dealt with under specialized administrative regimes instead of adversarial litigation. See W. Wadlington and J. Warren Wood III, 'Two "No-Fault" Compensation Schemes for Birth Defects in the United States' (1991) 7 *Professional Negligence* 40.

[26] e.g. *Whitehouse* v. *Jordan* [1980] 1 All ER 650, 655: 'special pleading rather than an impartial report', *per* Lord Denning; *Hotson* v. *Fitzgerald* [1985] 3 All ER 167, 183: 'I find myself unattracted to, and finally unable to accept, either of the competing extreme views', *per* Simon Brown J.

not alone in resenting a legal framework rooted in confrontation, which tends to generate hostility and to reinforce any anger or distress which patients (and their doctors) feel. Compelling patients to adopt the hostile stance which the logic of the adversarial approach dictates invites further adverse effects on their health and makes well-intentioned doctors feel doubly aggrieved. It is an impediment to the maintenance of good doctor–patient relationships.

Given that 'neither scientists, engineers, historians nor scholars from any other discipline use bi-polar adversary trials to determine facts',[27] doctors may be forgiven for finding 'trial by battle' a dispiritingly crude way of resolving medico-legal disputes at the close of the twentieth century. The underlying assumption that the litigation belongs to the parties, giving them an all but exclusive right to determine its shape by the two opposing positions which they choose to present to the court, is perplexing to those whose own diagnostic methods are more open-ended and scientifically based. They are understandably uncomfortable about a form of inquiry in which medically significant information may not be revealed or even elicited. Thus, the privilege attached to matters disclosed 'in aid of litigation' can result in the existence and contents of objectively important evidence—such as unfavourable medical reports—being withheld from the court.[28] At the same time, limited resources and the exigencies of legal aid[29] may deny patients the expertise needed for thorough investigation of the medical evidence.

When courts decide whether or not to attach responsibility to conduct, the insights of psychiatry and scientific understanding of causation are apt to be displaced or traduced by the law's compromise with considerations of social policy. Such tendencies

---

[27] G. Goodpaster, 'On the Theory of American Adversary Criminal Trial' (1987) 78 *Journal of Criminal Law and Criminology* 118, 122.

[28] J. Havard, 'Privilege' (1987) 55 *Medico-Legal Journal* 206; and cf. Havard, 'the adversarial and confrontational aspects of the procedure in tort actions do little to ensure that the court is provided with the best available independent expert evidence, and there is a case for adopting the system introduced in Europe as long ago as the 13th century whereby expert evidence can be given only by those recognized by the court as competent to give it', in ' "No Fault" Compensation for Medical Accidents' (1992) 32 *Medicine, Science, and the Law* 187, 194.

[29] See 58 below.

are notoriously apparent in the criminal sphere.[30] To the extent that criminal trials are power struggles over how to resolve social problems, the conflicting priorities of those professionally concerned can be a potent source of mutual misunderstanding and antipathy. A diagnostic label and recommended treatment for delinquent behaviour may be medically defensible, but at variance with proclaimed social objectives of the criminal justice system and with the rights of individuals. The familiar tensions between law and psychiatry over when to attribute personal responsibility where the defence relies on some form of mental disorder amply demonstrate the point.[31]

However, such conflicts are by no means confined to the criminal law. One might consider, for example, the actions for 'nervous shock'—the survival of the unscientific terminology is itself instructive—brought by relatives and friends of the Hillsborough football disaster victims.[32] In rejecting the claims of those who had seen the disaster unfold on television, the appellate judgments revealed what was either a failure to grasp or to address dispassionately the causes of psychiatric illness. Shortly before the case reached the Court of Appeal, there had been two first instance decisions in which close attention had been paid to relevant medical evidence. In one, the judge had said: 'on the statistical and medical evidence before me, psychiatric illness resulting from nervous shock, whether received as a result of witnessing an accident involving a loved one or hearing about it, can be no more than the most remote of possibilities'.[33] In the other, the judge concluded: 'There is no diagnostic or medical difference in the anxiety state caused through witnessing the accident itself or through being present at the aftermath or through simply learning about it from another'.[34] Scant regard was

[30] Where the psychiatrist is in danger of being 'alternately seduced by the power of the adversarial system and assaulted by it': A. Stone, 'The Ethical Boundaries of Forensic Psychiatry', *Bulletin of the American Academy of Psychiatry and the Law* 12 (1984), 209; cf. R. Smith, 'Forensic Pathology, Scientific Expertise, and the Criminal Law' in R. Smith and B. Wynne (eds.) *Expert Evidence: Interpreting Science in the Law* (London: Routledge, 1989), ch. 2.

[31] For recent examples relating to alcoholism and diminished responsibility, consider *R.* v. *Tandy* [1989] 1 WLR 350 and *R.* v. *Inseal* [1992] *Criminal Law Review* 35. Cf. S. Dell, *Murder into Manslaughter* (Oxford: Oxford University Press, 1984), 60.

[32] *Alcock* v. *Chief Constable of South Yorkshire Police* [1992] 1 AC 310.

[33] *Hevican* v. *Ruane* [1991] 3 All ER 65, 72.

[34] *Ravenscroft* v. *Rederiaktiebolaget Transatlantic* [1991] 3 All ER 73, 79.

to be paid to these findings in the *Hillsborough* appeals. Both decisions were 'seriously doubted' and misconceived fears of limitless liability led the judges to adopt artificial distinctions and perpetuate restrictive principles that belie the 'progressive understanding of mental illness' which their judgment is supposed to reflect. Thus the House of Lords endorsed the early case law's unscientific insistence on immediacy of reaction to traumatic stimulus—'the sudden appreciation by sight or sound of a horrifying event, which violently agitates the mind'[35]—despite the fact that such primary responses are usually transient and rarely result in psychiatric illness.[36] In fact, the House of Lords judgment in the *Hillsborough* case did not contain a single explicit reference to the medical determinants of such illness.

Whether one is addressing areas such as drug or vaccine damage,[37] environmental contamination,[38] or run-of-the-mill medical negligence cases, the 'mismatch of legal and scientific notions of causation'[39] is calculated to leave expert witnesses convinced that legal standards of proof are not as rigorous as scientific ones, and that legal analysis of scientific data is compromised by social pressures. There are, of course, intelligible grounds of social policy that explain divergences between legal and scientific reasoning. For present purposes, it is not so much their respective virtues which concern us. Rather it is the effect on doctors of having to accommodate their conception of the truth-finding process to the premises of the adversary system. That justifications can be advanced for the law's compromises or that the objectivity of expert evidence is itself open to question in the light of competing scientific approaches[40] and the personal or

[35] *Alcock*, above, n. 32, at 401, *per* Lord Ackner.

[36] Cf. 'it is highly artificial to imprison the legal cause of action for psychiatric injury in an outmoded scientific view about the nature of its origins', *Campbelltown City Council* v. *Mackay* (1989) 15 NSWLR 501, 503, *per* Kirby P. See, further, H. Teff, 'Liability for Negligently Inflicted Nervous Shock' (1983) 99 *Law Quarterly Review* 100, 104–8, and 'Liability for Psychiatric Illness after Hillsborough' (1992) 12 *Oxford Journal of Legal Studies* 440.

[37] See *Loveday* v. *Renton and Wellcome Foundation Ltd* [1990] 1 Med LR 117.

[38] *Reay* v. *British Nuclear Fuels plc; Hope* v. *British Nuclear Fuels plc* [1994] 5 Med LR 1: unsuccessful claim that radiation caused cancer in children of workers at Sellafield.

[39] R. Lee, n. 23 above, 56.

[40] e.g. the statistical methodology of epidemiology as against the empiricist model of clinical diagnosis: see e.g. *Brock* v. *Merrell Dow Pharmaceuticals Inc*, 874 F 2d 307 (5th Cir, 1989).

institutional values of the experts involved is not to the point. Nor is it relevant that the adversarial process is deeply entrenched, integral to our legal profession's current organizational structure, and supposedly responsive to community sentiment.[41] For in seeking to understand doctors' perceptions of the law as unscientific, intrusive, and unduly confrontational, it is how they experience it that counts. From this perspective, it suffices if they take exception to an accusatorial setting in which their views are liable to be discarded or distorted and ultimately made subservient to the 'demands of society' as legally perceived.

Most doctors then seek to minimize their professional contact with the law. Except for the small minority who regularly engage in court work, legal involvement on behalf of others is at best an occasional inconvenient necessity; at worst a positively alienating experience. It is potential involvement as defendant in a negligence action, with reputation and livelihood at risk, as well as possible exposure in the media, that is the doctor's ultimate phobia and a persistent source of anxiety.[42]

The fear that such an action might be *initiated* is far from irrational, particularly in certain specialties, such as obstetrics.[43] Though there may be room for debate about what would constitute an 'appropriate' level of claims, there can be no doubt that the absolute number has risen dramatically in recent years.[44]

• The sense of grievance felt within the profession at large, and by individual doctors whose conduct has been impugned, is only marginally assuaged by the fact that many cases are not ultimately substantiated. It has been argued that the absence of direct medical input into the deliberations of legal aid committees has resulted in unmeritorious and time-consuming claims getting off the ground, fuelling considerable frustration and stress among doctors, the more so if they do not appreciate how remote are the

---

[41] J. Jacob, *The Fabric of English Civil Justice* (London: Stevens, 1987), 15. Goodpaster, 'On the Theory of American Adversary Criminal Trial', n. 27 above.
[42] Cf. Dickens, n. 20 above, 179–82.
[43] See M. Ennis and C. Vincent, 'Obstetric Accidents: A Review of 64 Cases' *British Medical Journal* 300 (1990), 1365–7; J. Capstick and P. Edwards, 'Trends in Obstetric Malpractice Claims' *The Lancet* 336 (1990); 931–2. And see B. Markesinis, 'Litigation-Mania in England, Germany and the USA: Are we so very different?' (1990) 49 *Cambridge Law Journal* 233. [44] See 17–18 below.

prospects of actual proceedings.[45] Their concerns about the mounting frequency of malpractice claims are unlikely to be allayed by the recent structural, not to say cultural, change in the organization of the NHS.[46]

The vast majority of medical negligence claims concern hospital patients.[47] Before 1990, the cost of successful negligence claims against hospital doctors was met by the doctor's defence organization and the relevant health authority in proportion to their agreed share of responsibility.[48] An NHS indemnity scheme was then introduced,[49] under which health authorities and NHS trusts are obliged to indemnify hospital doctors fully for any liability incurred in the course of their employment. Several concerns underlay this development. Consultants and junior doctors resented having to pay a third of their rising subscription costs[50] and doctors working, or contemplating working, in high risk specialties were alarmed by differential rates being introduced.[51] It was also anticipated that dispensing with dual representation would prove cheaper and more efficient. But the new system signifies more than a changed financial mechanism for handling claims. Whereas the previous arrangement could be seen as a concession to hospital doctors' professional autonomy, NHS indemnity highlights the fact that in legal terms they are directly

[45] See C. Hawkins and I. Paterson, 'Medicolegal Audit in the West Midlands Region: Analysis of 100 Cases' *British Medical Journal* 295 (1987), 1533.

[46] See, further, Ch. 3.

[47] A few years ago, prior to the introduction of NHS Indemnity, the Medical Protection Society (MPS) produced the following figures: Hospital practitioners constituted 46% of their membership, but accounted for 80% of claims; GPs, 47% of the membership, but only 14% of claims. Obstetricians, who constituted 3% of the membership, accounted for 29% of claims: 'Medical Negligence: Addressing the Issues' MPS Symposium (13 Dec. 1988). Cf. 'malpractice actions against general practitioners are rare and barely more than a handful of reported cases exist': M. Brazier, *Medicine, Patients and the Law* (2nd edn.) (Harmondsworth: Penguin Books, 1992), 354. Cf. P. Weiler, *Medical Malpractice on Trial* (Cambridge, Mass.: Harvard University Press, 1991), 225–6, citing a 1984 survey on claims in the United States: 'Less than 13 per cent of malpractice claims are now brought for events that occur in physicians' offices.'

[48] HM (54) 32 and HM (54) 43. Where they failed to agree, they each paid 50%.

[49] HC(89)34; see also National Health Service and Community Care Act 1990, s. 21.

[50] In the case of hospital doctors, the other two-thirds of their indemnity cover was reimbursed. GPs were, and are still, fully reimbursed.

[51] Introduced in 1989 by the Medical Protection Society and then under consideration by the Medical Defence Union.

employed by health authorities and in principle subject to the same legal regime for claims as other hospital staff. The conception of the hospital doctor as an employee, rather than an independent professional with extensive clinical autonomy, is becoming more pronounced within the increasingly managerial and commercialized structure of the post-1990 NHS. Before the 1980s the Service had no designated 'managers'; in 1989–90 it had 6,091, and by 1992–3, 20,478![52] It would not be surprising if health service managers, constrained by tight budgets, were to prove less amenable than medical defence organizations to contesting claims when settlement seems on balance the cheaper option. By the same token, one might expect them to become increasingly selective about the services and procedures on offer and increasingly to direct which doctors undertake them, as well as perhaps seeking to impose clinical guidelines.[53]

It is obviously disturbing for doctors, patients and society at large if the quality of treatment suffers because the medical profession feels under threat from the law. Doctors commonly assert that they are forced to practise 'defensive medicine'—to the detriment of patients and the health service budget—either by carrying out expensive, medically inappropriate procedures or by not doing what is clinically justified, in order to avoid ending up in the courts.[54] Over many years judges have also voiced concern about the risks of defensive medicine.[55] Sometimes, as was particularly evident in the Court of Appeal judgments in *Sidaway*,[56] they have exaggerated the dangers by invoking the ills of American medicine and malpractice litigation.[57] Such warnings

---

[52] Parliamentary Questions: A. Milburn MP, HC Parl Deb, vol. 231, no. 239, col. 459. Figures supplied by Alan Milburn MP.

[53] M. Brazier, 'NHS Indemnity: The Implications for Medical Litigation' (1990) 6 *Professional Negligence* 88; F. Miller, 'Malpractice Liability and Physician Autonomy', *The Lancet* 342 (1993) 973.

[54] Cf. Dickens, n. 20 above, 184.

[55] e.g. *De Freville* v. *Dill* [1927] LJKB 1056, 1062; *Roe* v. *Minister of Health* [1954] 2 QB 66, 86–7, *per* Denning LJ; *Whitehouse* v. *Jordan* [1980] 1 All ER 650, 659, *per* Lawton LJ; *Sidaway* v. *Board of Governors of the Bethlem Royal Hospital and the Maudsley Hospital* [1985] AC 871, 887, *per* Lord Scarman and 893, *per* Lord Diplock.

[56] e.g. *Sidaway* [1984] 2 WLR 778, 791 (CA), *per* Lord Donaldson MR, 795, *per* Dunn LJ and 801, *per* Browne-Wilkinson LJ.

[57] Cf. 'that [damages for negligence] is a field in which the law has properly applied policy restrictions *is justified* by a glance at the position reached on the

have often taken insufficient account of major differences between the two countries, as regards the operation of the legal system and the structure of health care and social security provision, not to mention cultural and demographic differences. Thus if, in America, doctors feel so threatened by the prospect of being sued that it materially affects the way they practise, this is partly because there juries determine both liability and damages, and in assessing damages may be mindful that lawyers operating on a contingency fee basis typically receive some 30 per cent of a successful plaintiff's award. The predominant fee-for-service basis of remuneration for doctors, in the context of a private insurance-based system, virtually invites excessive testing. It also seems likely that the more explicitly commercial nature of medical transactions makes people more disposed to sue. In the absence of a national health service and with access to very limited welfare provision many patients are practically obliged to do so.

Since these conditions do not obtain in England,[58] medical litigation is more containable. Yet it has still increased dramatically in recent years. Are we then to conclude that there has been a massive intrusion of the law into medical practice, dictating its form, hampering the work of the medical profession, and subjecting its members to undue strain and anxiety? Does the situation in England manifest what one American authority has described as the 'pervasive, unwelcome, crushing embrace of medicine by law'?[59] In what respects and to what extent are the various fears of English doctors about legal encroachment justified?

THE INCREASING INVOLVEMENT OF LAW WITH MEDICINE

That doctors' decisions increasingly involve the courts is incontrovertible. But involvement is not the same as encroachment, or even engagement, and the precise impact of additional litigation

---

other side of the Atlantic where damages awarded in respect of medical and surgical negligence is, *it is believed*, affecting the proper execution by surgeons and others of their professional tasks to the detriment of their patients': *Greater Nottingham Co-operative Society Ltd* v. *Cementation Pilings and Foundations Ltd* [1988] 3 WLR 396, 409, *per* Purchas LJ (emphasis added).

[58] On the introduction of a conditional fee option, see 58 below.

[59] Rosenberg, 'Medicine under Siege', n. 2 above, 3.

on medical practice is far from clear. Certainly the recent proliferation of cases has given the judges ample opportunity to explore the ambit of medical law, especially in the area of negligence. In addition, court authorization is more commonly sought nowadays when difficult questions arise about the appropriateness of proposed treatment for patients who either lack competence to decide for themselves or whose competence is in doubt. Across a wide spectrum of cases, there have been judicial pronouncements which at first sight cast the law as authoritative decision-maker, if not moral arbiter, on matters once considered the exclusive province of the medical profession. To the extent that the judgement of doctors is thereby overridden, the law's involvement could intelligibly be characterized as encroachment. However it will be contended that this very rarely happens. Any impression that courts are dictating the medical agenda is more a matter of rhetoric than substance. Concrete interference with medical practice by the law is more likely to emanate from legislative enactments which directly address the issue of health care delivery,[60] or from statutory provisions of more general application which have repercussions for the medical profession.[61]

Charting the Recent Growth of Medical Litigation

In the late nineteenth and early twentieth centuries it was very unusual for patients to sue their doctors. Conventionally considered an almost presumptuous thing to do, it was in any event beyond the means of all but a tiny minority.[62] Reporting in 1978, the Pearson Commission observed that whereas fifty or sixty years previously claims against doctors had been rare, this had changed since the introduction of the NHS, reaching some 500 claims a year against doctors in the mid-1970s.[63] Some 60 per cent of them were abandoned, 34 per cent settled and a mere 5 per cent

---

[60] e.g. the National Health Service and Community Care Act 1990.

[61] e.g. data protection legislation: see ch. 3, n. 20, below.

[62] See C. Hawkins, *Mishap or Malpractice* (Oxford: Basil Blackwell, 1985), 12, 41. Cf. in the Scottish context, 'this action is certainly one of a particularly unusual character. It is an action of damages by a patient against a medical man. In my somewhat long experience I cannot remember having seen a similar case before': *Farquhar* v. *Murray* (1901) 3 F. 859, 862, *per* Lord Young (Sc).

[63] Royal Commission on Civil Liability and Compensation for Personal Injury (London: HMSO, 1978), Cmnd 7054, 282, para. 1318.

went to trial. Of the twenty-five that ended up in court, as many as twenty were won by the defendants. Overall, the value of compensation paid was approximately £1 million.[64] From the late 1970s, actions for medical malpractice became increasingly common, the number of cases and the size of awards rising sharply towards the end of the 1980s.[65] Between 1986 and 1988 alone, the subscriptions paid by doctors to medical defence organizations tripled. In 1989–90, the NHS spent approximately £45 million on an estimated 7,000 cases;[66] in 1991–92, £80 million; and in 1992–3, £100 million with anticipated growth of some 25 per cent in future years.[67] There are also indications that more use is being made of NHS complaints procedures to obtain information with a view to litigation.[68]

There are good grounds for believing that the momentum of medical litigation will be maintained. The explanations proffered for its increased incidence have, if anything, become more cogent with the passage of time. The sheer volume of additional treatment made possible by advances in modern medicine is an important factor. However beneficial in the long run, innovation has always proved a fertile source of injury, as witness the casualties of the novel forms of orthopaedic treatment, obstetric surgery, and X-ray equipment developed in the nineteenth century. Nowadays, when suing is a relatively more practical proposition, medical technology permits intricate but sometimes risky procedures that require levels of skill and concentration not always available in the prevailing conditions of hospital practice.[69]

[64] Ibid. See C. Ham *et al.*, *Medical Negligence: Compensation and Accountability* (London: King's Fund Institute, 1988), 8, Table 2.

[65] See P. Fenn and C. Whelan, 'Medical Litigation: Trends, Causes, Consequences' R. Dingwall (ed.), *Socio-Legal Aspects of Medical Practice* (London: Royal College of Physicians of London, 1989), ch. 2.

[66] Of which all but 5% or so would have been settled out of court: Department of Health, *Arbitration for Medical Negligence in the National Health Service* (London: Department of Health, 1991), 4.

[67] *The Economist*, 13 Nov. 1993, 35. Department of Health figures cited in J. Harris, 'The Price of Failure', *Health Service Journal* (14 Apr. 1994), 9.

[68] Department of Health, *Being Heard: The Report of a Review Committee on NHS Complaints Procedures* (London: Department of Health, 1994), 14.

[69] Especially in obstetrics. Complaints about obstetric and gynaecological practice account for some 30% of all negligence claims against UK health authority doctors: M. Ennis, A. Clark, and J. Grudzinskas, 'Change in Obstetric Practice in Response to Fear of Litigation in the British Isles', *The Lancet* 338 (1991), 616. Acheson, n. 24 above, estimated that the total number of claims filed for

In some settings it can almost seem as if the ingredients for negligent treatment have been consciously built into the system. The combination of budgetary constraints, overworked and sometimes inexperienced medical staff under pressure to cut waiting lists, and continued growth in the number of referrals is a recipe for litigation.[70]

As the scope of medical treatment constantly expands, accounts in the media of 'miracle' drugs, new forms of transplant surgery and other such advances reveal how conditions once seen as divinely ordained or untreatable can be cured or alleviated. Infertility treatment and the advent of gene therapy, for example, hold out the promise of overcoming disabilities until recently presumed irremediable. Such developments not only tend to make people less resigned to adverse medical outcomes, but also less disposed to accept them without recourse to the law,[71] at least when the wider institutional context is sufficiently supportive of legal remedies.[72] A better-educated public is less inclined to take on trust assurances about medical care and more disposed to question the adequacy of information provided. In the age of the Citizen's and Patient's Charters, it is also officially discouraged from doing so. More information about health care provision and the rights of patients is available, from Community Health Councils, consumer organizations, and a variety of patient support groups. There is more effective and systematic campaigning by pressure groups, most notably, in the legal context, by Action for the Victims of Medical Accidents (AVMA).[73] Founded in 1982,

---

negligence in respect of brain-damaged infants increased from about 75 in 1983 to 200 in 1989.

[70] See *Johnstone* v. *Bloomsbury HA* [1991] 2 All ER 293; *Wilsher* v. *Essex AHA* [1987] QB 730. Cf. *R* v. *Prentice* [1993] 3 WLR 927, and see G. Williams, 'Misadventures of Manslaughter' (1993) 143 *New Law Journal* 1413; C. Dyer, 'Manslaughter Convictions for Making Mistakes', *British Medical Journal* 303 (1991), 1218. See also E. Campling *et al.*, *The Report of the National Confidential Enquiry into Perioperative Deaths 1991/92* (London: National Confidential Enquiry into Perioperative Deaths, 1993).

[71] See D. Dewees, M. Trebilcock and P. Coyte, 'The Medical Malpractice Crisis: A Comparative Empirical Perspective' (1991) 54(1) *Law and Contemporary Problems* 217, 250: 'this growth must arise less from isolated doctrinal changes in one country than from changes in medical practice and social mores, which occur roughly simultaneously in most Western countries'.

[72] Cf. M. Galanter, 'Law Abounding: Legalisation around the North Atlantic' (1992) 55 *Modern Law Review* 1, 8–10.

[73] See AVMA, *10th Anniversary Report* (London: AVMA, 1992).

AVMA has been influential in prompting procedural reform,[74] complementing the advisory and campaigning work of the Patients Association and of single-issue action groups.[75] It has also helped to redress the imbalance in access to appropriate legal and medical expertise, which used to be overwhelmingly concentrated towards doctors and health authorities.

The sense that there is more scope for pursuing medical actions is underscored by the growth of legal practitioners specializing in claims on behalf of patients. As the legal profession has developed more effective techniques of organization and of information exchange, the profile of personal injury work generally, and medical negligence in particular, has been rising and has found institutional expression. The Association of Personal Injury Lawyers, founded in 1990, augments the work of AVMA in seeking to promote the interests of victims of accident and disease through better-quality legal provision and law reform. At the same time, the recent decision of the Law Society to complement its personal injury panel by establishing a specialist panel for medical negligence lawyers[76] attests to the widely held belief among practitioners that this is a sub-specialty destined to grow, not least through the co-ordinated efforts of firms undertaking large-scale multi-party actions.

In the late 1980s and early 1990s, vigorous and systematic pursuit of mass drug injury claims helped to ensure that allegations of negligence by pharmaceutical companies would be continually exposed to scrutiny in the media. Occasionally the medical profession is directly implicated. Doctors and hospitals were among those initially sued in the massive action launched on behalf of tranquillizer victims; negligence has been alleged against doctors and nurses for giving pertussis vaccine injections to young children who subsequently suffered severe brain damage.[77] But even when medical staff are not defendants in such litigation, it

---

[74] Most notably by helping to co-ordinate the claims in *Naylor* v. *Preston AHA* [1987] 1 WLR 958, which led to reform of the rules on disclosure. See text at n. 90 below.

[75] The Patients Association was founded in 1963. It has recently published the *Health Address Book*, containing details of more than 1,000 national self-help and support organizations: L. Lamont, 'Why Patients don't Sue Doctors', *Journal of the Medical Defence Union* 9 (1993), 39, at 40. See also A. Simanowicz, 'Agencies' in Powers and Harris, *Medical Negligence*, n. 24 above, ch. 6.

[76] See (1993) 90(32) *Law Society Gazette* 34.

[77] *Loveday* v. *Renton* [1990] 1 Med LR 117.

does indirectly have a bearing on their vulnerability to legal action. For the publicity which these often long-drawn-out battles attracts stimulates public awareness of legal processes as a potential means of redress, in much the same way as the regular reporting and dramatization of substantial medical negligence awards. Few campaigns in living memory can have made a more lasting impression on the general public than that waged on behalf of the thalidomide victims in the 1970s. In the late 1980s, the publicity surrounding the physical injuries and legal obstacles endured by victims of the anti-arthritis drug Opren conveyed a similar message.[78] The combination of pressure-group campaigning and convoluted legal proceedings[79] revived memories of thalidomide and the largely unfulfilled hopes of reform which it had prompted.

The scale of some of these actions and their cumulative impact have provided an added incentive for lawyers to develop expertise in medical litigation. More than 260 firms of solicitors were involved in the *Opren* case, representing some 1,600 plaintiffs. The documentation ran into millions of pages.[80] The tranquillizer suit at one stage involved over 17,000 would-be claimants, making it by far the largest personal injury action ever launched in England,[81] though, at the time of writing, it has all but collapsed. Not long after the Court of Appeal's decision that, in group litigation, actions may be struck out where any potential benefit to the plaintiffs would be extremely modest as against the astronomical expense of defending the claims,[82] the Legal Aid Board withdrew funding, having concluded that only a very small proportion of the 5,000 or so claims still being pursued could succeed. The plaintiffs' firms had collaborated to form the Benzodiazepine Solicitors Group, under the aegis of the disaster co-ordination service set up by the Law Society in 1987. This

---

[78] See K. Oliphant, 'Innovation in Procedure and Practice in Multi-Party Medical Cases' in A. Grubb (ed.), *Choices and Decisions in Health Care* (Chichester: John Wiley & Sons, 1993), 183.

[79] There were 13 separate hearings in the English courts prior to the settlement of the case. Ibid. 184.

[80] *Davies* v. *Eli Lilly & Co* (1987) 137 *New Law Journal* 1183, 1184, *per* Hirst J.

[81] 'there are six lead firms and, astoundingly, 1,553 feeder firms of solicitors representing the 10,800 or so claims notified to one defendant alone . . . Of this total, 2,336 claimants served writs' D. McIntosh, 'When the Only Winners are the Lawyers', *The Times*, 6 Apr. 1993.

[82] *AB and Others* v. *John Wyeth & Brother Ltd, Roche Products Ltd* [1994] 5 Med LR 149.

facility, in keeping with the more proactive ethos of the modern legal profession,[83] encourages potential claimants to come forward by issuing a press release and establishing a 'hot-line' telephone number for enquiries.[84] Like the enlisting of media support for clients' causes, this practice is becoming a familiar feature of medical litigation, despite the protestations of the British Medical Association. Co-ordination of vast and technically complex actions has also become more manageable as a result of advances in information technology. In some instances they are not feasible at all without a high-capacity computerized litigation support system. The indications are that such developments in efficient case management, by cutting costs considerably and enabling firms to cope with a substantially heavier caseload, have in themselves facilitated the growth of litigation.[85]

Admittedly, mass drug actions also graphically illustrate the substantive, procedural, and financial barriers which can confront plaintiffs seeking to establish a medical injury claim. Some of the difficulties are peculiar to, or magnified in, multi-party actions; others, such as proving causation and establishing the defendant's failure to satisfy the requisite standard of care, are common to medical litigation, where they are typically more onerous than in other personal injury actions. However, partly because of the compelling way in which they expose the deficiencies of the existing system, medical cases, and in particular mass drug disasters, have been a major catalyst for change aimed at easing the plaintiff's path in the quest for compensation.[86] It is often in

---

[83] Cf. the controversy over a reputable London personal injury firm which advertised its services to potential victims of wrong cancer diagnoses at a Birmingham hospital: Comment, 'Ambulance Chasers in the UK', *Solicitors Journal*, l0 Sept. 1993.

[84] See Supreme Court Procedure Committee, *Guide for Use in Group Actions* (London: Supreme Court Procedure Committee, 1991), App. 1.

[85] L. Mounteer, 'Cutting Costs Using Computerised Litigation Support Technology', (1991) 2(3) *Computers and Law* (NS) 22. Among issues currently under consideration for co-ordinated litigation and pooled data is that of smoking and cancer, which could involve claims against the Government and health authorities regarding the adequacy of health warnings, following the US Supreme Court ruling that such warnings do not confer automatic protection: *Cipollone* v. *Liggett Group Inc*, 112 S Ct 2608 (1992). See also *Haines* v. *Liggett et al.* CA 84–67 (DNJ) 1992.

[86] e.g. *Cartledge* v. *Jopling (E.) & Sons Ltd* [1963] AC 758: pneumoconiosis and the Limitation Act 1963; Thalidomide and the Consumer Protection Act 1987; Opren and the Supreme Court Procedure Committee's *Guide for Use in Group Actions*, n. 84 above.

the context of medical injury that judges have been most scathing about the difficulties of pursuing personal injury claims and most active in initiating or advocating reform.

Judicial recognition that pursuing a medical claim can be too much of an uphill struggle has led to changes aimed at reducing the tendency of the adversarial process to hinder prompt clarification of the issues and early settlement. In *Wilsher* v. *Essex Area Health Authority*, Mustill LJ trenchantly criticized the practice of not exchanging experts' medical reports before trial: 'practitioners do their clients and the interests of justice no service by continuing to pursue this policy of concealment . . . To me it seems wrong that in this area of the law, more than in any other, this kind of forensic blind-man's buff should continue to be the norm'.[87] Building on the calls for reform in *Wilsher*,[88] the Court of Appeal in *Naylor* v. *Preston Area Health Authority*[89] expressly sought to ease the plaintiff's path by ordering early disclosure of evidence that was to be relied on at the hearing, indicating that this should become standard practice. The Rules of the Supreme Court were subsequently amended accordingly.[90] In addition, claims for less than £50,000[91] are now normally heard in the County Court,[92] avoiding the more expensive and lengthier High Court process. In these various respects, the still-demanding task of preparing medical injury claims has become somewhat easier, especially now that the necessary legal and medical expertise is more widely available.

Obviously pursuing a medical claim in any court can still be prohibitively expensive and no amount of procedural reform will avail people who cannot afford to use the system. Their numbers have increased considerably since the radical cuts to the legal aid budget in 1993. We will shortly consider the issue of cost as a disincentive to taking legal action.[93] Meanwhile, in exploring the

---

[87] [1987] QB 730, 773–4.

[88] Cf. ibid. 776, *per* Glidewell LJ and 780–1, *per* Browne-Wilkinson LJ.

[89] [1987] 1 WLR 958.

[90] RSC Ord. 38 r. 37(1): SI 1989/2427. Plaintiffs must now serve a medical report together with their statement of claim and there is provision for early exchange of experts' reports as well as of witness statements.

[91] The vast majority of medical claims—of the £45 million awarded in 1990, the damages exceeded £300,000 in only some 35 cases, totalling £17m. The remaining £28 million went on some 7,000 cases at an average cost of £6,500: *Arbitration for Medical Negligence in the National Health Service*, n. 66 above.

[92] Courts and Legal Services Act 1990 and the High Court and County Courts Jurisdiction Order 1991 (SI 91/724).   [93] See 58 below.

factors which have contributed to the upward trend in medical litigation, it should be noted that the effect of the general reduction in legal aid provision has been partially offset by children under 16 now being assessed for eligibility solely by reference to their own resources. They already account for a substantial proportion of medical claims, partly due to the incidence of injury related to obstetric treatment. Genetic counselling and gene therapy may also prove to be significant sources of litigation. Governmental determination to deal with rising legal aid costs and persistent criticism of the tort system's expense and delay have prompted numerous proposals for less elaborate, low-key forms of dispute resolution, mostly favouring an inquisitorial model centred on documentary evidence and including the suggestion that medical negligence claims be removed entirely from the remit of the ordinary courts.[94] Though the medical profession would be likely to welcome a more investigative and less confrontational approach, it is by no means clear that the overall number of cases would decline were some such scheme to be implemented.

Suing Hospital Authorities

A central element in the growth of medical litigation is the altered conception of the hospital as an institution and the legal changes which this has prompted. In this respect, too, one might reasonably anticipate an increasing disposition to sue. As the relationship of patients and the NHS is redefined in terms of 'value for money', patients are in effect encouraged by government to use market remedies, of which recourse to the law is a prime example.

Doctors are inevitably affected by these developments. To begin with, they are frequently implicated in litigation against hospital

[94] e.g. Lawton LJ in *Whitehouse* v. *Jordan* [1980] 1 All ER 650, 661–2; Department of Health, *Arbitration for Medical Negligence in the National Health Service*, n. 66 above; Association of Community Health Councils for England and Wales and Action for Victims of Medical Accidents, *A Health Standards Inspectorate* (London: ACHCEW/AVMA, 1992); British Medical Association, *Report of the Working Party on No Fault Compensation for Medical Injury* (London: British Medical Association, 1987 and 1991); Royal College of Physicians, *Compensation for Adverse Consequences of Medical Intervention* (London: Royal College of Physicians, 1990).

authorities. Though it is almost invariably the employing authority that injured patients will look to for compensation, they will commonly name the doctor or doctors involved as parties if only to draw attention to their alleged responsibility. More generally, major alteration in the structure and organization of health care delivery also alters the way doctors and their work are perceived, by hospital managers as well as by patients. For what is in issue here is the historical transformation of the hospital from mere venue *for* treatment to provider *of* treatment, on terms increasingly driven by commercial considerations. This radical shift naturally signifies a diminution in the authority and status of doctors in the hospital setting. The formerly independent practitioner, who often provided hospital services gratuitously, is recast as a salaried employee constrained by managerial and administrative directives, with all that that implies for the dominance of the traditional paternalistic model.

For hundreds of years the hospital was essentially the location where surgeons came to train and practise their skills. Well into the twentieth century, the most that was required of the hospital authority was to provide a properly equipped facility. To this end, it was under an obligation to take care in selecting competent staff and could be held vicariously liable for 'purely ministerial or administrative duties.'[95] But as far as treatment was concerned, doctors were seen as professionals exercising independent judgement, not employees subject to the authority's control. Consequently, the courts would not hold the authority vicariously liable for negligent treatment,[96] something which they would have been reluctant to do anyway, since hospitals were often poorly funded charitable or public undertakings.[97] In short, just as in the absence of legal aid most patients could not afford to bring an action for medical negligence at all,[98] the few who could were not only disinclined for social and psychological reasons to sue their doctors, but legally unable to sue the hospital authority.

Even before the NHS came into being, the Medical Defence Union, the leading organization responsible for advising and

---

[95] *Hillyer* v. *Governors of St. Bartholomew's Hospital* [1909] 2 KB 820, 829.
[96] Ibid.
[97] *Cassidy* v. *Ministry of Health* [1951] 2 KB 343, 361, *per* Denning LJ.
[98] At least without trade union support, which was mainly provided for ordinary personal injury cases.

indemnifying members of the profession in respect of legal proceedings, had observed that it was becoming somewhat easier to prove negligence against doctors.[99] The growth of medical defence societies, it argued, had encouraged judges to take a more lenient view of claims for medical injuries and to begin to view them as in effect an insurable risk, akin to road accidents and accidents at work. But the main impetus for change came with the establishment of the National Health Service as a comprehensive system in 1948 and the introduction of legal aid two years later. The dual shift in the nature of hospitals, from charitable and voluntary status to state-financing and from treatment location to organized provider of services, facilitated piecemeal development of vicarious liability in the medical sphere.[100] The previous resistance to its imposition was progressively eroded, and health authorities were to become liable for all full-time and part-time hospital staff.[101] The introduction of legal aid in 1950 meant that pursuing a legal claim had become a feasible financial proposition for some 70–80 per cent of the population, the less inhibiting in that it was an action against an impersonal state institution.[102] The creation of the NHS, legal aid, and expanded vicarious liability were widely seen as key causes of the rise in the number of claims from the 1950s onwards.[103]

Direct Liability of Hospitals?

The more hospitals came to be seen as actively controlling the provision of medical services, the more plausible it became to think of them as not just vicariously responsible for negligent treatment, but directly or 'personally' liable; that is, over and

[99] Medical Defence Union Annual Report, 1947–8 (London: MDU, 1948). See Hawkins, *Mishap or Malpractice?*, n. 62 above, 41.

[100] *Gold* v. *Essex County Council* [1942] 2 KB 293; *Collins* v. *Hertfordshire County Council* [1947] KB 598; *Cassidy* v. *Ministry of Health* [1951] 2 KB 343; *Roe* v. *Minister of Health* [1954] 2 QB 66.

[101] Under the new arrangements for NHS indemnity, see 14–15 above, visiting consultants and agency staff are also expressly covered.

[102] Against 'the State Hospitals' rather than 'Our Hospitals': J. Eddy, *Professional Negligence* (London: Stevens & Sons, 1955), 79.

[103] Ibid. 79–80; cf. P. Addison and P. Baylis, 'The Malpractice Problem in Great Britain', in United States Department of Health, Education and Welfare, *Secretary's Commission on Medical Malpractice* (Washington DC: Department of Health, Education and Welfare, 1972), Report No. SCMM–PA–GB, 854, 859.

above any direct liability they might have had for not providing adequate and competent staff. It was precisely such a primary, non-delegable, duty which Denning LJ asserted when he said that 'hospital authorities are themselves under a duty to use care in treating the patient'.[104] Moreover, a hospital authority's statutory duty to provide medical services to patients[105] has been held to be a primary duty.[106] The potential reach of direct liability for hospitals is apparent from a recent Canadian decision imposing a non-delegable duty to ensure that informed consent[107] is obtained from patients prior to medical treatment being performed.[108] Today we have extensive debate about the setting of priorities in health service provision, and a host of proactive managers and administrators immersed in the planning and delivery of health care. There is accordingly more scope for arguing that the basis on which hospital authorities might be held directly liable for organizational deficiencies should be broadened, a view which has begun to attract greater sympathy in the case law. In *Wilsher*, Browne-Wilkinson LJ said:

In my judgment, a health authority which so conducts its hospital that it fails to provide doctors of sufficient skill and experience to give the treatment offered at the hospital may be directly liable in negligence to the patient. Although we were told in argument that no case has ever been decided on this ground and that it is not the practice to formulate claims in this way, I can see no reason why, in principle, the health authority should not be so liable if its organisation is at fault.[109]

---

[104] *Cassidy*, n. 97 above, 362–3. Cf. 'the hospital undertakes the care, supervision and control of patients who are in special need of care': *Kondis* v. *State Transport Authority* (1984) 58 ALJR 531, 537. And again 'a duty to use reasonable care in treatment' ibid. 536.

[105] See now National Health Service Act 1977, s. 3(1).

[106] *Razzell* v. *Snowball* [1954] 1 WLR 1382.

[107] See Introduction, n. 18 above.

[108] *Lachambre* v. *Nair* [1989] 2 WWR 749. And see *Ellis* v. *Wallsend District Hospital* (1989) 17 NSWLR 553. Cf. J. Bettle, 'Suing Hospitals Direct: Whose Tort was it Anyhow?' (1987) 137 *New Law Journal* 573; J. Montgomery, 'Suing Hospitals Direct: What Tort?' (1987) 137 *New Law Journal* 703; W. Whippy, 'A Hospital's Personal and Non-delegable Duty to Care for Its Patients—Novel Doctrine or Vicarious Liability Disguised?' (1989) 63 *Australian Law Journal* 182.

[109] [1987] QB 730, 778; cf. Glidewell LJ, 775. See further C. Newdick, 'Rights to NHS Resources after the 1990 Act' (1993) 1 *Medical Law Review* 53; J. Montgomery, 'Medicine, Accountability, and Professionalism' (1989) 16 *Journal of Law and Society* 319, especially 331–6.

As Newdick points out, 'the 1990 Act, which establishes an "internal market" for health, creates a system which significantly increases the likelihood of litigation concerning NHS resources'.[110] There had previously been indications that the courts could begin to look more critically at attempts by health authorities to avoid liability on grounds of financial stringency, at least as regards patients who have already been accepted for treatment. Thus, in *Bull* v. *Devon Area Health Authority*, Mustill LJ considered that there might be circumstances in which public medicine could be likened to other public services 'in respect of which it is not necessarily an answer to allegations of unsafety that there were insufficient resources to enable the administrators to do everything which they would like to do'.[111] So, too, in *Knight* v. *Home Office*, Pill J said that 'It is for the court to say what standard of care is appropriate . . . It is not a complete defence for a government department . . . to say that no funds are available for additional safety measures.'[112]

Of course, for the law to scrutinize the organization of hospital practice is very different from impugning the conduct of individual doctors. Indeed, some of the judicial analysis has been prompted by a desire to prevent individual practitioners from being made scapegoats when inordinate demands are made of them, whether in the form of unattainable levels of skill or workload, or because their unit is inadequately equipped. The point was made in terms by Browne-Wilkinson LJ in *Wilsher* v. *Essex Area Health Authority*: 'the law should not be distorted by making findings of personal fault against individual doctors who are, in truth, not at fault in order to avoid such questions'.[113]

The effective removal of legal responsibility from the hospital doctor, with whom the patient may have a personal relationship of sorts, not only makes it psychologically easier for patients to sue but could prompt doctors to encourage them to do so, as allies in their quest for compensation. However, any such support would no doubt be tempered by inhibitions about managerial come-back. If, in addition to greater emphasis on managerial and financial accountability, hospital authorities were to be subjected to closer judicial scrutiny of their procedures, it would be naïve to imagine

---

[110] Above, n. 109.   [111] [1993] 4 Med LR 117, 141 (case decided 1989).
[112] [1990] 3 All ER 237, 243.   [113] See above, n. 109.

that this would not have repercussions for the medical staff who are called upon to implement them. The BMA has estimated that, by 1996, no less than 13 per cent of the total resources available to an average health authority will go towards paying compensation for medical negligence claims.[114] Risk-averse and cost-conscious health service managers, especially in NHS Trust hospitals, which have to bear their own losses from such claims, will be loath to provide treatment of a kind considered either uneconomic or prone to generate litigation, and more inclined to exercise control over the allocation of duties as between particular doctors.

Judicial 'Interventionism'

Though the vast majority of medical actions are either settled or withdrawn, the mere fact that a much larger number than before do reach the courts has presented the judiciary with more opportunities to flesh out established principles and to formulate new ones. Where once there was little judicial involvement with medical practice, and a corresponding dearth of legal authority, now the range of liability is visibly expanding and courts seem to be more willing to scrutinize medical conduct or, to be more precise, the actions and decisions of medical practitioners. For several aspects of the doctor–patient relationship which English judges have begun to probe primarily concern decisions that are not strictly speaking 'medical' in nature, or not centrally so; rather they involve a range of moral, economic, or other considerations that arise in a medical context or in circumstances which have conventionally been regarded as within the province of medicine. The fact that, in keeping with the spirit of medical paternalism, the judgement of doctors about the appropriateness of almost all treatment decisions went largely unchallenged by the courts until well into the 1980s helps to explain doctors' resentment of *any* judicial involvement, and their tendency to interpret it as unwarranted intrusion.

In the course of the 1980s one could detect a distinct change of tone in judicial observations about the obligations of doctors towards their patients. It finds its clearest expression in the difference between the rhetorical stance of Lord Donaldson,

[114] (1991) HC Deb., vol. 184, col. 1234.

Master of the Rolls from 1982 until 1992, and that of his predecessor, Lord Denning. In a number of influential judgments spanning much of the post-War period, Lord Denning had shown himself notoriously reluctant to question medical standards or to find doctors negligent.[115] He laid great stress on the fact that their professional reputation was perpetually at risk. Concerned that fear of being sued would inhibit good medical practice, including the use of innovative techniques, he maintained that it was not in the interests of the community for the courts to scrutinize the conduct of doctors too closely. Since several of these judgments were delivered when he presided over the Court of Appeal, they had the dual effect of discouraging medical litigation and inhibiting the development of legal principle in the sphere of medical liability.[116] Lord Donaldson appeared to convey a very different message. In *Sidaway* v. *Governors of Bethlem Royal Hospital*, the leading decision on the extent of the duty to inform patients about the risks of treatment, he stated that '[the courts] cannot stand idly by if the profession, by an excess of paternalism, denies their patients a real choice. In a word, the law will not permit the medical profession to play God'.[117] In similar vein, he was to say that doctors owe patients a 'duty of candour,' so that when treatment has gone wrong they should explain frankly what happened and advise the patient to take independent medical and legal advice.[118]

In the House of Lords decision in *Sidaway*, Lord Scarman would have incorporated into English law the doctrine of 'informed consent' which prevails in many United States jurisdictions, giving the patient 'an opportunity to evaluate knowledgeably the options available and the risks', at least to the extent that the doctor must disclose such information as would be deemed material by a reasonable person in the patient's position. Though he was

---

[115] e.g. *Roe* v. *Minister of Health*, n. 100 above; *Hatcher* v. *Black*, *The Times*, 2 July 1954; *Davidson* v. *Lloyd Aircraft Services* [1974] 1 WLR 1042; *Whitehouse* v. *Jordan* [1980] 1 All ER 650.

[116] 'Individual senior judges may exert an apparently disproportionate influence on the relationship between the law and medical practice during their limited terms of high office': J. Mason, 'Master of the Balancers; Non-Voluntary Therapy under the Mantle of Lord Donaldson' [1993] *Juridical Review* 115.

[117] [1984] 2 WLR 778, 791.

[118] *Naylor* v. *Preston Area Health Authority* [1987] 1 WLR 958, 967. Cf. *Lee* v. *South West Thames Regional Health Authority* [1985] 1 WLR 845, 850; and see M. Jones, *Medical Negligence* (London: Sweet & Maxwell, 1991), 128–9.

expressing a minority view, Lord Scarman was not alone in emphasizing the importance of patients' rights and *Sidaway*, in drawing attention to the development in other jurisdictions of informed consent, provided a basis for elaborating on the extent of the duty to disclose risks and discuss options. In the field of reproductive medicine, for example, there have been several such cases concerned with failed voluntary sterilization,[119] which had rarely been a source of litigation in the past.

The courts have also become more involved in the complexities of decision-making for patients whose competence is in question. Thus in *Gillick* v. *West Norfolk and Wisbech Area Health Authority and the DHSS*,[120] where it held that children under 16 with sufficient understanding and intelligence to appreciate what is entailed may validly consent to medical procedures, the House of Lords specified the circumstances in which contraceptive advice and treatment may lawfully be given to under-age girls without parental consent. The decision appeared to epitomize a new era of judicial readiness to address the mores of the medical profession, not least in that Mrs Gillick's challenge to the Department of Health and Social Security (DHSS) guidance on contraception was deemed justiciable at all. For there were serious doubts, acknowledged by the House itself, as to the technical propriety of her claim. Given that it raised highly controversial and sensitive issues of social policy, and could in its outcome have exposed the judiciary to the charge of effectively condoning under-age sexual intercourse, it would not have been altogether surprising had the courts declined to adjudicate.

Even if her claim could properly be viewed as having raised an issue of *public law*—in that she was challenging the legal validity of action taken by a public authority—its procedural soundness remains doubtful.[121] The guidance in the DHSS circular on family

---

[119] e.g. *Eyre* v. *Measday* [1986] 1 All ER 488; *Thake* v. *Maurice* [1986] QB 644; *Gold* v. *Haringey Health Authority* [1988] QB 481.

[120] [1986] AC 112.

[121] Mrs Gillick was allowed to bring her action in the form of an ordinary *private law* writ. Yet it seems clear that she was not really seeking to vindicate a private right or some special damage which she had personally suffered (or even anticipated) in respect of her own children. Her essential aim was to establish *as a matter of general principle* that doctors could not prescribe the Pill to girls under 16 without parental consent. It is not however the normal practice of the courts to sanction private actions to establish hypothetical propositions of law.

planning to which Mrs Gillick objected was merely advisory. It
had no statutory force, and it is far from clear that in issuing it the
DHSS was exercising the kind of power which is open to judicial
review.[122] Yet not only did all nine judges involved treat the claim
as justiciable, but the House of Lords proceeded to debate the
substantive issue at considerable length and detailed guidelines
were proffered by Lord Fraser on the conditions under which
doctors could legitimately provide contraceptive advice.

Gillick was decided in 1985, the same year as *Sidaway*. In 1989,
the House of Lords tackled the controversial issue of involuntary
sterilization of the mentally handicapped, again setting out
guidelines for the medical profession. In *Re F*,[123] it conceded that
there was no legal obligation on doctors to seek court approval
before sterilizing a mentally incompetent adult woman at risk of
becoming pregnant. However, the House was at pains to say that
this would be highly desirable as a matter of good practice. 'The
court's jurisdiction', said Lord Bridge, 'should be invoked when-
ever such an operation is proposed to be performed'.[124] In fact,
Lord Griffiths, on grounds of 'public interest', would have
preferred such approval to be mandatory.[125] The House specified
a range of factors to be taken into account and the procedure to be
followed by a doctor or health authority seeking a declaration by a
court that the proposed operation was lawful. Shortly afterwards,
the Official Solicitor was to issue a Practice Note[126] in broadly
similar terms, asserting that 'the sterilization of a minor or a
mentally incompetent adult (the patient) will in virtually all cases
require the prior sanction of a High Court judge'. The procedure
envisaged was to be a summons for directions before a High Court
judge, to be followed by a full adversarial hearing.

In the wake of the House of Lords' holdings in *Gillick* and *Re F*,
courts have adjudicated on a number of highly charged cases
concerning the autonomy rights of seriously ill teenagers and of
mentally handicapped women for whom sterilization has been
proposed. The law would thus appear to have assumed a pivotal
role in declaring how some of the most complex dilemmas
surrounding medical treatment should be resolved. By the early
1990s, courts were issuing guidance on how to reconcile the

---

[122] [1986] AC 112, 192–4, *per* Lord Bridge.   [123] *Re F* [1990] 2 AC 1.
[124] [1990] 2 AC 1, 51.   [125] Ibid. 70.
[126] *Practice Note (Official Solicitor: Sterilization)* [1989] 2 FLR 447.

respective claims of patient autonomy and patient welfare, and pronouncing on the propriety of medical procedures for patients with grave or life-threatening conditions, to an extent scarcely imaginable a mere decade before.[127] It would seem that doctors, and the health authorities or NHS trusts which employ them, increasingly act at their peril in not seeking prior judicial authorization.

Moreover, it is not just the courts with which they have to contend. When doctors complain of legal interventionism, it is normally the role of the courts that they have in mind, but the law is currently making its presence felt in medicine by other means. Of major significance has been the fundamental reorganization of the health care delivery system, within a legislative framework signalling tighter management and more medical accountability as key objectives, as well as adding substantially to the administrative workload of doctors.[128] Important statutory developments of general application in the areas of consumer and data protection are also beginning to impose additional burdens on them, partly as a consequence of European Community legislation. More specifically, the legislature has at times intervened directly in medical practice, for example by restricting the range of drugs which doctors may prescribe under the National Health Service[129] and by introducing indicative drug budgets for individual practices.[130] And in view of recent and prospective advances in biomedicine, there have been legislative changes and continued pressure for stricter statutory controls in respect of medical experimentation, as concern persists over the legitimacy of certain types of research and the way some trials are conducted.[131]

---

[127] See, further, ch. 4.

[128] i.e. the creation of an 'internal market' under the National Health Service and Community Care Act 1990, which made provision for NHS contracts, NHS trusts, and fund-holding practices. The 1990 Act comprises both new provisions and amendments to the National Health Service Act 1977, which had consolidated the National Health Service Acts 1946 to 1976.

[129] National Health Service (General Medical and Pharmaceutical Services) Amendment Regulations 1985 (No 290).

[130] National Health Service and Community Care Act 1990, s. 18; National Health Service (Indicative Amounts) Regulations, SI 1991 No 556.

[131] Human Fertilisation and Embryology Act 1990. In 1991, the Nuffield Council on Bioethics was established to examine these issues. See, e.g. Nuffield Council on Bioethics, *Genetic Screening: Ethical Issues* (London: Nuffield Council on Bioethics, 1993).

THE LIMITED DESIGNS AND IMPACT OF LAW ON MEDICINE

It is thus not difficult to see why doctors might perceive the law, if not necessarily as an 'insatiable cormorant', as more than mere sporadic predator. In so far as this perception relates to what the courts do, it is misconceived. On all the issues which we have just addressed, medical negligence, competence, and consent to treatment, as well as health policy at the macro-level, the instincts of the judiciary and their actual decisions reveal a marked preference for leaving the medical world to its own devices. At the heart of all this is the '*Bolam* test',[132] and much of what follows is about how its application and influence in the medical sphere have served to buttress the paternalistic tradition in medical practice. Though it might appear that we have entered a new era of judicial interventionism in medical affairs, we would do well to suspend judgement about both the extent and likely effects of such intervention. Recent inroads into clinical freedom in matters of health care provision are more attributable to legislation than to the courts, and though some statutory developments undoubtedly have an effect on the way doctors treat patients, Parliament has rarely sought to interfere directly in medical relationships and dictate the terms. As far as the civil liability of the medical profession is concerned, over many centuries it has been the law's lack of engagement with medicine which is most noteworthy.

Medical Negligence

English law has to an unusual degree been content to let doctors set their own standards for treatment and determine unilaterally what decisions are within the remit of 'medical judgement'.[133] Most cases are decided in negligence and the touchstone of medical negligence is the failure to exercise the care of the ordinary, competent medical practitioner professing skill in the relevant field. Whether or not a doctor has fallen below that standard is almost invariably attested to, and for most practical

---

[132] *Bolam* v. *Friern Hospital Management Committee* [1957] 1 WLR 582. See xvii above and chs. 5 and 6 below.

[133] Cf. D. Giesen, 'Vindicating the Patient's Rights' (1993) 9 *Journal of Contemporary Health Law and Policy* 273.

purposes determined by, *medical* opinion. A doctor who has acted 'in accordance with a practice accepted as proper by a responsible body of medical men skilled in [the] particular art' is not negligent.[134] It is in this respect that the basis of liability in medical negligence appears to part company with the general principle that negligence consists in falling below the standard of care which the law deems reasonable in the circumstances.[135] The 'accepted medical practice' or '*Bolam*' test is, in the words of Lord Scarman, 'a totally medical proposition erected into a working rule of law'.[136] As a member of the Medical Defence Union Council recently put it:

The paranoia of surgeons may lead them to believe that the law is a predator which has created its own unrealistic ethical standards. This is not so . . . it is the natural and gradual evolution of ethical standards in medicine which has led to standards which are acceptable to the courts. This is so particularly in legal systems which depend largely upon 'case law' rather than upon 'statute law'. Since the courts will inevitably be guided by medical evidence, factual or expert, the medical profession plays a large part in the evolution of case law.[137]

The relatively undemanding nature of the *Bolam* test is apparent from the willingness of English courts to condone diagnostic practices and methods of treatment which have obtained only a modicum of acceptance within the medical profession and which may be widely regarded as inferior or outmoded.[138] As confirmed by the House of Lords in *Maynard* v. *West Midlands Regional Health Authority*, courts are not entitled to impose liability because of a preference for one 'body of competent professional opinion' over another.[139] When one adds to this the relative lack of rigour in determining what counts as a 'respectable body of professional opinion', it can be seen that the defendant is typically at a distinct advantage.

---

[134] *Bolam* v. *Friern Hospital Management Committee* [1957] 1 WLR 582, 586.
[135] See further ch. 5, below.
[136] 'Law and Medical Practice' in P. Byrne (ed.), *Medicine in Contemporary Society* (London: King Edward's Hospital Fund for London, 1987), 134.
[137] J. Garfield, 'Ethico-Legal Aspects of High-Risk Neurosurgery', *Journal of the Medical Defence Union* 8 (1992), 76, reproduced from *Acta Neurochirurgica* (Vienna) 118 (1992), 2–6.
[138] See e.g. *Robinson* v. *Post Office* [1974] 1 WLR 1176.
[139] [1984] 1 WLR 634, 638.

In the medical sphere, expert evidence on what suffices as accepted practice has been treated as more legally conclusive than in commercial[140] or, it would seem, other professional contexts.[141] Normally such evidence is admissible only to indicate what *constitutes* an accepted practice, conformity with which may or may not be deemed by the court to rule out negligence. In medical cases such conformity will almost invariably preclude liability. In theory, the courts reserve the right to decide that a diagnosis or treatment has fallen below the requisite standard; in practice they very rarely conclude that this has happened, though naturally the more egregious the error the less likely is it to be fully litigated.

Even as regards the ambit of the doctor's duty to disclose risks, where considerations other than those calling for a purely clinical judgement can be crucial, judges are unusually reluctant to take issue with professional opinion. In *Sidaway*, Browne-Wilkinson LJ observed that where a consulting engineer was aware of material risks, the duty to disclose them 'would be determined by the general law, not by the standard of the profession',[142] but that 'in relation to doctors the duty to disclose should be approached on a different basis from that applicable to ordinary professional men'.[143] In medicine, 'all questions of disclosure will be decided by reference to the practice of the profession', subject only to evidence of the plaintiff's circumstances having been taken into account.[144]

When one bears in mind the range of acceptable procedures for many conditions, the scope for variation within procedures, and the range of medical opinion and practice as regards information disclosure, the scale of the task facing many plaintiffs becomes apparent. Though a misplaced sense of loyalty to the profession on

---

[140] The difference of approach has been more marked in the English courts, though not confined to them: cf. A. Linden, 'Custom in Negligence Law' (1968) 11 *Canadian Bar Journal* 151, 157: 'Evidence of general practice is accorded more respect in medical matters than it receives in other types of cases because there is greater judicial trust in the reasonableness of the practices of a sister profession than there is in the methods of commercial men'.

[141] Contrast the approach taken in *Thompson* v. *Smiths Shiprepairers (North Shields) Ltd* [1984] QB 405 (industrial practice); *Corisand Investments Ltd* v. *Druce & Co.* (1978) 248 EG 315 (surveyors); *Lloyds Bank* v. *E. B. Savory & Co.* [1933] AC 201 (bankers), and *Edward Wong Finance Co Ltd* v. *Johnson Stokes & Master* [1984] AC 1296 (solicitors). See R. Buckley, *The Modern Law of Negligence* (London: Butterworths, 1988), 283–4.   [142] [1984] 2 WLR 778, 799.

[143] Ibid. 799–800.   [144] Ibid. 800.

the part of experts may not influence their attitude to the extent that it once did,[145] plaintiffs can take no comfort from the relative ease with which medical experts can usually be found to attest that the doctor's conduct attained the level of *an* acceptable practice. In England, unlike some other EC jurisdictions, no specified qualification is required for acting as a medical expert. This encourages the parties to indulge in the dubious activity of 'shopping around' until a sympathetic expert is found, a practice more likely to be feasible for the defence, as most plaintiffs are legally aided and frequently restricted to a single expert's opinion. It is of interest that, as recently as 1992, the eminent consultant and medico-legal authority, Nigel Harris, observed:

My experience in trauma and orthopaedic negligence claims for which I receive instructions in over 300 cases a year, leads me to believe that the Bolam test strongly favours the Defence. It may well have been appropriate when medicine and particularly surgery was much less complex and sophisticated than it is today.

There is good evidence from experienced medical experts that deserving Plaintiffs lose their claims—not so much on the facts and their interpretation, but because unfortunately there is a minority of expert witnesses who are willing to say that they would support the doctor's action and that what was done is accepted practice. Enquiry will often indicate that the expert's evidence is not supported by his own clinical practice; nevertheless his evidence is generally accepted by the court without question.[146]

Harris makes the interesting suggestion that, during the pre-trial exchange of medical reports, defence experts should be required to give evidence from their own practice in support of their opinion. Failure to do so might then be taken into account by the court when seeking to determine whether the doctor's practice was, in Lord Donaldson's words, '*rightly* accepted as proper'.[147]

In fact, Lord Donaldson's own superficially strong disavowal of medical paternalism in *Sidaway*—'the law will not permit the medical profession to play God'—was substantially qualified. Describing the content and manner of information disclosure as 'very much a matter for professional judgement', he also appeared

---

[145] See *Rahman* v. *Kirklees Area Health Authority* [1980] 1 WLR 1244, 1246–7.
[146] 'Medical Negligence Litigation: The Need for Reform' (1992) 60 *Medico-Legal Journal* 205, 206.
[147] *Sidaway* v. *Bethlem Royal Hospital* [1984] 2 WLR 778, 792.

to assume, without more, that the doctor was best placed to judge the patient's 'true wishes'. On appeal, though (Lord Scarman apart) the Law Lords formally preserved the Court's role as ultimate arbiter, they reasserted the primacy of the *Bolam* test in its essentials and expressly rejected the doctrine of informed consent. Subsequent Court of Appeal decisions have reiterated the orthodox approach, if anything extending its reach. The *Bolam* test has been held to apply just as much to disclosure of risks in the non-therapeutic context of voluntary sterilization as to therapeutic procedures.[148] It has also been said to govern situations where the patient asks for information.[149] As it operates in practice, and as uniquely applied to the medical profession, the test hardly seems to justify allegations of undue interventionism on the part of the courts.[150]

The Courts and Consent to Treatment: Non-Interventionism

The courts have shown a not dissimilar reluctance to question medical judgement as regards the competence of patients to consent to treatment, whether they be under-age children or adults who are either clearly incapable of making decisions about treatment, or whose capacity to do so is in question. In these circumstances, too, medical perceptions of the patient's best interests are often decisive. Despite occasional dicta which might convey a contrary impression, this is one of the underlying themes of *Gillick*, *Re F*, and many other relevant cases decided in the last few years.

Thus, though the case has proved to be a source of substantial and continuing controversy,[151] *Gillick* did confirm that there are circumstances in which doctors have a discretion to give contraceptive advice and treatment to under-age children without the consent or knowledge of their parents. Moreover, the scope for exercising that discretion is considerable. It is true that Lord Fraser and, to a lesser extent, Lord Scarman purported to lay

---

[148] *Gold* v. *Haringey Health Authority* [1988] QB 481.

[149] Possibly even when a quite specific request is made: *Blyth* v. *Bloomsbury Area Health Authority* [1993] 4 Med LR 151 (case decided 1987).

[150] See further, Ch. 6.

[151] For Lord Donaldson's controversial interpretation of *Gillick* regarding refusal of treatment by a competent child see Ch. 4 below.

down specific criteria for doctors to apply in determining when a child is competent to consent independently to such treatment. But in practice, hard-pressed GPs and family planning clinic staff commonly fail to explore the maturity and understanding of young patients with the thoroughness envisaged by a judgment with which few of them will have more than a passing familiarity.[152] Though stressing that his judgment was not to be read as giving doctors a free hand to disregard the wishes of parents, Lord Fraser concluded that the only practicable course was 'to entrust the doctor with a discretion to act in accordance with his view of what is best in the interests of the girl who is his patient'.[153] Lord Scarman said that the doctor would 'have to satisfy himself' that she had 'sufficient maturity to understand what is involved'.[154] The net result is that where the doctor is unable to persuade a girl to involve her parents, the doctor's 'clinical' judgement is all but dispositive.[155]

On one level, then, not unlike *Sidaway*, *Gillick* signified a vindication of clinical freedom; it symbolized the primacy of the 'doctor's right' to exercise judgement and discretion over the alleged 'parental right' to prior consultation. Anticipating the criticism that his view would 'leave the law in the hands of the doctors', Lord Scarman said:

I accept that great responsibilities will lie on the medical profession. It is, however, a learned and highly trained profession regulated by statute and governed by a strict ethical code which is vigorously enforced . . . The truth may well be that the rights of parents and children in this sensitive area are better protected by the professional standards of the medical profession than by 'a priori' legal lines of division between capacity and lack of capacity to consent.[156]

In the event, the propriety of the DHSS guidance was endorsed and Lord Scarman, in common with Lord Fraser, conceded the

---

[152] See Institute of Population Studies, *Sexual Health and Family Planning Services in General Practice* (London: Family Planning Association, 1993).

[153] *Gillick* v. *West Norfolk and Wisbech Area Health Authority and Department of Health and Social Security* [1986] AC 112, 174.

[154] Ibid. 189.

[155] In the words of one commentator, 'It is one thing for the courts to overrule a parent's decision . . . It is another matter for the House of Lords to take power away from parents and give it to doctors without any real means of reviewing a doctor's discretion': P. Parkinson, 'The Gillick Case—Just What Has It Decided' (1986) 16 *Family Law* 11, 14.   [156] [1986] AC 112, 191.

practical limitations of the law in this sensitive area. They observed that such control over medical judgement as was attainable was more likely to be derived from professional expectations and the disciplinary authority of the General Medical Council (GMC). However, there has been considerable dissatisfaction with the Council's performance and priorities as a disciplinary body. Critics point to its overwhelmingly medical composition, convoluted screening procedures, lack of an inspectorate or investigating unit, and apparent reluctance to assume powers to deal effectively with cases involving inadequate professional performance not amounting to serious professional misconduct.[157] Moreover, it is a body with which the courts have for long been singularly loath to interfere, adding a further layer to judicial unwillingness to regulate the profession.[158] Only in the most tenuous and formalistic of senses could *Gillick* itself be characterized as a case of judges dictating medical behaviour.

In *Re F*, as in *Gillick*, the nature of the House of Lords' involvement was also more formal than real. In the first place, though the House considered it desirable, as a matter of good practice, that doctors seek court authorization before sterilizing mentally-handicapped adult women for non-therapeutic purposes, it did not make it mandatory. The Official Solicitor's Practice Note

---

[157] See J. Robinson, *A Patient Voice at the GMC: A Lay Member's View of the General Medical Council* (London: Health Rights Report, 1988); M. Stacey, 'Medical Accountability: A Background Paper' in A. Grubb (ed.), *Challenges in Medical Care* (Chichester: John Wiley & Sons, 1992), 109; R. Smith, 'Profile of the GMC: Discipline II: The Preliminary Screener—A Powerful Gatekeeper', *British Medical Journal* 298 (1989), 1632. Some of these criticisms are currently being addressed. See further Ch. 7.

[158] 'the jurisdiction of the domestic tribunal which has been clothed by the Legislature with the duty of discipline in respect of a great profession must be left untouched by Courts of Law': *Leeson* v. *General Council of Medical Education and Registration* (1890) 43 Ch 366, *per* Bowen LJ. Cf. 'the Medical Acts have always entrusted the supervision of the medical advisers' conduct to a committee of the profession, for they know and appreciate better than anyone else the standards which responsible medical opinion demands of its own profession': *McCoan* v. *GMC* [1964] 3 All ER 143, 147 *per* Lord Upjohn. See also D. Feldman, 'Public Law Values in the House of Lords' (1990) 106 *Law Quarterly Review* 246, 256–8, and J. Montgomery, n. 109 above, 320–1. Similarly, it has been held that the BMA's ethical code is not justiciable: *Cox* v. *Green* [1966] 1 All ER 268, and that the courts should be slow to intervene to compel an Ethical Committee to investigate or advise on a problem: *R* v. *Ethical Committee of St Mary's Hospital, ex parte Harriott* [1988] 1 FLR 512. See also *Colman* v. *GMC* [1989] 1 Med LR 23.

on procedure in such cases is at most advisory. Moreover, *J* v. *C*[159] indicated that in apparently 'straightforward' cases and where there is 'a real degree of urgency' the matter may be disposed of at the initial summons for directions, without a subsequent full hearing,[160] prompting the claim that 'Thorpe J has in fact opened the door to sterilisations on convenience grounds'.[161] Later cases have decided that court involvement is not even desirable or good practice when the procedure is 'medically indicated' or 'therapeutic'.[162]

The residual significance of *Re F* as an exercise of judicial authority was diminished by the readiness to rely on the *Bolam* test to decide whether the operation was in the 'best interests' of the patient. In Lord Bridge's words, 'if the professionals in question have acted with due skill and care, judged by the well known test laid down in *Bolam* . . . they should be immune from liability'.[163] That in a matter of such fundamental social and individual concern as sterilization, 'best interests' should be determined by reference to a relatively undemanding medical criterion of whether a doctor has acted negligently is indicative of the extent to which courts will defer to 'clinical freedom'.[164] A few years later, the same test was to be utilized in the case of Anthony Bland to decide on the legitimacy of ending life itself.[165]

'Treatment in the "*best*" interests" of the patient' sounds like a very reassuring criterion; deceptively so, when one appreciates that it can be satisfied by a medical judgement which the court and even the preponderance of expert medical opinion would have rejected.[166] It was precisely this concern which had led all three members of the Court of Appeal in *Re F* to reject the *Bolam* test as not 'sufficiently stringent' for deciding whether or not to authorize operations on incompetent adults. Instead they would have defined 'best interests' by reference to the general body of medical

---

[159] [1990] 3 All ER 735.

[160] The Practice Note was amended accordingly: [1990] 2 FLR 530.

[161] J. Shaw, 'Regulating Sexuality: A Legislative Framework for Non-Consensual Sterilisation' in S. McVeigh and S. Wheeler (eds.), *Law, Health and Medical Regulation* (Aldershot: Dartmouth, 1992), 85.

[162] See 142 below.   [163] [1990] 2 AC 1, 52.

[164] See I. Kennedy, 'Patients, Doctors and Human Rights,' in R. Blackburn and J. Taylor (eds.), *Human Rights for the 1990s* (London: Mansell, 1991), 81, 88–108.

[165] *Airedale NHS Trust* v. *Bland* [1993] AC 789. And see *Official Solicitor to the Supreme Court—Practice Note on Persistent Vegetative State* [1994] 1 FLR 654.

[166] *Maynard* v. *West Midlands Regional Health Authority* [1984] 1 WLR 634.

opinion in the particular specialty.[167] However, the House of Lords unanimously reaffirmed the applicability of the *Bolam* test, content in Carson's telling phrase, that this group of people 'could have their *best* interests restated as merely the right not to have others make negligent decisions in relation to them'.[168] For good measure, Lord Brandon also asserted that, at common law, the 'best interests' principle permits doctors to treat adult patients incapable (for whatever reason) of giving consent, in order 'to ensure improvement or prevent deterioration in their physical or mental health'.[169] This formulation provides rather more scope for medical intervention without consent than earlier cases, which had only clearly sanctioned emergency treatment necessary to save the life or preserve the health of the patient.

If the courts are disinclined to intervene when doctors wish to treat, they categorically rule out ordering (as distinct from authorizing) them to do so. In *Re J (A Minor) (Child in Care: Medical Treatment)*,[170] the local authority responsible for a severely brain-damaged child obtained an interim order which would have required the health authority to provide artificial ventilation if needed to prolong his life. The order was granted despite the doctors' clinical judgement that his prospects of life were so poor that it was not in his best interests to undergo the additional stress and pain involved. The Court of Appeal, in unanimously setting aside the order, could hardly have been more emphatic. Leggatt LJ said that he could 'envisage no circumstances in which it would be right directly or indirectly to require a doctor to treat a patient in a way that was contrary to the doctor's professional judgement and duty to the patient'.[171] Balcombe LJ could 'conceive of no situation where it would be a proper exercise of the [court's] jurisdiction';[172] and in the view of Lord Donaldson MR,[173] it would be 'an abuse of power as directly or indirectly [i.e.

---

[167] In *T* v. *T*, Wood J. went further still, suggesting that treatment should be authorized only 'where based on good medical practice there are really no two views of what course is for the best': [1988] 1 All ER 613, 621.

[168] D. Carson, 'The Sexuality of People with Learning Difficulties' [1989] *Journal of Social Welfare Law* 355.

[169] *Re F (Mental Patient: Sterilization)* [1990] 2 AC 1, 55.

[170] [1992] 3 WLR 507.   [171] Ibid. 520.   [172] Ibid. 518.

[173] Who had made the same point, *semble obiter*, in *Re J (A Minor) (Child in Care: Medical Treatment)* [1991] Fam 33 and in *Re R (A Minor) (Wardship: Consent to Treatment)* [1991] 3 WLR 592.

through the health authority] requiring the practitioner to act contrary to the fundamental duty which he owes to his patient . . . to treat the patient in accordance with his own best clinical judgement'.[174]

Clearly, as well as the practical problems which would arise were the courts to compel doctors to treat, there are profound ethical issues at stake. Counsel for the health authority in *Re J* argued that to make such an order would be 'a challenge to the fundamental relationship that should or ought to exist between patient and doctor'. For present purposes it is the categorical tone of the judgments in deferring to the clinial judgement of the individual doctor concerned which is important.[175] Subsequent decisions such as *Re S*[176] and *Bland*[177] also demonstrate just how pronounced judicial reluctance to take issue with professional medical judgement can be.

When the judges stress the value of court authorization for medical procedures, they often appear to be more concerned with appearances and assuaging public concern than with the desire to exercise substantive control. In some instances they have voiced a positive distaste for their role. In *Bland*, Lord Mustill said, 'I have felt serious doubts about whether this question is justiciable, not in the technical sense, but in the sense of being a proper subject for legal adjudication',[178] and Lord Browne-Wilkinson observed that 'In the past, doctors exercised their own discretion, in accordance with medical ethics, in cases such as these. *To the great advantage of society*, they took the responsibility of deciding whether the perpetuation of life was pointless.'[179] As things now stand, there is a certain arbitrariness about the way that PVS and certain sterilization procedures have been singled out as belonging to a 'special category' for which court involvement is deemed desirable. In *Re F* there was some suggestion that other procedures such as abortion and organ donation might be subject to similar scrutiny. It is of interest that the Law Commission has recently

[174] See n. 170 above, 516.

[175] One might add that Lord Donaldson was equally concerned that health authorities should not be subject to undue judicial control. Ibid.

[176] [1992] 3 WLR 806: court-authorized caesarian. See Ch. 4, below.

[177] [1993] AC 789: persistent vegetative state. Cf. *Frenchay Healthcare NHS Trust* v. *S* [1994] 1 WLR 601, where the Court of Appeal's decision that treatment could be withheld was arguably precipitate and unduly influenced by the medical evidence recommending that it be discontinued.

[178] Ibid. 891.   [179] Ibid. 880, emphasis added.

proposed the establishment of a 'judicial forum' to authorize
treatment, or its withdrawal, in difficult or disputed cases.[180] At a
time of growing pressure for more efficient dispatch of court cases,
any judicial desire to preserve a largely formal role on decision-
making in matters of life or death is tempered by the realization
that the courts could easily become inundated. In the leading
United States case of *Saikewicz*,[181] 'a Massachusetts court seemed
to imply that all termination of treatment cases required judicial
approval. But after a brief experiment in which judges found
themselves interrupted and awakened by frequent and insistent
demands to rule on one case or another, a second Massachusetts
court quickly overruled the lower court.' [182]

'Clinical' Judgement

As further evidence of judicial reluctance to dispute the effective
authority of the medical profession, cases like *Sidaway*, *Gillick*,
and *Re F* and, for that matter, *Bland*, are notable for the tendency
to assume that decisions taken by medical practitioners are *ipso
facto medical* decisions. They are often either designated 'clinical'
decisions or it is simply accepted that they are naturally within the
doctor's province. But several key questions surrounding such
matters as disclosure of risks, the provision of contraceptive advice
and treatment, the appropriateness or otherwise of sterilization
and withdrawal of artificial feeding are only marginally, if at all,
related to medical expertise.[183] In *Bland*, Lord Goff said that there
was 'overwhelming evidence that, in the medical profession,
artificial feeding is regarded as a form of medical treatment; and
even if it is not strictly medical treatment, it must form part of the
medical care of the patient'.[184] Defining the form of feeding in this
question-begging way[185] enabled the Court to characterize its

---

[180] The Law Commission, *Mentally Incapacitated Adults and Decision-Making:
Medical Treatment and Research* (London: HMSO, 1993), part IV, 68–83.
    [181] *Superintendent of Belchertown State School* v. *Saikewicz*, 370 NE 2d 417
(1977).   [182] Zussman, n. 6 above, 176.
    [183] Cf. J. Keown, *Abortion, Doctors and the Law* (Cambridge: Cambridge
University Press, 1988), showing how the concept of 'therapy' has been exploited to
assimilate human activities within the medical profession's domain.
    [184] [1993] AC 789.
    [185] Cf. 'the application of a medical technique': ibid., *per* Lord Keith. Though
Lord Browne-Wilkinson noted that 'Within the medical profession itself, there are

withdrawal as a technical professional judgement of what was in the patient's best interests, rather than as murder by starvation. By such means, the profound social and moral issues raised by the case, though not remaindered,[186] perhaps featured less prominently and openly in the judgments than was merited by the gravity of the decision to be made. In his revealing study of the dynamics of treatment in intensive care units, Zussman demonstrates how in dealing with the wishes of patients and their families, doctors become adept at 'moving decisions from the realm of values to the realm of technique'.[187] However well motivated, these 'claims for the domain of the technical are, at the very least, convenient, for they allow physicians to reconcile two otherwise irreconcilable values. They allow physicians to acknowledge the rights of patients in matters of values while, at the same time, preserving their own ability to make decisions.'[188]

As regards contraceptive advice for under-age girls, Lord Fraser observed that:

The medical profession have in modern times come to be entrusted with very wide discretionary powers going beyond the strict limits of clinical judgement and there is nothing strange about entrusting them with this further responsibility which they alone are in a position to discharge satisfactorily.[189]

In similar vein, Lord Scarman has said that '*Gillick* . . . indicates, within a very different context from *Sidaway*, how medical practice now requires, as a matter of law, that doctors should concern themselves with values and rules outside the limits of clinical judgement'.[190] Plainly, the impetus and scope for active judicial regulation of medical conduct are much reduced if one defines the doctor's remit in such broad terms and, at the same

those, including one of the very distinguished doctors who gave evidence in this case, who draw a distinction between withholding treatment on the one hand and withholding food and care on the other, the latter not being acceptable': (ibid. 381–2).

[186] See especially the judgment of Hoffman LJ in the Court of Appeal: [1993] 2 WLR 316, 349.　　　　　　　　　　　　[187] *Intensive Care*, n. 6 above, 141.
[188] Ibid. 152.
[189] *Gillick* v.*West Norfolk & Wisbech Area Health Authority* [1986] AC 112, 174.
[190] Extra-judicially: 'Law and Medical Practice' in Byrne (ed.), *Medicine in Contemporary Society*, n. 136 above, 138–9.

time, regards any contravention of judicial guidelines as more
appropriately dealt with by the GMC than by the courts.

Reluctance to Interfere with Health Policy

In the prevailing climate of health care delivery, increasing resort
to the courts might be anticipated from patients challenging health
policies determined at a national or local level, either by way of
judicial review, or alternatively by seeking redress directly from an
institutional provider. As policy decisions about the allocation of
resources are made more explicit and attract greater publicity,
they are more likely to be challenged over a wide range of issues—
if, for example, priority is inappropriately accorded to particular
kinds of treatment, or to the patients of fund-holding GPs, or if a
hospital bowing to commercial pressure ceases to provide a
'comprehensive service'.[191] Were the courts to act on the
occasional hints that they might scrutinize more closely the way
health authorities deploy their resources, it would naturally have
important policy implications for hospitals and would lead to
further allegations of judicial interference in medical practice.

By definition, the role of the courts in litigation is reactive,
though, of course, judicial decisions and pronouncements may
encourage people to sue. Judges respond to the claims of litigants
and their legal advisers; they do not initiate them. Moreover, it
should be borne in mind that some litigation of the kind referred to
above has been instigated or encouraged by doctors. On several
occasions surgeons have themselves advised patients to seek the
assistance of the courts, to contest delay or denial of treatment
resulting from a health authority's priorities in the allocation of
resources. In such circumstances the judges have been conspicu-
ously reluctant to intervene and have expressed their reluctance in
no uncertain terms. This was graphically demonstrated in 1987,
when a health authority decided that it could not immediately
provide urgently needed heart surgery for two babies. In both
cases, not only was the parents' application for judicial review
firmly rejected, but it was made clear that the courts had no
intention of investigating the authority's options or the reasons for

---

[191] See C. Newdick, 'Rights to NHS Resources after the 1990 Act' (1993) 1
Medical Law Review 53.

their decisions. Judicial review was to be used 'extremely sparingly'.[192] 'The courts of this country', it was said, 'cannot arrange the lists in the hospital'.[193] The court 'has no role of general investigator of social policy and of allocation of resources'.[194] This stance reflects the conception of judicial review in English law as fundamentally concerned with procedural fairness as distinct from the merits of substantive decision-making, and in particular the resistance to detailed analysis of policy decisions taken by public bodies in allocating scarce resources.[195] In the absence of *prima facie* evidence of unreasonableness to the point of irrationality, the courts are most reluctant to intervene on matters of substance.[196] As regards health care provision, the tone had been set in the late 1970s by the leading case concerned with policy at national level. Patients waiting for orthopaedic surgery, encouraged by their doctors, sought a declaration and damages, claiming that the Secretary of State had not fulfilled his duty to provide a comprehensive service. It was held that his duty to maintain 'a comprehensive health service . . . to such extent as he considers necessary to meet all reasonable requirements' was impliedly subject to the availability of resources.[197]

In the longer term, it is possible that the resistance to substantive judicial review of such decisions will diminish. There are signs that several senior members of the judiciary are troubled by the lack of room for manœuvre that the principle of '*Wednesbury* unreasonableness'[198] allows them when policy

---

[192] *R.* v. *Central Birmingham Health Authority, ex parte Walker, R.* v. *Secretary of State for Social Services, ex parte Walker* (1992) 3 BMLR 32, 36 *per* Lord Donaldson MR (case decided 1987).

[193] *R* v. *Central Birmingham Health Authority, ex parte Collier* (CA 1988, unreported), *per* Brown LJ.

[194] Ibid. *per* Gibson LJ. Cf. *R.* v. *Central Birmingham Health Authority, ex parte Walker, R.* v. *Secretary of State for Social Services ex parte Walker*, n. 192 above; *R.* v. *Ethical Committee of St. Mary's Hospital, ex parte Harriott* [1988] 1 FLR 512.

[195] *Rowling* v. *Takaro* [1988] AC 473, 501, *per* Lord Keith. Cf. *Ross* v. *Secretary of State for Scotland* [1990] 1 Med LR 235, 240, *per* Lord Milligan.

[196] *Associated Provincial Picture Houses Ltd* v. *Wednesbury Corporation* [1948] 1 KB 223, 229, *per* Lord Greene MR. Cf. R. Jackson and J. Powell, *Professional Negligence* (3rd edn.) (London: Sweet & Maxwell, 1992), 493. See, further, D. Longley, *Public Law and Health Service Accountability* (Buckingham: Open University Press, 1993), 81 ff.; F. Miller, 'Informed Consent in English and American Law' (1992) 18 *American Journal of Law and Medicine* 37, 46–8.

[197] *R* v. *Secretary of State for Social Services, ex parte Hincks* (1992) 1 BMLR 93, 95, *per* Lord Denning MR (case decided 1980).

[198] See text at n. 196 above.

decisions of Ministers and governmental bodies are challenged.[199] There has been growing talk of the merits of the 'proportionality' test, recognized under EC law, whereby substantive decisions of public authorities can be quashed when, though not wholly irrational, they are adjudged to interfere with fundamental rights by means of a disproportionate response in the particular circumstances.[200] One might, for example, envisage such an approach being adopted when a hospital authority pursued a resource allocation policy that was rational in terms of the profitability of the enterprise, but which deprived patients of previously available and beneficial forms of treatment.

However, that day still seems a long way off. In *Re J*, Lord Donaldson said that 'The court when considering what course to adopt in relation to a particular child has no knowledge of competing claims to a health authority's resources and is in no position to express a view as to how it should elect to deploy them'.[201] This reluctance to intervene stems in part from a concern not to encroach on what most judges instinctively feel is not their terrain. The issues involve questions of policy on which they are not self-evidently well qualified to pronounce. They operate within a legal analytical framework which is unsuited to the purpose, and they cannot relish the invidious and exacting task of determining whether or not heroic treatment should be continued, which is effectively what many of the cases are about. In *Re J*, for example, Leggatt LJ felt moved to state that 'since our decision was announced it has been rendered in headlines such as "Court gives doctors right to refuse life support". But the reality is that the court has not given to doctors any right that they did not

---

[199] D. Rose, 'Silent Revolution', *Observer*, 9 May 1993.

[200] e.g. 'We should apply differential standards in judicial review according to the subject-matter, and to do so deploy the tool of proportionality, not the bludgeon of *Wednesbury*': Sir J. Laws J, 'Is the High Court the Guardian of Fundamental Constitutional Rights?' [1993] *Public Law* 59, at 78, and see 71–5. See also, J. Jowell and A. Lester, 'Beyond *Wednesbury*: Substantive Principles of Judicial Review' [1987] *Public Law* 369; Lord Mackenzie Stuart, 'Recent Developments in English Administrative Law—The Impact of Europe' in F. Capotorti *et al.* (eds.), *Du Droit International au Droit de l'Integration: Liber Amicorum Pierre Pescatore* (Baden-Baden: Nomos, 1987), 411.

[201] *Re J (A Minor)(Child in Care: Medical Treatment)* [1992] 3 WLR 507, 517; cf. Balcombe LJ, 519. See also *R. v. North West Thames Regional Health Authority* [1993] 4 Med LR 364.

previously have: it has merely declined to deprive them of a power which it is for them alone to exercise'.[202]

We have argued that the judiciary has been no more disposed to challenge the policies of health authorities than the decisions of individual doctors. Where the two are in conflict in a case which reaches court, it is in the nature of the *Bolam* test that the doctor's view will be deemed to prevail over that of the authority. This is so because, as we have seen, actions involving hospital doctors are almost invariably resolved on the basis of the authority's vicarious liability for the conduct of individual doctors, as itself determined by the test. Precisely because of the extent to which the courts have countenanced the Hippocratic view that the doctor's over-riding duty is to the individual patient, cases like *Bland* can proceed on the unreal assumption that resources are unlimited, just as the doctor's clinical-cum-value judgement of the 'best interests' of a profoundly handicapped child[203] would legally take precedence over hospital policy.

In the wider debate outside the courts, the plight of Tony Bland stimulated considerable discussion about the resourcing implications of treating the patient who is 'a passive prisoner of medical technology'.[204] There was much reference in the press to the Do Not Resuscitate (DNR) orders which are a daily occurrence in hospitals. It was pointed out that the cost of treating patients in a persistent vegetative state was more than £2,000 a week and that an estimated 1,000 or more such patients were being kept alive for years[205] at a cost of some £20 million per annum. These are disturbing figures leading to unpalatable considerations. If there was a consensus that in the harrowing circumstances of the particular case a compassionate and humane decision was arrived at, there was also much soul-searching, as well as the predictable vitriol of a committed minority for whom the decision 'paves the

---

[202] *Re J*, 520.
[203] *Re J*. Cf. the debate on selective treatment in cases of severe spina bifida: J. Lorber, 'Ethical Problems in the Management of Myelomeningocele and Hydrocephalus', *Journal of the Royal College of Physicians* 10 (1975), 47; cf. R. Zachary, 'Life with Spina Bifida', *British Medical Journal* 2 (1977), 1460.
[204] *Cruzan* v. *Director, Missouri Dept. of Health* 110 S Ct 2841, 2864 (1990) *per* Brennan J.
[205] 'Some survive for 10, 20 or even 30 years': B. Jennett, 'The Persistent Vegetative State: Medical, Ethical and Legal Issues' in Grubb (ed.), *Choices and Decisions in Health Care* n. 78 above, 139.

way to "medical cleansing" of the long-stay wards'.[206] As Bland's consultant pointed out, however, 'Ten years ago the US and Canadian Supreme Courts permitted doctors to withdraw treatment from PVS patients and euthanasia has not taken any steps nearer in those countries.'[207]

In most of the judgments in the case there was relatively little explicit analysis, as distinct from acknowledgement, of its ethical and philosophical implications, and even less mention of the allocation of resources. Lord Browne-Wilkinson said that he was very conscious of having reached his conclusions on narrow, legalistic grounds. In a sense, and to a degree inevitably, the proceedings in court were sanitized by their very legal characterization. Could artificial feeding be deemed 'medical treatment'? Could removal of the nasogastric tube legally be said to 'cause' death? There was no examination of the Trust's resource allocation policy. In the Court of Appeal, Hoffmann LJ indicated that the Trust had:

> invited us to decide the case on the assumption that its resources were unlimited and we have done so. But one is bound to observe that the cost of keeping a patient like Anthony Bland alive is very considerable and that in another case the health authority might conclude that its resources were better devoted to other patients. We do not have to consider such a case, but in principle the allocation of resources between patients is a matter for the health authority and not for the courts.[208]

For our purposes, the point is that while in the House of Lords some of the judges, briefly and with understandable restraint, alluded to the issue of resources, they again emphatically declared the matter to be beyond their remit. Lord Mustill, for example, after saying that 'the large resources . . . now being devoted to Anthony Bland might in the opinion of many be more fruitfully employed in improving the condition of other patients', added, 'this argument was never squarely put, although hinted at from time to time. In social terms it has great force, and it will have to

---

[206] Dr P. Norris of Alert, an anti-euthanasia organization: *The Times*, 5 Feb. 1993.

[207] *Guardian*, letters col. 10 Feb. 1993. By 1993, American courts had agreed to withdrawal of food and water in about 80 similar cases.

[208] *Airedale NHS Trust* v. *Bland* [1992] 2 WLR 316, 357.

be faced in the end. But this is not a task which the courts can possibly undertake.'[209]

What all of this suggests is that English law, particularly judge-made law, has few designs on medical practice and its practitioners. Such impact as it does have derives more from an image of legal encroachment than from the reality. Nothing makes this clearer than the pervasive dominance of the *Bolam* test, a potent symbol of judicial acquiescence in traditional medical mores.

The Pivotal Role of Bolam

Whether the decision concerns the most commonplace of medical procedures, or is an essentially non-medical one about the ethics of communication when cancer has been diagnosed or the propriety of controversial forms of involuntary or heroic intervention, the *Bolam* test plays a key role. In many cases there is also a disturbing and puzzling readiness to assume that medical conduct which conforms to the test automatically serves the 'best interests' of the patient. As Gostin notes, commenting on *Re F*:

The House of Lords used loose and confusing terminology in setting a standard for deciding what medical treatment should be provided in the absence of consent. Throughout their opinions, several inconsistent standards were enunciated: necessity, absence of negligence (the *Bolam* test) and best interests. Although the Lords defined these terms almost interchangeably, they are, in plain English three quite different standards.[210]

The same point arises in *Bland*, a classic instance of making doctors moral arbiters, in effect if not in form. Whereas the Court of Appeal seemed to consider the *Bolam* test insufficiently exacting, the House of Lords applied it. In the Court of Appeal, Butler-Sloss LJ said that 'the *Bolam* test may not by itself be an adequate basis for this grave decision . . . The principle of the best interests of an incompetent patient in the present circumstances

---

[209] Ibid. 397. Cf. Lord Browne-Wilkinson, 'it is not legitimate for a judge in reaching a view as to what is for the benefit of the one individual whose life is in issue to take into account the wider practical issues as to allocation of limited financial resources': (ibid., 382).

[210] L. Gostin, 'Consent to Treatment: The Incapable Person' in C. Dyer (ed.), *Doctors, Patients and the Law*, (Oxford: Blackwell Scientific Publications, 1992), 82.

encompasses wider considerations, including some degree of monitoring of the medical decision.'[211] But the House of Lords' virtual identification of 'best interests' with *Bolam*[212] means that what might be a relatively low standard of care, as represented by conformity with one merely acceptable medical approach, satisfies the commitment to optimal treatment implicit in 'best interests'. Lord Browne-Wilkinson, for example, said in terms that for incompetent patients, it 'can be deduced from *In re F*' that 'the right to administer invasive medical care is wholly dependent upon such care being in the best interests of the patient. Moreover, a doctor's decision whether invasive care is in the best interests of the patient falls to be assessed by reference to the test laid down in *Bolam*'.[213] Not only does this view in practice imply a derogation from optimal treatment, but it sanctions a disturbing degree of arbitrariness in conceding that, on an issue as serious as whether or not to continue life support, 'the doctor's answer may well [legitimately] be influenced by his own attitude to the sanctity of human life. . . . *the court's only concern will be to be satisfied that the doctor's decision to discontinue is in accordance with a respectable body of medical opinion and that it is reasonable*'.[214] Lord Goff's suggestion that, in situations of conflict between the patient's relatives and the doctor, 'the solution could be found in a change of medical practitioner'[215] merely drives home the arbitrary nature of the test, with its ready acceptance of private ordering in a matter of fundamental ethical concern. As a commentator cryptically observed, 'to argue that a course of action is right because a lot of doctors agree with it is bizarre'.[216] One might think it even more bizarre that the courts would condone such action even if they themselves and most doctors *did not* agree with it![217] The reality is that the test of 'best interests' for

---

[211] *Airedale NHS Trust* v. *Bland* [1993] 2 WLR 316, 344: cf. Hoffman LJ, 358–9, Lord Bingham MR, 339.

[212] Apart from Lord Mustill's doubts: ibid. 399.　　　　　[213] Ibid. 385.

[214] Ibid. 386.　　　　　[215] Ibid. 377.

[216] M. Phillips, *Guardian*, 5 Feb. 1993.

[217] Cf. L. Doyal and D. Wilsher, 'The true criticism of the *Bland* decision lies in the fact that the House of Lords abdicated responsibility for the solution of these ethical questions to the medical profession. To pretend that they had no more to contribute to the debate than persistent references to "professional standards" can only be called an act of judicial cowardice': *Guardian*, letters col. 11 Feb. 1993.

incompetent patients depends on the substituted judgement of the doctor, subject only to cosmetic judicial control.[218]

The spirit of *Bolam* has largely survived the critical onslaught on medical paternalism. It continues to be invoked by judges naturally disposed to endorse a medical ethic that used to be taken for granted. Typical of the tendency is an observation of Lord Justice Dunn in *Sidaway*: '[most patients] prefer to put themselves unreservedly in the hands of their doctors. This is not in my view "paternalism", to repeat an evocative word used in argument. It is simply an acceptance of the doctor/patient relationship as it has developed in this country'.[219] The bulk of the modern case law fluctuates between this kind of passive acquiescence and an overtly instrumental approach. The latter, most evident in Lord Denning's judgments, was also apparent in *Sidaway*. There the Court of Appeal, in particular, seemed fearful that the very notion of 'informed consent' constituted a threat to the professional authority of the doctor—an inevitable recipe for undermining medical practice, encouraging unduly defensive medicine, and fostering needless, costly litigation.[220] At times it has seemed as if a bare

[218] See M. Brazier, 'Competence, Consent and Proxy Consents' in M. Brazier and M. Lobjoit (eds.), *Protecting the Vulnerable* (London: Routledge, 1991), 35. See also *Frenchay Healthcare NHS Trust* v. *S* [1994] 1 WLR 601.

[219] [1984] 2 WLR 778, 795. Cf. Browne-Wilkinson LJ, 'most people want to know the material risks in taking a particular course of action before they take it': ibid. 800. Dunn LJ's vision of the doctor–patient relationship is not unknown in the more rights-conscious jurisprudence of the US Supreme Court: 'In our society, the doctor/patient dialogue embodies a unique relationship of trust. The specialised nature of medical science and the emotional distress often attendant to health-related decisions requires that patients place their complete confidence, and often their very lives, in the hands of medical professionals. One seeks a physician's aid not only for medication or diagnosis, but also for guidance, professional judgement, and vital emotional support. Accordingly, each of us attaches profound importance and authority to the words of advice spoken by the physician': *Rust* v. *Sullivan* 111 S Ct 1759, 1785 (1991), *per* Blackmun J (dissenting).

[220] See text at n. 56 and 57 above. Lord Bridge, if more covertly, was voicing similar concerns when approving the decision in *Bly* v. *Rhoads*, 222 SE 2d 783 (1976): *Sidaway* v. *Governors of Bethlem Royal Hospital* [1985] AC 871, 899. In addition, during oral argument the Law Lords repeatedly spoke of the need to protect the medical profession and its status. See R. Schwartz and A. Grubb, 'Why Britain can't Afford Informed Consent' (Aug. 1985) 15 *Hastings Center Report*, 19, 21.

allusion to the presumed preference of patients for decision-making to be left to doctors, or to the American 'medical malpractice crisis' and 'defensive medicine' could be taken to conclude the argument.

Such assertions are unsubstantiated and unwarranted. It is not appropriate for doctors to presume what a given patient wants any more than it is safe to extrapolate from the American experience. The claim that fear of litigation breeds defensive medicine has a superficial appeal, but it has rightly been pointed out that 'it is difficult to isolate the effect of the threat of legal action on medical practice, because clinical decision-making is influenced by many factors, including the payment system, training, work environment, peer culture, and the physical stress or fatigue of the doctor'.[221] In any event, 'defensive medicine' is an ambiguous concept, which does not necessarily imply attempting a 'legal' diagnosis. It may simply reflect appropriate quality assurance procedures, signifying commendable caution and careful monitoring of the patient's condition. We seldom hear comparable concern expressed about the 'aggressive medicine' of the surgeon who is too predisposed to cut.

To the extent that doctors do engage in inappropriate defensive medicine through fear of being held negligent, it argues inadequate appreciation of the substantive law which affords the profession substantial protection against unfounded negligence claims. It is inherent in the *Bolam* test that doctors cannot be held liable for failing to carry out procedures which competent professional opinion considers undesirable or unnecessary, or for taking medically justifiable risks. On the other hand, seriously inappropriate defensive medicine, as well as being unethical and a waste of scarce resources, could itself constitute negligence.[222] For most practical purposes, a doctor whose conduct is endorsed by only a single expert witness has little reason to fear being found negligent, even if other experts are critical.[223] In its substantive

---

[221] R. Dingwall, P. Fenn, and L. Quam, *Medical Negligence* (Oxford: Centre for Socio-Legal Studies, 1991), 49.

[222] In some American States it has been prohibited by statute: W. Wadlington, 'Legal Responses to Patient Injury: A Future Agenda for Research and Reform' (1991) 54(2) *Law and Contemporary Problems* 199, 207.

[223] At first instance in *Bland*, the judge said, '*because of the gravity of the decision . . . I would expect that in all similar applications there would be* not

principles, medical malpractice law is neither unduly intrusive nor a reason for engaging in defensive medicine. In fact it stands out as a rare exception to the general expansion of liability for negligence which has been the most distinctive feature of twentieth century tort law.

None of this is meant to suggest that a degree of judicial empathy with the medical profession is out of place. Doctors are continually subject to exacting pressures: understandably they resent the image of 'neglect' so easily conjured up by a single finding of 'negligence'. Their 'negligence' is not infrequently the kind of momentary inadvertence which we all display fairly often. The predicament of the surgeon with a record of dedicated service effectively on trial for one alleged lapse of judgement or oversight—in the very process of providing well-intentioned treatment—properly invites our sympathy. It would be surprising if it did not inspire some fellow-feeling in the legal clinician called upon to pass judgment. As the judge in a recent medical manslaughter case put it, 'you are far from being bad men; you are good men who contrary to your normal behaviour on this one occasion were guilty of momentary negligence'.[224] Such sentiments doubtless played some part in Lord Denning's benign view of 'error of judgement' in *Whitehouse* v. *Jordan*, and in earlier cases which toyed with the notion of 'gross' negligence as a threshold requirement for professional liability. What is none the less noticeable in medical case law is the unusual extent of the affinity, at times deference, revealed in judicial dicta, the sheer resilience of the *Bolam* principle, and, in particular, the mechanical way in which it has been used to justify highly controversial procedures.

This stance is not adequately explained by the relatively narrow scope for judicial creativity in a common law system, since several other common law jurisdictions have shown much more flexibiity in departing from *Bolam* or limiting its application.[225] It is, of

---

merely one medical opinion but at least two responsible medical opinions' (*Airedale NHS Trust* v. *Bland* [1993] 2 WLR 316, 331–2. Emphasis added).

[224] See G. Korgaonkar and D. Tribe, 'Medical Manslaughter' (1992) 136 *Solicitors Journal* 105; and see *R.* v. *Prentice* [1993] 3 WLR 927. Cf. *Wilsher* v. *Essex Area Health Authority*, n. 70 above, 746–7, *per* Mustill LJ.

[225] Most recently, the High Court of Australia's strong disavowal of it as a basis for determining the doctor's duty to disclose risks: *Rogers* v. *Whitaker* [1992] ALJR 47. See further, 222–4 below.

course, true that litigation generally is not conducive to a wide-
ranging debate about appropriate standards of care in medicine.
Arguments about competing models of the doctor–patient
relationship, common enough in medical ethics and social scientific
discourse, are not the stuff of which our legal judgments are made.
Geared to resolving individualized disputes, generally about
isolated, one-off incidents, within the constraints imposed by legal
precedent, the court is not an ideal vehicle for establishing
comprehensive and systematic guidelines for medical practice. The
specificity of adversarial proceedings and traditional techniques of
legal reasoning do not lend themselves to extended .analysis of
medical relationships at the best of times. The position is further
complicated by the need for urgent resolution in some of the
gravest cases, of which *Re S*[226] is only the most graphic example.

Courts, like doctors' surgeries, are not primarily designed to
cure social ills. Such general principles as have emerged from the
cases are rooted in analyses and attitudes that long predate
modern controversies over medical relationships and contemporary
modes of health care delivery. It is of interest in the latter context
that although in *Sidaway* the plaintiff was an NHS patient, Lord
Templeman's analysis was couched in terms of contract law, that
is, in a form appropriate to the legal framework for private
medicine.[227] In the same case, Lord Diplock tersely observed, in a
manner suggestive of a total failure to comprehend the hospital
setting as experienced by the bulk of the population, that the
patient who wants information has only to ask.[228] That a major
social debate has been taking place about doctor–patient relationships and the regulation of medicine generally is not readily
apparent from the English case law on medical negligence. It
conveys little sense, for example, of the scale of political and
economic controversy surrounding the organization and delivery
of health care, or of the current ferment within the National
Health Service.

The fact that the law reports do not dwell at length on such
matters reflects the general tendency for any modification of
established common law principles to be a piecemeal process

---

[226] *Re S (Adult: Refusal of Treatment)* [1992] 3 WLR 806; see further 152–6
below.
[227] *Sidaway* v. *Bethlem Royal Hospital* [1985] AC 871, 904.
[228] Ibid. 895.

dictated, and restricted, by the particular issues which happen to be at stake in the litigation. Also, in England there is no basis for an appeal to rights or expectations embodied in a written constitution or bill of rights.[229] Instead, the scope of medical liability has been circumscribed, if not fettered, by judicial adherence via a relatively strict doctrine of precedent to the limited range of duties historically imposed on doctors. In Germany, by contrast, the courts have adopted a much more patient-centred approach to the doctor's duty of disclosure. This reflects legal appeal to entrenched human rights protecting self-determination, formulated in response to the experience of the Nazi era, including the 'medical' experiments which prompted the Nuremburg Code. Similarly, there has been no equivalent in England of the United States' explicit constitutional articulation of democratic ideals, expressing the conviction that the 'right to know' and formal accountability are integral to the democratic process.

The Impact of Litigation

The legal characteristics, then, of the doctor–patient relationship in England are shaped by a judiciary generally well-disposed towards the medical profession, relatively free of the kind of constitutional constraints that have altered the 'balance of power' between doctors and patients in a number of jurisdictions, and somewhat insulated from the turmoil within the health service and the way medical encounters are routinely experienced. As regards the substance of the legal principles which govern medical litigation, their application and the outcome of most fully litigated cases, doctors can have few grounds for complaint. To the extent that they perceive the *courts* as intrusive they have chosen the wrong target.

On the other hand, it is understandable that for doctors any allegation of negligence is a source of concern, whatever the outcome and regardless of whether the claim is fully litigated or dropped at a fairly early stage. No doctor can relish the prospect of being embroiled in a legal dispute, the anxiety and possible self-doubt generated by a complaint, the threat to reputation and the

---

[229] Beyond the limited opportunities afforded by the possible applicability of the European Convention on Human Rights on some issues, with the inordinate delays involved.

diversion of time and effort. In a substantial number of cases the injuries are in fact attributable to natural causes or unavoidable risks, prompting the suggestion that legal aid panels should have medical assistance to help weed such cases out.[230] In so far as this proposal was based on the assumption that it is relatively easy to initiate a claim, it has lost some of its force due to the recent erosion of access to legal aid and advice. In April 1993, the qualifying disposable income limit for free civil legal aid was reduced to income support levels.[231] The limited funding available under the legal aid system for vital but expensive items, such as the written advice and oral evidence of medical experts, remains a major drawback for legally aided plaintiffs. As an added disincentive to applicants eligible subject to making a contribution, the (increased) contributions are now payable for every year that a case lasts, instead of for one year only. As a result of the changed eligibility levels and the substantial, rising cost of much medical litigation, there are also many more people caught in the 'legal aid trap', that is, being marginally outside the eligibility limits they are either unable to make a claim or feel constrained to accept inadequate offers.[232] The proposed conditional fee arrangement, under which solicitors would not be able to charge unsuccessful litigants but could charge a mark-up of 100 per cent for those who win their case, would probably not be used extensively. Losing plaintiffs would still be liable for the defendant's costs and normally for their own experts' fees. Overall, expense and the other considerations which inhibit most people from initiating litigation continue to present a serious stumbling block to launching a medical claim.

That this must be the case is borne out by a moment's reflection on such evidence as we have about the incidence of medical litigation relative to the sheer number of medical encounters that

[230] C. Hawkins and I. Paterson, n. 45 above, 1533–6: in 16 of the cases 'adverse events' were found to be the result of minor unavoidable risks of treatment and, in 39, natural causes.

[231] Then £2,294. Free legal *advice* under the 'green form' scheme was limited to people with a weekly income of £61 or less. 47% of households are eligible for civil legal aid in 1994–95: *Hansard* (HC) vol 241, no. 88, Written Answers, cols. 588–9; 21 April 1994. In 1993–94 10,844 legal aid certificates were issued to plaintiffs in medical negligence cases: Legal Aid Board, *Annual Report* (1993–94) (London: HMSO, 1994) 68. For 1991–92 the figure was 18,658: Legal Aid Board, *Annual Report* (1991–92) (London: HMSO, 1992) 53.

[232] See e.g. Harris, n. 146 above, 205.

take place. If one considers the annual amount of diagnosis, testing, advice, and treatment and seeks to extrapolate from available data on medical injury, it is the relative paucity of litigation that is most striking. Reporting in 1978, the Pearson Commission noted that 'each year some six million in-patients are treated in National Health Service hospitals and some 19 million people attend out-patient or accident and emergency departments. Yet in a year probably no more than 1,000 claims are made against doctors, dentists, pharmacists or health authorities in respect of negligence.'[233] In 1991, there were some 7.7 million in-patient treatments and 24.4 million out-patient.[234] These figures take no account of the medical treatment provided in nursing homes or, for that matter, of diagnosis and treatment in the course of the 200 million or so annual consultations with GPs.

Nearly twenty years ago, Fried said 'it is universally agreed that the rate of [medical] malpractice litigation in the United States is excessive . . . I am inclined to believe that the British rate is inadequate. It is hard for me to believe that there are as few negligently caused medical accidents as the statistics would indicate.'[235] In fact there are good grounds for believing that the litigation rate was, and continues to be, low in proportion to the incidence of medically negligent behaviour in *both* countries. The recent highly sophisticated Harvard Study,[236] based on evaluation by medical researchers of the records of more than 31,000 in-patients from fifty-one hospitals, provides an interesting insight into the rate for New York State. It found that 1 per cent of the patients suffered injury as a result of negligence. Only one in eight sued, and of these claimants only half obtained any damages. In other words, in what is arguably the most litigious setting in the world, only one in sixteen negligently injured patients is compensated through the tort system. Put another way, on average there is

---

[233] *Report of the Royal Commission on Civil Liability and Compensation for Personal Injury*, n. 63 above, I, para. 1323. Only some 5% of the claims would have reached court.
[234] Central Statistical Office, *Social Trends* (London: HMSO, 1994), Table 7.23, 102, and Table 7.24, 103, respectively.
[235] C. Fried, 'The Future in the USA,' in C. Wood (ed.), *The Influence of Litigation on Medical Practice*, (London: Academic Press, 1977), 192.
[236] Harvard Medical Practice Study Group, *Patients, Doctors and Lawyers: Medical Injury, Malpractice Litigation, and Patient Compensation in New York* (Cambridge, Mass.: Harvard University, 1990).

no more than a 6 per cent risk of a New York doctor who has been negligent being held negligent.

The editor of the *British Medical Journal* has estimated that if the findings of the Harvard Study are applicable in Britain,[237] 'about 300,000 patients a year may experience an adverse event while in hospital, 45,000 may die in part because of the event, and 75,000 cases of potential negligence may arise from hospital admissions'. Observing that 'these numbers do not include the problems that arise from outpatient encounters or consultation in general practice', he concluded that 'clearly, few cases of negligence in Britain result in a claim and even fewer in compensation'.[238]

Any raw extrapolation from American findings must naturally be viewed with caution, and we still await reliable figures for medical negligence claims in England. However, given the nature of the differences between the respective health and legal systems,[239] one might reasonably expect the litigation rate to be lower still in England. Granted that a significant proportion of negligence claims are not substantiated, 'it seems likely . . . that there are far more patients who suffer medical injury as a result of negligence who do not sue their doctors, than patients with spurious claims who do. From the patients' perspective it could be argued that the malpractice "crisis" arises from too few patients being able to litigate, rather than too many doctors becoming defendants'.[240] Though this conclusion is of little comfort to doctors whose conduct has been wrongly impugned, it remains a valuable corrective to assumptions of legal overreach. One of the more interesting findings of the Harvard Study was that the perceived risk by doctors of being sued in a given year was three times the actual risk.

STIRRINGS OF LEGAL CHANGE?

One would hardly expect the courts to be in the forefront of an attack on the more paternalistic features of medical practice. But,

---

[237] An earlier Californian study produced substantially similar results: California Medical Association, *Medical Insurance Feasibility Study* (San Francisco: Sutter Publications, 1977).

[238] R. Smith, *British Medical Journal* 301 (1990), 621.

[239] See 15–16 above.   [240] Jones, *Medical Negligence*, n. 118 above, 4.

despite the tenacity with which English law has clung to the *Bolam* test, there are signs, as yet perhaps only straws in the wind, of greater judicial readiness to deploy legal principles that reflect changing notions of what is appropriate in medical relationships. Naturally, judge-made rules will be less significant in determining the future shape of those relationships than governmental policy or change from within the profession, whether or not prompted by a felt need to assuage critics. But this is not to say that the courts are without influence in the matter. Judicial decisions and pronouncements on medical issues, and *a fortiori* legislative requirements, have a kind of influence denied to social and moral theory, as authoritative sources for action capable in some measure of affecting medical behaviour.

Judicial analysis, not ethical debate, still less the medical schools or medical scholarship, inspired and gave content to the idea of informed consent in the United States.[241] The publicity resulting from applications for judicial review of health authorities' resourcing policies helped to trigger the review of the NHS which culminated in the most radical structural reform of the health service since its inception.[242] It was the legal action brought by the father of Libby Zion, who died in 1984 following mis-diagnosis by exhausted house officers, that precipitated America's nation-wide reform of the conditions and hours of work for doctors in training. In England, too, the campaign by junior doctors for a reduction in hours was boosted by the Court of Appeal decision that doctors whose health is put at risk by having to work for excessively long periods may sue the health authority.[243] Health authorities were subsequently required to reduce the hours to a maximum of seventy-two a week on-call and fifty-six full shift by the end of 1994.[244] However, in 1993, against the wishes of other Member

---

[241] See R. Faden and T. Beauchamp, *A History of Informed Consent* (New York: Oxford University Press, 1986), 88–91.

[242] See 108–111 below. Cf. F. Miller, 'Informed Consent in English and American Law'(1992) 18 *American Journal of Law and Medicine* 37, 54–5.

[243] In *Johnstone* v. *Bloomsbury Health Authority* [1991] 2 All ER 293, the period in question was of up to 88 hours a week. Stuart Smith LJ said, 'I have no doubt that it is a matter of grave public concern that junior doctors should be required to work such long hours without proper rest that not only their own health may be put at risk but that of their patients as well': ibid. 301.

[244] NHS Management Executive, *Junior Doctors: The New Deal* (London: Department of Health, 1991).

States, Britain negotiated the exemption of doctors in training from the draft directive on working hours for community workers,[245] and this still contentious issue may ultimately fall to be resolved by the law, via the European Court of Justice.[246]

Even when altered medical behaviour is prompted by false perceptions of legal requirements, it argues that 'the law' is acknowledged within the profession as a force which does influence the conduct of doctors. The effects can be both subtle in form and dramatic in impact. Discussing the use of respirators in intensive care units, Zussman noted that 'physicians avoid beginning those treatments they believe the law proscribes them from withdrawing'.[247] More generally, if doctors gain the impression that informed consent is required by law,[248] this in itself provides an incentive to be more communicative. It is not without irony that, in a recent Scottish case which vigorously reaffirmed the *Bolam* approach to the duty of disclosure, the judge commented that 'movement towards more openness has seemingly been prompted by medico-legal as much as by purely medical reasons'.[249] Similarly, at least *some* wasteful defensive medicine presumably reflects exaggerated fears of being sued that result from misconceptions about the legal standard of care.[250] The argument should not however be pushed too far. The Harvard study, though it found that New York doctors believed the risk of being sued was three times higher than it actually was, also concluded that 'doctors saw the effect of the tort system as a

---

[245] Council of the European Communities, *Common Position adopted by the Council with a view to the Adoption of a Directive concerning Certain Aspects of the organisation of Working Time* (Brussels: EC, 1993 (7253/93, soc 196, PRO-COOP 27)).

[246] J. Poulsen, 'Junior Doctors and the EC Draft Directive on Working Hours', *British Medical Journal* 307 (1993), 1158.

[247] See n. 6 above, 138.

[248] Perhaps strengthened in the belief by misleading claims in the Patient's Charter. See 106–8 below.

[249] *Moyes* v. *Lothian Health Board* [1990] 1 Med LR 463, 468, *per* Lord Caplan. Cf. G. Robertson, 'Informed Consent Ten Years Later: The Impact of *Reibl* v. *Hughes*' (1991) 70 *Canadian Bar Review* 423, 439–40; B. Dickens, 'The Effects of Legal Liability on Physicians' Services' (1991) 41 *University of Toronto Law Journal* 168, 213.

[250] See D. Tribe and G. Korgaonkar, 'The Impact of Litigation on Patient Care: An Enquiry into Defensive Medical Practices' (1991) *Professional Negligence* 2–7; cf. M. Jones and A. Morris, 'Defensive Medicine: Myths and Facts', *Journal of the Medical Defence Union* 5 (1989), 40.

psychological distraction rather than a factor which influenced the way they practised'.[251] A postal survey suggested that the increased use of tests was due as much to scientific and technological advances as to defensive medical practice by doctors, who believed that they were significantly at risk of being sued whether or not they had been negligent.[252]

In England, at the highest levels of judicial decision-making, the general picture has been one of increasing involvement in medical conduct, but with few signs of a desire to shape it. The three leading medical negligence cases of the 1980s to reach the House of Lords—between them covering the three functions of diagnosis, treatment, and advice[253]—left medical standards all but immune from judicial control, by their obeisance to the *Bolam* principle of 'accepted medical practice'. The Court of Appeal has endorsed this stance in several subsequent decisions. In *Gold*[254] it asserted that *Bolam* applies just as much to the non-therapeutic context of voluntary sterilization as to therapeutic procedures; in *Blyth*[255] that it would often apply even when a patient has asked for information. Moreover in each of these instances the case concerned advice and disclosure, the very areas in which the criterion of 'accepted medical practice' is most open to question. Recent Scottish decisions have reiterated the primacy of *Bolam* in even stronger terms.[256] By and large, the same judicial reluctance to invade 'medical territory' can be seen in the recent spate of cases on the 'best interests' of incompetent patients, in matters as controversial as involuntary sterilization and the withdrawal of life support, not to mention the authorization of a caesarean for a competent woman against her will and denial of the right to refuse treatment to *Gillick*-competent adolescents.[257]

It is true that in some of these selfsame decisions we find occasional rhetorical appeals to patients' rights and expressions of

---

[251] D. Harris, 'Evaluating the Goals of Personal Injury Law: Some Empirical Evidence' in P. Cane and J. Stapleton (eds.), *Essays for Patrick Atiyah* (Oxford: Oxford University Press, 1991), 302–3.   [252] Ibid. 303–4.

[253] Respectively, *Maynard* v. *West Midlands Regional Health Authority* [1984] 1 WLR 634; *Whitehouse* v. *Jordan* [1981] 1 WLR 246, and *Sidaway* v. *Board of Governors of Bethlem Royal Hospital* [1985] AC 871.

[254] *Gold* v. *Haringey Health Authority* [1988] 1 QB 481.

[255] *Blyth* v. *Bloomsbury Health Authority* [1993] 4 Med LR 151 (case decided 1987).

[256] See, especially, *Moyes* v. *Lothian Health Board* [1990] 1 Med LR 463, 471. Cf. *Gordon* v. *Wilson*, 1992 SLT 849.   [257] See, further, ch. 4.

unease about the consequences of adhering mechanically to the *Bolam* test. Plainly some judges are uncomfortably aware that in emotionally fraught and complex situations bearing on fundamental rights, such adherence is an inadequate response to the gravity of what is at stake. Also, in *Sidaway*, to add to Lord Scarman's lone approval of informed consent, the majority of the Law Lords did assert that in the last analysis the courts have the right to decide that non-disclosure of risks amounts to negligence, even when it was not condemned by any of the medical expert witnesses. But they did so in such a tentative and heavily-qualified fashion[258] that one is left with the overriding impression of a Court still incapable of renouncing a doctor-centred view of medical relationships and medical law.

The influence that the *Bolam* test has exerted on medical law is the more remarkable when one considers both its apparent deviation from the orthodox negligence standard of reasonable care in the circumstances[259] and its lowly origins as part of the direction in what must have been one of the last decisions on medical negligence to come before a jury. As will later become apparent, in the United States, the ascendancy of the 'professional practice' test seems to have been the culmination of a process discernible in the case law from about the mid-nineteenth century onwards when, instead of directing juries to view customary professional standards as merely *relevant* to an assessment of reasonable care in the circumstances, courts began to *equate* such standards with reasonable care.[260] The shift was perhaps a measure of the prestige acquired by the profession during a period of substantial scientific advance and institutional development.[261] The English cases of the time are less demonstrably explicable in these terms, but the modern position crystallizing with *Bolam* made for a similar outcome, without the kind of modifications which have since been introduced in the United States and in several Commonwealth jurisdictions. *Bolam* is a decision which, by virtue of its general

---

[258] See Ch. 6 below.   [259] See Ch. 5 below.

[260] T. Silver, 'One Hundred Years of Harmful Error: The Historical Jurisprudence of Medical Malpractice' [1992] *Wisconsin Law Review* 1193. See, further, Ch. 5.

[261] M. Larson, *The Rise of Professionalism* (Berkeley: University of California Press, 1977); I. Waddington, *The Medical Profession in the Industrial Revolution* (Dublin: Gill and Macmillan, 1984).

tone and through over-literal interpretation, has had a deadening effect to this day, by more or less closing off discussion of the interests at stake in medical treatment. It obviated any need for the courts to explore the concerns of patients except as perceived by doctors.

In the mid-1950s this was understandable. But once the notion began to take root that professional medical judgement does not have to be dispositive, it became easier to see that there is a range of possible perspectives on how decisions about medical treatment should be arrived at. Now we are directly exhorted by government and attuned by cultural and institutional change to pay more attention to the patient's voice. As patients become better informed and more actively engaged in their health care, as they become more exposed to a commercial conception of the medical exchange, which implies a degree of de-professionalization, the tensions between the *Bolam* legacy and new expectations of doctor–patient relationships are coming to the fore in ways which seem to call for resolution along fresh lines. It remains to be seen what consequences the erosion of medical paternalism will have for medical practice itself and for its legal framework. Will it lead to enhanced patient autonomy, a more commercial approach, more collaboration between doctor and patient, or perhaps a model which combines various aspects of these approaches?

As yet, as far as the legal framework is concerned, these are but the stirrings of change. For the most part the law has been neither insatiable cormorant nor benign instrument for improving the doctor–patient relationship. It has largely and deliberately remained disengaged, save to endorse a medical model increasingly seen as outmoded within medicine itself and a legal test at odds with mainstream negligence theory. Considerable room thus exists for judicial manœuvre. There are concepts available for use, and scope for what might be considered enlightened encroachment. But before we can assess how legal principles might be more fruitfully utilized in the medical sphere, it is necessary to explore the various models of medical relationships discernible in traditional conceptions of medical practice and in the current challenges to them.

PART TWO

The Doctor–Patient Relationship

2

Resilient Paternalism

THE RESILIENCE OF THE TRADITIONAL ETHIC

In his classic study, *The Silent World of Doctor and Patient*, Katz declared that 'if a conspiracy of silence exists, it takes place in the consulting room, right in front of the patient'.[1] In *Sidaway*, the plaintiff referred to her neurosurgeon as a man of 'very, very few words'. The trial judge found him to be 'a reserved, slightly autocratic man of "the old school" '.[2] Non-disclosure and deference have been among the hallmarks of the paternalistic tradition which has dominated orthodox medical practice over a period of some 2,500 years.[3] It is only in the last thirty years or so that paternalism's credentials as the appropriate model for medical relationships and as the best guarantor of patient welfare have been seriously challenged. There have, of course, always been other traditions and alternative images, complementary systems of medicine, and individual physicians averse to the dominant model. Equally, for many centuries the vast bulk of the population had little or no alternative to reliance on self-diagnosis, home remedies, and family support; while bitter experience made people sceptical about orthodox medicine's curative powers. But paternalism has always been prominent in Western medicine, and remarkably resilient considering the strong countervailing social and cultural changes which have shaped modern society.

The charge-sheet is by now very familiar: paternalism prevents doctors from appreciating how illness is actually experienced. By paying insufficient attention to genuine communication with

---

[1] J. Katz, *The Silent World of Doctor and Patient* (New York: The Free Press, 1984), 56.

[2] *Per* Skinner J. See R. Schwartz and A. Grubb, 'Why Britain can't Afford Informed Consent', 15 *Hastings Center Report*, Aug. 1985, 19.

[3] See, generally, E. Pellegrino and D. Thomasma, *A Philosophical Basis of Medical Practice* (New York: Oxford University Press, 1981).

Reasonable Care

patients, they have failed both to encourage their active involvement and to respect their autonomy. The modern tendency to view patients as biological machines has only made things worse. Medical practice, it is said, focuses too much on the relief of organic symptoms and too little on the patient. So frequently have such accusations been made in recent years that they risk being dismissed as tired clichés, or ill-intentioned exaggerations, put about by people reluctant to admit that any positive changes have occurred and insensitive to the pressures that doctors face. But though some inroads into the traditional ethic are evident in medical theory, education, and practice, the main impact has been in primary health care. It has not been very pronounced in the hospital context. Nor, merely because many doctors share popular misgivings about the 'usurpation of solicitude by technology',[4] does it follow that communicative competence is the norm in medical exchanges. The regularity with which the above concerns continue to be voiced in leading *medical* journals is testimony to their endurance.[5] It is also indicative of the medical world's relative self-sufficiency and its capacity to withstand or neutralize critics, despite sustained, vigorous, and diverse attack.

At first sight it seems odd that effective communication with patients has not always been seen by the profession as a central concern. Medical codes of ethics have invariably accorded a special status to the doctor–patient relationship. Its pastoral overtones and intimate, potentially intrusive nature have made it almost sacrosanct. The exposure of one, often vulnerable, person's physical and mental condition to the scrutiny and judgement of another is an inherently delicate and fraught matter.[6] Though it may not be easy to specify with precision the

---

[4] G. Silver, 'A Threat to Medicine's Professional Mandate', *Lancet* 2 (1988), 787.

[5] See e.g. L. Fallowfield, 'Giving Sad and Bad News', *Lancet* 341 (1993), 476; D. Kerrigan *et al.*, 'Who's Afraid of Informed Consent?' *British Medical Journal* 306 (1993), 298.

[6] Cf. F. Peabody, 'The treatment of a disease may be entirely impersonal: the care of a patient must be completely personal. The significance of the intimate personal relationship between physician and patient cannot be too strongly emphasized, for in an extraordinarily large number of cases both diagnosis and treatment are directly dependent on it': 'The Care of the Patient', *Journal of the American Medical Association* 88 (1927), 877. And again, 'the secret of the care of the patient is in caring for the patient': ibid., 882.

legitimate expectations of the parties in a medical encounter, it is self-evidently desirable to avoid, or at least minimize, misunderstanding between them. What then explains the resilience of the traditional ethic?

At the level of individual encounters, it is sustained by powerful psychological needs. Many patients do have a strong urge to place their trust in the 'expert'. Whether from natural disinclination, lack of medical expertise or the loss of autonomy which their condition induces, they may show little or no desire to be instructed in the mysteries of Gray's *Anatomy*. And because modern medicine does have an unprecedented capacity to effect cures and alleviate symptoms, unquestioning compliance with 'doctor's orders' would normally be more rational than in the past. It is also easy to see the attractions of such a model for doctors. They may often be tempted to avoid a potentially stressful or time-consuming dialogue by following familiar routines, proffering bland words of reassurance, or resorting to a placebo, the ultimate symbol of the efficacy of trust. Sheer pressure of work, as well as considerations of convenience and efficiency, will often lead them to adopt the clinical and conversational methods with which they feel most comfortable. In addition, they may feel compelled to project an image of self-confidence and authority, whether to raise patient morale or to dispel self-doubt.[7]

Patients want to 'get better' and often prefer the doctor to decide what that entails. Strictly speaking, such a preference does not imply a paternalistic relationship, as it does not involve any *overriding* of patient autonomy. Nevertheless, the awareness of doctors that many patients do want them to decide adds to the temptation to act paternalistically as a matter of course. As one commentator has put it, 'practitioners are trained to make decisions for patients, and to put those decisions in the form of advice . . . The emphasis on giving advice rather than explanation has led practitioners (doctors, nurses and paramedics) to be more skilled at persuasion than at discussion, more dependent on authority than on rationale. And it has sometimes tempted them to take short cuts in gaining or assuming consent'.[8] Consciously or

---

[7] See Katz, n. 1 above, especially chs. 4 and 7.
[8] C. Williamson, *Whose Standards?* (Buckingham: Open University Press, 1992), 110–111.

otherwise, both parties often incline towards a broadly paternalistic relationship, if not necessarily one in which patients 'put themselves *unreservedly* in the hands of their doctors'.[9]

The Hippocratic Tradition

Most doctors no longer formally take the Hippocratic Oath, and may have only a passing familiarity with it and other Hippocratic writings. In its historical context, the Oath seems to have been more of a declaration of loyalty concerning the terms on which physicians could practise their craft than a source of ethical obligations towards patients. This emphasis was also to be a feature of subsequent codes of ethics. 'Medical ethics', said Berlant, 'though ostensibly pertaining to the doctor–patient relationship, have, in fact, addressed the structuring of relationships among doctors'.[10] Significantly, the oath accords pride of place to the 'profession' in the form of a pledge of allegiance to the new physician's teacher and fellow-practitioners.[11] But conventionally portrayed as a precursor of modern ethical codes, it remains a powerful symbol of doctors' responsibilities. When it does address the issue of treatment, a key passage reads: 'I will apply measures which according to my ability and judgement, I consider to be for the benefit of my patients'. This principle sounds unexceptionable, even laudable. It seems to befit the members of a caring profession and to encapsulate the dedication, high ethical standards, and genuine sense of obligation to serve the interests of patients which most doctors maintain. Yet in a curious way it is also a root cause of the tension between practitioners and their critics. For, as Veatch has pointed out,[12] the articulated concern for the patient and the evident worthiness of the sentiment are disarming. One can easily overlook its undiluted subjectivism and

---

[9] *Sidaway* v. *Board of Governors of the Bethlem Royal Hospital and the Maudsley Hospital* [1984] 2 WLR 778, 795, *per* Dunn LJ.

[10] J. Berlant, 'Medical Ethics and Professional Monopoly', (1978) 437 *Annals of the American Academy of Political and Social Science* 49, 50.

[11] See L. Edelstein, 'The Hippocratic Oath: Text, Translation and Interpretation' in *Ancient Medicine: Selected Papers of Ludwig Edelstein* (Baltimore: Johns Hopkins University Press, 1967), 3, cited in C. Chapman, *Physicians, Law, and Ethics* (New York: New York University Press, 1984), ch. 2, especially 22–6.

[12] R. Veatch, *A Theory of Medical Ethics* (New York: Basic Books, 1981), ch. 6.

indifference to any available *medical* consensus about treatment, let alone consideration of the patient's own views or any conception of the public interest. When Hippocratic 'beneficence' enjoined physicians 'to help, or at least to do no harm',[13] it was proclaiming an obligation to serve the 'best [medical] interests' of the individual patient as perceived by the individual doctor. The essential message is clear. Doctors decide; patients need only comply. Clinical freedom is of the essence and overrides any claim the patient might make to a right of self-determination or even to a share in decision-making.

It is in the same spirit that *Decorum XVI* of the Hippocratic Corpus advised physicians to reveal 'nothing of the patient's future or present condition' and to conceal most things from their patients because, when given information 'many patients . . . have taken a turn for the worse'.[14] This is naked paternalism, if to some extent altruistically inspired. When it is condemned as oppressive and self-serving, the feeling pervasive within the medical profession of being at once embattled and unjustly maligned is intensified. The sense of grievance is all the more keenly felt in that the pejorative label 'paternalism' is often unthinkingly attached to behaviour more appropriately explained by inadequate communicative skills than by any conscious desire to assume authority. In either case, however, the patient tends to be cast in the role of passive recipient of treatment.

In ancient times, the oracular nature of 'medicine', with its heavy reliance on magical powers and ritual, served both to conceal ignorance and to foster the mystique of the healer. It conferred authority to divine and determine the true interests of patients and, if need be, override their wishes. 'Medicine and magic became associated because the earliest medical practitioners were herbalists who accumulated facts and experience. Finding that their skill had a market value, they guarded their secrets from the vulgar by surrounding them with mystery.'[15] In the course of time, in England as elsewhere, a not dissimilar authority was to vest in physicians. They were the medical *élite*, with a status

---

[13] *Epidemics*, X1, in W. Jones (trans.) *Hippocrates*, 4 vols. (Cambridge: Harvard University Press, 1923–31), i. 165.

[14] Ibid., 'Decorum', ii. 297–9.

[15] W. Sanderson and E. Rayner, *An Introduction to the Law and Tradition of Medical Practice* (London: H. K. Lewis, 1926), 45.

appreciably higher than that of surgeons and apothecaries, their main rivals as healers under the elaborate guild system. According to the statutes of the College of Physicians,[16] in terms which echo the priorities of the Hippocratic Oath, members were called upon to 'determine all things to the credit, honour, and perpetuity of the Society', and to 'do all things in the practice of [the] profession for the honour of the college and the good of the public'.[17]

The same order of priorities was also to be found in Percival's *Medical Ethics*, written at the end of the eighteenth century. Originally intended to be called *Powers, Privileges, and Employments of the Faculty*, it was much concerned with enhancing the reputation, status, and monopolistic position of the guild as a corporate entity, encouraging secrecy, deploring criticism by doctors of doctors, and explaining how they might best 'inspire the minds of their patients with gratitude, respect, and confidence'. Proper patient care could then confidently be expected to ensue. It is true that not long before Percival's Code was published there had been occasional appeals to the patient's perspective, notably in the work of Gregory and Gisborne. Gregory considered it the responsibility of the profession to help create a public better-educated and more discriminating in medical matters, as an incentive for doctors to improve their skills. He espoused the more radical Enlightenment view that encouraging greater medical awareness among the public, in a climate of free inquiry, would enhance people's welfare. Gisborne similarly counselled physicians to avoid 'all affectation of mystery'.[18] But their views had little impact on medical mores. Both in England and the United States, Percival's Code proved far more influential in this respect, though by comparison with its elaborate attention to intra-professional conflict in matters such as the poaching of patients and the protocol for conducting consultations, it had relatively little to say about doctor–*patient* relationships.

The physician, as member of a 'learned profession' was widely perceived to be the custodian of abstruse knowledge not communicable to the laity, and, at least for difficult cases, Percival

[16] Founded in 1518, to become in 1551 the prestigious Royal College of Physicians of London.

[17] C. Chapman, *Physicians, Law, and Ethics*, n. 11 above, 67.

[18] Ibid. 83.

reiterated the traditional view that patients should be kept unaware of their condition.[19] In reality, of course, extensive ignorance about diseases and how to cure them meant that until recent times doctors had little in the way of hard, accurate information to impart. For one thing, they 'hardly examined patients before the middle of the nineteenth century'. Instead, physicians engaged in 'long, detailed history-taking with elaborate classification of symptoms; diagnosis using a purely theoretical system of pathology; and symptomatic treatment of a frequently elaborate nature'.[20] Being very much in the dark themselves, they must have found it hard to resist obfuscation and benign reassurance, whether consciously resorting to such tactics as a control device, or unthinkingly adhering to traditional modes of practice. But in Percivalean ethics the refusal to reveal the mysteries of the craft was partly dictated by the fear that such disclosure would undermine the market position of professionals 'who sought to maximize the distance between medical man and patient, using secrecy and systematic ignorance to accentuate the disadvantageous position of the patient'.[21]

Though Percival's work has often been portrayed as laying the foundations for modern medical ethics, and Hippocratic thinking featured prominently in it, it should not be assumed that there was uniform or continuous acceptance of the Hippocratic tradition. The Oath, in particular, had a somewhat chequered existence, acquiring renewed vitality in the nineteenth century, when invoked to buttress claims of professional authority based on ancient scientific and ethical lineage.[22] Ironically, the stress that was to be laid on the natural sciences from the late nineteenth century onwards, together with the enormous technical advances

[19] See R. Faden and T. Beauchamp, *A History of Informed Consent* (New York: Oxford University Press, 1986), ch. 3; cf. M. Pernick, 'The Patient's Role in Medical Decision-making: A Social History of Informed Consent in Medical Therapy' in *Making Health Care Decisions: The Ethical and Legal Implications of Informed Consent in the Patient–Practitioner Relationship* (Washington: President's Commission for the Study of Ethical Problems in Medicine and Biomedical and Behavioral Research, 1982), Vol. 3, App. E.

[20] R. Downie and B. Charlton, *The Making of a Doctor* (Oxford: Oxford University Press, 1992), 13.

[21] J. Berlant, 'Medical Ethics and Professional Monopoly', n. 10 above, 55.

[22] I. Thompson, 'Fundamental Ethical Principles in Health Care', *British Medical Journal* 295 (1987), 1461.

in medical instruments and laboratory findings which have shaped modern medicine, have meant that 'therapy is principally directed towards the correction of laboratory-defined abnormalities'.[23] The primacy of the biomedical model provided fresh justification for maintaining that it was unnecessary to engage patients actively in their treatment.

The Limited Horizons of Medical Education

Medical training and institutionalization have helped to sustain and promote this attitude. If the medical profession perceives a largely acquiescent legal system as threatening and intrusive, one might expect it to be even less favourably disposed towards disciplines which have seriously questioned the nature of the medical enterprise, the authority of scientific medicine, and the methods of those who practise it. It is important to appreciate what a major shift in professional attitudes, training, and conduct is implicit in making effective communication central to medical treatment. In this respect, as in the matter of medico-legal education, both the ethos and teaching methods of the medical schools have been important factors. It has been argued that 'in taking over licensing the universities would seem to have taken over the ethos appropriate for apprenticeship and training'.[24] Relentlessly overloading students with information to be memorized and regurgitated in multiple choice examinations, the medical schools, with few exceptions, have not been receptive to the study of medical ethics and the behavioural sciences[25]—to say nothing of practical training in communication and counselling,[26] or, for that matter, basic instruction in first aid which has traditionally been seen as best left to nurses.

There is some evidence to suggest that both empathy with patients and the ability to communicate with them are *adversely*

---

[23] Downie and Charlton, n. 20 above, 14.

[24] Ibid. 51.

[25] See e.g. Institute of Medical Ethics, *Report of a Working Party on the Teaching of Medical Ethics* (the 'Pond Report')(London: IME Publications, 1987), ch. 1.

[26] L.Frederikson, 'Designing a Doctor: Do They have the "Strong Silent Type" in mind' (paper presented to the British Psychological Society, London: 18 Dec. 1991).

affected by this narrowly conceived form of medical education,[27] which does little either to sensitize students to the patient's perspective or to encourage a critical approach. As recently as 1992, when the GMC was still bemoaning the 'progressive disenchantment of many [students] as they work their way through the course',[28] Downie and Charlton concluded that, 'It is scandalous that preclinical students are force-fed facts for seven hours a day, that a consultant's teaching ward-round—the major method of clinical teaching—can be accurately encapsulated as "shifting dullness", that the "best years" of a young doctor's life may be spent sitting (and re-sitting) postgraduate exams of unknown validity and doubtful utility'.[29]

Traditionally, familiarity with expected standards of conduct has been acquired through a combination of osmosis and the passing reference to professional codes and guidelines, supplemented by the BMA since 1980 by means of its *Handbook of Medical Ethics*. The 1988 edition of this work, renamed *Philosophy and Practice of Medical Ethics*,[30] purported to provide an approach to the subject 'completely different from that in all previous editions' by setting out competing ethical positions. Yet, despite some background material primarily concerned with religious influences on medical ethics, and the substitution of the term 'professional behaviour' for 'etiquette', in its essentials the text remained a traditionally conceived manual on professional ground rules. Its frequent references to patients' 'needs' and 'best interests', coupled with its definition of 'ethical' as that which is 'currently acceptable and proper to the group of which the reader is a part',[31] somewhat undermined the claim that 'we are now experiencing a change from paternalism into partnership'.[32] It is symbolically significant that the latest volume produced in 1993, entitled *Medical Ethics Today*,[33] is a substantially recast and greatly expanded work,

---

[27] T. Marteau *et al.*, 'Factors Influencing the Communication Skills of First Year Clinical Medical Students', *Medical Education* 25 (1991), 127, 128; J. Firth-Cozens, 'Stress in Medical Undergraduates and House Officers', *British Journal of Hospital Medicine* 41 (1989), 161.
[28] General Medical Council, *Undergraduate Medical Education. The Need for Change* (London: GMC, 1991). See also S. Lowry, *Medical Education* (London: BMJ Publishing Group, 1993), 19–26.   [29] See n. 20 above, 200.
[30] London: British Medical Association, 1988.   [31] Ibid. p. iii.
[32] Ibid. 8.
[33] *Medical Ethics Today* (London: BMJ Publishing Group, 1993).

containing a powerful statement of patient-centred medical ethics. Pursuing the introductory themes of partnership and effective communication, it tells us, for example, that 'doctors should attempt to enter into continuing dialogue with patients about decisions which affect their well-being. Trust will only grow from frankness. Patients should control the amount and timing of information'.[34] Nowadays many patients will welcome these sentiments, but to what extent can it be said that medical education equips students to act in accordance with them?

In the medical schools there has to this day been little formal instruction in professional ethics. Until recently there was no teaching at all of medical ethics in the sense of systematic inquiry into moral problems raised by the practice of medicine. Despite increasing efforts to remedy this situation and notable achievements in certain medical schools, many others have shown a signal lack of commitment. In 1989 one could, for example, still qualify at one London school after attending only two one-hour lectures in medical ethics over the entire course[35] and in most institutions it remains a fringe area with no provision for compulsory attendance or assessment. In 1993, the *Lancet* published an article by a prominent physician, largely disparaging of what he termed 'academic ethics,' which culminated in the following peroration: 'and, in our anxiety not to be arrogant, let us not lose our self-confidence and self-esteem. If we hand over the teaching of medical ethics to outsiders, as some seem to think we should, we send the wrong message to society. For we hand over the core, the kernel, the very heart of good medicine'.[36] It is not without interest that, earlier on, he had asserted that 'the wishes of patients are sovereign and always have been. There is nothing new in that concept'.[37]

In formal terms at least, the teaching of sociology as applied to medicine appears to be more established. Over twenty years ago, a Royal Commission recommended that it should constitute part of the curriculum, in response to concern that the way people

---

[34] *Medical Ethics Today* 33, para. 1:10 (3).

[35] S. Burling *et al.*, 'Review of the Teaching of Medical Ethics in London Medical Schools', *Journal of Medical Ethics* 16 (1990), 206, 208.

[36] T. Brewin, 'How Much Ethics is Needed to Make a Good Doctor?' *Lancet* 341 (1993), 161, 163.   [37] Ibid. 162.

experience illness and its social setting were being neglected. A training mainly geared to producing an 'expert engineer of the body' offers little insight into the dynamics of encounters with individual patients, the broader environmental determinants of ill-health or the institutional organization of health care provision. Actively encouraged by the GMC's Education Committee, by 1980 most British medical schools had introduced sociology courses.

However, the commitment of many individual institutions to such courses has been far from wholehearted. Students quickly perceive the denigration of sociology in medical institutions and are themselves mostly hostile, suspicious, or at best indifferent. They do not take kindly to its methodologies or to the doubts which it raises about the way medicine is routinely practised. In such an environment, courses in sociology, as well as in medical ethics, are effectively marginalized. They will survive in some form, if only because they are not expensive to teach; but their already precarious existence within medical education remains vulnerable. They are competing for the time and resources needed to cater for an exponential growth of material in mainstream courses, new high technology specialties and sub-specialties. At the same time, it is advances in 'hi-tech', including the advent of computerized diagnosis and treatment, that contribute to the widespread belief that the practice of medicine has become too impersonal. Consequently the case for a more serious commitment to subjects which explore doctor–patient relationships, 'the culture of the ward',[38] and the broader social context of medicine, is more compelling than ever.

It is not however as clear as is sometimes assumed that to provide a grounding in the social sciences will suffice. Training and entry requirements tend to restrict admission to people from a comparatively narrow social range, including a significant, if declining, proportion from 'medical families'.[39] If greater under-standing of patients as people enhances the capacity of doctors to treat them, ideally we need medical schools to take account of this concern in their admissions policies, and to construct a model of

[38] R. Zussman, *Intensive Care* (Chicago: University of Chicago Press, 1992), 12.
[39] I. Allen, *Any Room at the Top?: A Study of Doctors and Their Careers* (London: Policy Studies Institute, 1988), 9.

medical education that aspires to foster compassionate insight into the way individual patients experience illness. As Downie and Charlton have pointed out, though exposure to the social sciences can, in principle, sensitize students to the roles which people have in society and to general patterns of human behaviour, it may not make much impact on their own attitudes towards, or empathy with, individual patients. It is, they argue, rather the arts or humanities which, with their immediacy and particularity of focus, have the power to engage our feelings in such a way that we can understand a case history from the subject's perspective and can thus make a contribution to the ideal of humane doctoring.[40]

The apparent reluctance of medical schools to change the nature of the traditional curriculum in part reflects the minimal control exercised by the GMC over their day-to-day organization. Though its Education Committee has a statutory responsibility to 'determine the extent of the knowledge and skill which is required' for a student to qualify,[41] the GMC cannot enforce its recommendations, short of outright refusal to recognize an institution's qualifications. In a discussion document published in 1991,[42] the Council 'hints at its frustration at the failure of the schools to implement the educational reforms proposed by the Council in 1980 when it called for a reduction of the factual overload in the curriculum and the promotion of self-education and critical thought'.[43] It remains to be seen how far recommendations to like effect in its latest report will be acted upon.[44]

Among the more glaring deficiencies has been the lack of effective training in communication skills. 'Unfortunately, traditional medical education at all levels is generally ineffective in teaching clinical communication. Medical education is a stressful and sometimes abrasive experience that can produce cynicism and callousness . . . although some important advances have occurred, there is extensive variability in the quality and intensity of courses

---

[40] *The Making of a Doctor*, n. 20 above, ch. 7.

[41] Medical Act 1983, s. 5(2)(a).

[42] General Medical Council, *Undergraduate Medical Education. The Need for Change*. See n. 28 above.

[43] S. Lowry, 'What's Wrong with Medical Education in Britain?' *British Medical Journal* 305 (1992), 1277, 1279.

[44] General Medical Council, *Tomorrow's Doctors* (London: GMC, 1994). See also S. Lowry, 'A Model for British Medical Education' (1993) 307 *British Medical Journal* 1021.

offered.'[45] Few medical schools require demonstrations of ability
to communicate for graduation or certification. Though the
acquisition of communication skills is among the stated aims of
medical training as set out by the GMC, and is indispensable if the
BMA's conception of the doctor–patient relationship is to become
a reality, as yet there are no specified forms of training or required
standards for it and there must be serious doubts about the level of
commitment in the majority of medical schools. A recent survey of
twenty-seven UK medical schools[46] revealed that nearly three-
quarters of them devoted less than 5 per cent of the total course to
communication skills, commonly incorporating them into the
already skeletal sociology or psychology modules, and that only six
schools formally assessed the ability of students to communicate
effectively. The survey concluded that 'medical education pays lip
service to communication skills and interpersonal relations while
remaining disease oriented in its approach'[47] and that 'the overt
display of positive attitudes is not backed up by appropriate
behaviour in all the institutions charged with providing basic
medical education'.[48] The GMC's recommendations for restructuring undergraduate medical teaching include the teaching
of communication skills as part of the core curriculum, but past
performance would seem to justify some scepticism about how any
such provisions will be implemented.

It is an integral feature of medical education that students are
treated as embryonic practitioners, encouraged from the outset to
adhere to established professional norms.[49] 'Applicants are
expected to make medicine their career. Candidates are asked
"Why do you want to be a doctor?" not "Why do you want to
study medicine?" '[50] It is, as it were, the continuation of the guild
by other means. 'To the outsider medical training looks very much
like a process of indoctrination—or professionalization, to give it a
more polite title. To the social scientist, the sheer length of the
training stems from the need to establish standards of conformity

---

[45] M. Simpson *et al.*, 'Doctor–Patient Communication: The Toronto Consensus
Statement', *British Medical Journal* 303 (1991), 1385, 1386.
[46] L. Frederikson, 'Designing a Doctor: Do They have the "Strong, Silent Type"
in mind?': n. 26 above.   [47] Ibid. 9.   [48] Ibid.
[49] S. Watkins, *Medicine and Labour : The Politics of a Profession* (London:
Lawrence and Wishart, 1987), 27–29.
[50] S. Lowry, 'Student Selection,' *British Medical Journal* 305 (1992), 1352.

to the group. It is often said that what follows is a progressive desensitization to the patient's point of view'.[51] Conventional medical wisdom, on the other hand, has it that such an approach is a practical necessity if student doctors are to cope with the pressures to come. Drawing mainly, but not exclusively, on the context of intensive care, Zussman points out that stressful intensity of work, in combination with great responsibility and fatigue, can have its positive side. It often fosters a strong sense of loyalty to other co-workers, which can advantage patients as well as work against their interests.[52]

The separate location of medical schools and hospitals re-inforces corporate identity, the feeling common among medical students of belonging to a self-contained world, almost a breed apart. It is a world which they are to inhabit for many years, yet most of them enter the hospital ward largely untutored in the complexities of its social organization and with little conception of how to relate to patients. The standard pre-clinical course studying basic medical sciences, followed by the three year 'apprenticeship' with consultants during clinical training, is simply not designed to attune them to the subtleties of communicating fruitfully with patients, or for that matter with other medical and nursing staff involved in patient care. Moreover, there is some evidence to suggest that those medical students who do not see communication skills as particularly relevant to medicine are more likely to prefer a career in hospital medicine or surgery, where such skills have not been greatly valued in the past[53] and are increasingly hard to deploy in institutions committed to more day surgery and shorter bed stays. Today, the environment of a busy hospital seldom lends itself to sensitive interaction by doctors with patients. All too often, organizational constraints, a lack of co-ordination, and the repetitive nature of most hospital treatment with its emphasis on episodic, organic disorder, induce a routinized focus on the disease rather than on the person whom it chances to inhabit.

This kind of distancing has traditionally been perceived and continues to be justified as a virtue, as a necessary defence mechanism against undue empathizing with patients. The judgement and performance of doctors who do not experience or exhibit

---

[51] Downie and Charlton, n. 20 above, 2.   [52] See n. 38 above.
[53] T. Marteau *et al.*, 'Factors Influencing the Communication Skills of First-Year Clinical Medical Students', n. 27 above.

intense emotional involvement are less likely to be impaired. That said, apart from the personal consequences for doctors that may flow from the suppression of their emotions, there are profound implications for the nature of medical relationships. In the words of a medical student at a London teaching hospital, describing how she was overcoming the problem, 'I feel myself beginning to separate patients from persons—people in hospital don't seem quite human any more.'[54] The line between authority and authoritarianism is not too difficult to cross, and one cannot readily accord rights to or collaborate with someone who 'doesn't seem quite human'.

Several accounts of medical training have criticized the extent to which the virtues of detachment, self-assurance, and robustness take pride of place over empathy with patients. The subsequent, notoriously gruelling regime of cheap labour imposed on the junior hospital doctor—for at least a further three years—has been attacked for fostering a degree of 'professional busyness' which, apart from dissipating nearly all available time and energy, can easily function as an avoidance mechanism inducing emotional distancing and authoritarian behaviour.[55] A survey conducted in 1987 revealed that junior doctors in the UK have longer hours of work than any others in western Europe.[56] Five years later, a *Times* editorial trenchantly observed that 'the sweated labour of hospital training, through which all doctors must pass, benefits neither doctors nor patients and plays a large part in junior doctor demoralization'.[57] A survey of 900 junior doctors in 1993 found that nearly six out of ten were still working more than their contracted hours.[58]

As a role model for the medical student in the crucial learning

[54] S. Spindler, 'Behind the Bedside Manner', *The Times*, 10 Nov. 1992. Cf. G. Harper, 'Breaking Taboos and Steadying the Self in Medical School', the *Lancet* 342 (1993), 913.

[55] See G. Bennet, *The Wound and the Doctor* (London: Secker & Warburg, 1987), chs. 1 and 6.

[56] Over 80 hours per week: S. Brearley, 'Medical Manpower' in T. Richards (ed.), *Medicine in Europe* (London: British Medical Journal, 1992), 45–6. Cf. 'In Denmark, Norway, and Sweden junior doctors work 37–45 hours a week': J. Poulsen, 'Junior Doctors and the EC Draft Directive on Working Hours', *British Medical Journal* 307 (1993), 1158.

[57] 'The Doctor's Dilemma', *The Times*, 2 Mar. 1992. Cf. J. Roberts, *British Medical Journal* 302 (1991), 225: 'Graduate medical education is a brutal enterprise in Britain'.   [58] *The Times*, 5 Oct. 1993.

environment of the ward round, the surgeon can all too easily reinforce traditional disregard for genuine dialogue with the patient. Evidence that the stereotypical surgeon with an authoritarian, non-communicative persona is far from a mythical figure can be found in a recent sociological study of surgery in England. Basing his conclusions on fieldwork conducted in the late 1980s, Fox[59] pointed to the prevalence of authoritarian behaviour in the highly structured setting of the ward round, an occasion which seems tailor-made for imposing the surgeon's point of view. In Fox's account, during these visits patients were often regarded in much the same way as defendants can be in busy magistrates courts: 'patients are disruptive elements, capable of challenging an otherwise shared discourse on surgical healing'.[60] 'The authority of the surgeon', he says, 'extends throughout the post-operative period, in her/his ascribed moral right to determine an appropriate date of discharge . . . the pleasure on the part of the patient which derives from this decision, in conjunction with the authoritarian nature of the discourse on recovery and discharge gives the air of a benevolent despotism to these interactions.'[61] Beyond any natural desire to achieve a successful outcome, Fox discerns a particular psychological mechanism at work in the strongly felt urge of many surgeons to pronounce the operation a success—the desire to cancel out, in a sense to deny or perhaps atone for, the surgical wound. The surgeon is, after all, a *wounding* healer. On those occasions when it is indisputable that healing has not occurred, it is the less surprising if silence should prevail.

The Maintenance of Authority through Prestige

Medicine is generally considered supreme among the professions—one of the very few walks of life in which people are so totally identified with their work that they are routinely addressed by their professional title, in and out of working hours. One does not say 'Good morning, solicitor'. Authoritative organizational apparatus has enabled the medical profession to combine an

[59] N. Fox, *The Social Meaning of Surgery* (Buckingham: Open University Press, 1992), ch. 4.

[60] Cf. P. Carlen, *Magistrates' Justice* (London: Martin Robertson, 1976); M. King, *The Framework of Criminal Justice* (London: Croom Helm, 1981).

[61] See Fox, n. 59 above, 88.

altruistic ideal of service enshrined in ethical codes with pronounced monopolistic practices.[62] The authority and prestige
which medicine acquired under the guild system were later
maintained and developed by the Royal Colleges and similar
bodies. Regulation under the Medical Act 1858 proved more of a
benefit than a hindrance to thĕ profession, as it conferred on
registered practitioners a status repeatedly denied to the homeo-
paths, osteopaths, and others who made up nearly two-thirds of
the healers then aspiring to the title of doctor.[63] Despite conveying
an outward impression of accountability, in practice the Act
allowed for substantial self-regulation and freedom to determine
health care delivery with minimal competition or external
monitoring.[64]

By making its mark in the upper reaches of public life, the
profession further enhanced its standing and influence. Strong
representation on public health schemes in the early nineteenth
century was to ensure it a secure foothold in the bureaucratic
apparatus of the state, to an extent that would have made the
absence of a major say on health care provision surprising. When
the National Health Service was established in 1948, the need to
accommodate opposition from within the profession meant that,
far from the statutory regime for regulating doctors being unduly
restrictive, 'the medical profession obtained a monopoly of
legitimacy among the health service providers: a unique position,
reflected in the participation of doctors in the running of the
NHS'.[65] Discretionary decision-making was to be the organizational hallmark. Commenting on the National Health Service Act
1977, Jacob observed that 'a characteristic running through the
legislation is the almost endless grant of discretionary power.
Despite numerous provisions for lay inputs, it is not unreal to
regard these powers as reflecting a legal reliance on the judgement

---

[62] Cf. J. Berlant, *Profession and Monopoly: A Study of Medicine in the United States and Great Britain* (Berkeley: University of California Press, 1975), pointing to the monopolistic rules on trust inducement, consultations, criticism, and fee-setting in Percival's 1803 code of ethics, as replicated and reinforced in the American Medical Association's codes from 1847 onwards.

[63] Although see now the Osteopaths Act 1993 (c.21).

[64] See M. Moran and B. Wood, *States, Regulation and the Medical Profession* (Buckingham: Open University Press, 1993), ch. 6.

[65] R. Klein, *The Politics of the National Health Service* (2nd edn.) (London: Longman, 1989), 28.

of the medical profession and its associated occupations . . . Time and time again, the statute provides that the profession will make and administer the rules (and judge their breach) and that the role of the state . . . is merely to confirm what has been done'.[66]

This kind of legislative endorsement has been a key element in medicine's capacity to withstand attack and deflect criticism. It reinforces the 'discipline effect' which, as Cotterrell has argued, enabled its exponents as a socially powerful group to rely on 'professional knowledge' as a self-sufficient rebuttal of critics, helping to maintain their autonomy and neutralize competition.[67] What counts as professional knowledge may cover a wide spectrum, sometimes embracing conflicting elements. Thus in medicine it includes both insistence on rigorous scientific method and what has been described as 'tacit' knowledge, or the intuition of professionalism.[68] Each of these approaches serves to nullify or fend off the claims of outsiders.

In particular, the ability to point to an impressive record of research based on scientific method has helped the profession to maintain its ascendancy over alternative and complementary therapies, many of which have not been subjected to rigorous testing and may not be amenable to it. Commenting on a BMA study in 1986, the *Lancet* observed that, 'the report's discussion sets up a dichotomy between the supremacy of modern medicine and what is virtually dismissed as witchcraft'.[69] Though it is, of

[66] J. Jacob and J. Davies (eds.), *Encyclopedia of Health Services and Medical Law* (London: Sweet & Maxwell, 1987), part 1, para. 1–010. Cf. 'substantive aims and powers are stated only in very general terms and their implementation is left to the relatively unstructured discretion of the Secretary of State, the Department of Health in its several manifestations and the various health authorities. The two major reorganizations prior to the present one did little to alter this structure, nor at first sight do the latest reforms appear to depart radically from the traditional format': D. Longley, *Public Law and Health Service Accountability* (Buckingham: Open University Press, 1993), 17.

[67] R. Cotterrell, 'Professional Autonomy and the Construction of Professional Knowledge: Sociology in the Professional Practice of Law and Medicine' (Paper to British Sociological Association Annual Conference, University of Durham, 1980). Cf. E. Freidson, *Profession of Medicine* (New York: Dodd Mead, 1970), 369 ff.: 'the critical flaw in professional autonomy' is that 'by allowing and encouraging the development of self-sufficient institutions, it develops and maintains in the profession a self-deceiving view of the objectivity and reliability of its knowledge'.

[68] R. Cotterrell, above, 6–7; cf. J. Montgomery, 'Medicine, Accountability, and Professionalism' (1989) 16 *Journal of Law and Society* 319, 327.

[69] (1986) 1 *Lancet* 1223.

course, wholly salutary that people should be warned against exploitation by the untrained and unregulated peddlers of false cures, there is a danger of this legitimate concern leading to a blanket condemnation of non-conventional treatments, some of which require the study of orthodox medical sciences and have a considerable following for particular conditions.

The classic case has been osteopathy, for years more or less confined to the sphere of private practice by virtue of statutes which severely restricted the expenditure of public funds, and only very recently accorded the status of a regulated profession under the Osteopaths Act 1993. In fact, a high proportion of doctors will on occasion delegate the care of a patient to complementary therapists,[70] and now that some positive scientific evidence has begun to emerge from controlled trials for specific conditions,[71] one can detect some change of attitude within the profession towards certain non-conventional forms of medicine. In its most recent report on the subject, the BMA welcomed closer collaboration with osteopaths and chiropractors[72] and was noticeably less critical than in the past about other 'discrete clinical disciplines', such as homeopathy and acupuncture,[73] for which it recommended that statutory self-regulation be considered. Interestingly, the presentation of reorganization in the NHS as a monument to 'patient choice'[74] enabled proponents of complementary therapies to press for their more extensive and explicit incorporation in health service provision, though ultimately without success.[75]

It might be thought that the consumerist and cost-cutting agenda of the latest NHS reforms would be bound to make major inroads into professional autonomy and supremacy in the health care field, not only because of new managerial pressures but also in response to the claims of paramedical professions seeking to enlarge the

[70] As many as 71.7% in one study: R. Wharton and G. Lewith, 'Complementary Medicine and the General Practitioner', *British Medical Journal* 292 (1986), 1,498.
[71] E. Ernst, 'Complementary Medicine: Scrutinising the Alternatives' (1993) 341 *Lancet* 1626.
[72] *Complementary Medicine: New Approaches to Good Practice* (Oxford: Oxford University Press, 1993) 6. The Chiropractors Bill received its Third Reading in the House of Commons on 6 May 1994.
[73] Ibid. 138–9 and 139–40, respectively.
[74] Department of Health, *Working for Patients* (London: HMSO, 1989).
[75] One such attempt failed by only 3 votes in the House of Lords: Hansard (House of Lords), vol. 520, Session 1989–90 (8th vol.) col. 217 (12 June 1990).

scope of their responsibilities.[76] Skilled nurses and midwives, for example, have long argued that the division of labour enshrined in various statutory provisions undervalues their potential contribution as patient-centred carers and is at odds with the realities of medical practice.[77] Though district nurses have been given a limited right to prescribe without reference to a medical practitioner,[78] it is uncertain whether recent statutory developments in nursing[79] will enhance self-regulation, given the increased regulatory powers granted to the Secretary of State, the reduction in the number of elected representatives on the United Kingdom Central Council for Nursing, Midwifery and Health Visiting and the provision for state-appointed non-Council members on professional conduct committees.[80]

A recent comparative study of state regulation and the medical profession concluded that 'the 1989–91 reforms were less than comprehensive. UK doctors retain the self-regulation of market entry and discipline exercised by the GMC . . . Their ability to work for both the public and private sectors; the self-employed status of GPs; the strict separation of hospital and general practice activity . . . and a great deal of clinical freedom . . . all remain scarcely if at all changed . . . the boundaries of the profession continue to hold secure, with virtually no intrusion by pharmacists or nurse prescribers, or by osteopaths, chiropractors or other providers of "alternative medicine". The state continues to recognize allopathic medicine as a legitimate monopoly, just as it did when it passed the 1858 Act. The very existence of the NHS thus actually strengthens the status of doctors by severely

---

[76] See the Professions Supplementary to Medicine Act, 1960, regularizing the position of several paramedical professions operating within the NHS, granting limited professional autonomy for physiotherapists, radiographers, and chiropodists.

[77] See e.g. J. Salvage, 'The Theory and Practice of the New Nursing', *Nursing Times* 86(4) (1990), 42. See, also, on the persistence of a restrictive legal approach, J. Montgomery, 'Doctors' Handmaidens: The Legal Contribution' in S. McVeigh and S. Wheeler (eds.), *Law, Health and Medical Regulation* (Aldershot: Dartmouth, 1992) 141, 155–8.

[78] The Medicinal Products: Prescription by Nurses etc. Act 1992.

[79] The Nurses, Midwives and Health Visitors Act 1992, modifying the Nurses, Midwives and Health Visitors Act 1979.

[80] See N. Fletcher, 'The Nurses, Midwives and Health Visitors Act 1992' (1992) 8 *Professional Negligence* 94.

restricting the ability of alternative providers to enter the market successfully.'[81]

This judgement, made only a short time after the introduction of the NHS reforms, may, at least in the longer term, prove to have been premature. Since the passage of the 1990 Act, we have seen the managerial threat to clinical freedom, the passing of the Osteopaths Act, and the modification of the BMA's attitude to several other complementary regimes. There is also the limited increase in nurses' prescribing powers which is part of a broader design, epitomized by the strategy known as Project 2000. Its stated aim is to reform nursing education by shifting the emphasis from apprenticeship towards an integrated approach involving more course-based learning, and by measures which would provide a clinical career structure. Clearly, however, in the present economic climate, radical reorganization of nursing work will not be implemented without cogent evidence of its cost effectiveness. Nor, if the historical development of nursing is any guide,[82] is it likely to be viewed with equanimity by doctors. As Beardshaw has noted, 'the extent to which doctors will be willing to exchange their traditional "handmaidens" for clinical partners is one of the most important questions posed by the new nursing'.[83]

SOME FORCES FOR CHANGE

The Emergence of the Patient's Voice

If genuine commitment to dialogue between doctors and their patients is essentially a modern idea, willingness to concede that meaningful consent to treatment could be a legitimate expectation owes much to the long-drawn-out historical process whereby civil,

---

[81] Moran and Wood, *States, Regulation and the Medical Profession*, n. 64 above, 135. Cf. M. Elston, 'The Politics of Professional Power: Medicine in a Changing Health Service' in J. Gabe, M. Calnan and M. Bury (eds.), *The Sociology of the Health Service* (London: Routledge, 1991).

[82] R. Dingwall, A. Rafferty, and C. Webster, *An Introduction to the Social History of Nursing* (London: Routledge, 1988).

[83] V. Beardshaw, 'Prospects for Nursing' in E. Beck *et al.* (eds.), *In the Best of Health?* (London: Chapman & Hall, 1992), ch. 6, 120.

political, and social rights came to be seen as individual entitlements.[84] Thus when, in the seventeenth and eighteenth centuries,
the notion of government by consent began to take root, medicine
was one of several spheres in which, by extrapolation, the case for
applying the concept was to surface.[85] In keeping with the spirit of
the Enlightenment, some eighteenth century political theorists and
physicians discerned a concrete link between autonomy and
patient well-being, contending that 'individual freedom directly
promoted human health'.[86] The eminent and erudite physician,
Benjamin Rush, himself a signatory of the American Declaration
of Independence, deplored the elements of mystique and obfuscation in medicine which made 'consent' a hollow formality. In
language reminiscent of Gregory (his former teacher), he urged
colleagues to 'strip [the] profession of everything that looks like
mystery'.[87]

However, Rush was far from advocating that patients should
override the views of their doctors. Not unlike Gregory, 'he
wanted patients to be sufficiently educated so that they could
understand physicians' recommendations and therefore be motivated to *comply*'.[88] It is in this limited sense, of informed patients
voluntarily deferring to the authority of the medical expert for
their own therapeutic benefit, that he was committed to their
'decisional autonomy'. His approach was ultimately rooted in
considerations of welfare based on beneficence.[89] Any disposition
to cultivate in the medical sphere the Enlightenment view about
the life-enhancing properties of liberty was increasingly held in
check by nineteenth century physicians, who maintained that
autonomy was normally detrimental to the health of most
patients.[90]

---

[84] See A. Barron and C. Scott, 'The Citizen's Charter Programme' (1992) 55
Modern Law Review 526, at 532–5.
[85] J. Fletcher, 'The Evolution of the Ethics of Informed Consent' *Progress in
Clinical and Biological Research* 128 (1983), 187, 198–202.
[86] See Pernick, n. 19 above, 5.
[87] B. Rush, *The Selected Writings of Benjamin Rush*, ed. D. Runes (New York:
Philosophical Library, 1947). 236.
[88] R. Faden and T. Beauchamp, *A History of Informed Consent* (New York:
Oxford University Press, 1986), 65.
[89] See T. Beauchamp, 'The Promise of the Beneficence Model for Medical
Ethics' (1990) 6 *Journal of Contemporary Health Law and Policy* 145, especially
147 and 150.   [90] Pernick, n. 19 above, 10.

Today, there are several strands to the argument that medical practice needs to be more sensitive to the concerns of patients. It is not only lawyers who have been depicted as 'insatiable cormorants'. Doctors have been accused of exploiting and expanding their own 'professional dominance',[91] of needlessly medicalizing our lives and inducing an unhealthy dependence on their palliatives.[92] They have been castigated for asserting a right to determine priorities in health care provision, as a corollary of their socially acknowledged control over the definition of illness.[93] And such challenges have not always come from outside medicine. The epidemiologist, McKeown, in stressing the importance of improved nutrition and environmental measures in combating disease, criticized a tendency within the profession to exaggerate the historical contribution of scientific medicine and to grant pride of place to high-technology intervention. This stance, he argued, helped to ensure that preventive measures and the provision of care for chronic conditions, for the mentally ill, and the handicapped have been under-resourced by comparison with curative medicine.[94] Support for this conclusion can be found in the work of yet more radical reformers, who condemn the 'commodification of health care' for diverting attention from endemic social and economic causes of ill-health.[95] At the same time, market economists and some advocates of consumerism have extolled the virtues of medicine as trade. Their preferred conception of health care provision has struck a chord with those academic lawyers who seek a legal framework for it based on private ordering, whereby patients could, in principle, strike bargains tailored to their individual wishes.[96] Advocates of complementary medicine also appeal to the virtues of consumer choice, emphasizing the importance of individualized treatment and of adopting a more sympathetic attitude towards lay conceptions of health and illness. Similar themes have surfaced in feminist writing that espouses a

---

[91] E. Freidson, *Professional Dominance* (New York: Atherton, 1970).
[92] I. Illich, *Medical Nemesis: The Expropriation of Health* (London: Calder & Boyars, 1975).
[93] I. Kennedy, *The Unmasking of Medicine* (London: Allen & Unwin, 1981).
[94] T. McKeown, *The Role of Medicine: Dream, Mirage or Nemesis* (London: Nuffield Provincial Hospitals Trust, 1976).
[95] e.g. V. Navarro, 'Work, Ideology and Science: The Case of Medicine', *Social Science and Medicine* 14 (1980), 191. [96] See 166–8 below.

model of health care less influenced by patriarchal assumptions about the treatment of women.[97] Mainly, but not exclusively, addressing itself to the field of obstetrics, the women's health movement has protested against widespread resort to invasive techniques and has also sought to promote strategies of self-care.

Plainly not all of these challenges to the dominant model are mutually compatible. As is evident from its prominence as an issue in the 1992 General Election and beyond, the future direction of health care provision remains highly contentious, leaving a number of unanswered questions about the place of doctor–patient relationships within the scheme of things. What seems clear is that we are witnessing the application to health care of an expansive notion of consumerism, which embraces the quality of services as well as of products. On one view, this concern about consumer choice can be adequately met by the provision of information alone. But there is a range of other possible implications, which include greater professional accountability, more patient participation in medical decision-making, and full-blooded self-determination. All such demands reflect the general social decline in deference, revealing scepticism on the part of a better-educated public about professional expertise and increasing resentment of the secrecy which often accompanies professional practices. There is growing resistance to claims by professional groups to monopolize decision-making in matters which either do not self-evidently require, or exclusively depend upon, their particular skills or judgement. In medicine, this is most clearly the case when issues other than technical proficiency in diagnosis and treatment are at stake, though it can also hold true in the purely clinical sphere.

If there is a general unifying thread in the above critiques of the dominant model, it is their concern that it dispenses with the patient's voice. Yet if advocates of medical paternalism stand accused of insensitivity to the moral, political, and therapeutic claims of the individual patient, they are also increasingly under attack for making that patient their exclusive focus. Seeking to promote the 'best interests' of the particular patient conjures up an

---

[97] M. Stacey, *The Sociology of Health and Healing* (London: Unwin Hyman, 1988).

archaic, almost self-indulgent vision of medical practice as a one-to-one pastoral relationship devoid of institutional constraints. It is a vision far removed from the realities of a beleaguered health service, where the scope for continuity of care is much diminished. It is not easy for doctors to sustain their commitment to individualized treatment in a hospital sector dominated by managerial notions of efficiency, where administrators are constrained by the imperative of cost containment, and where the demands of budget-holding GPs increasingly dictate the ground rules. Locally imposed age limits for expensive life saving procedures,[98] a perceptible retreat from the ideal of comprehensive provision[99] and the adoption of batch referral arrangements for hospital treatment do not promote deepening medical relationships or the pursuit of the individual patient's 'best interests'.

The Government sought to justify the recent restructuring of health care delivery on grounds of cutting costs and empowering patients. Undoubtedly, in the face of budgetary restrictions and the priorities of health administrators, the decision-making powers of *hospital* doctors are declining. Hospital managers are more inclined to defer to the purchasing power of budget-holding GPs than to the 'professional knowledge' of consultants or the principle of clinical freedom. There are signs that the new managerial ascendancy in the health service presents a much more immediate and direct threat to medical paternalism than less tangible criticisms about the need for dialogue. The orientation of the new-style NHS could prove to be the single most potent factor in the demise of a doctor-centred conception of health care provision. What remains unclear is how, to what extent and with what consequences it will permit the patient's voice to be heard.

[98] See e.g. N. Boon, 'New Deal for Old Hearts', *British Medical Journal* 303 (1991), 70.

[99] See e.g. D. Keeley, 'The Fundholding Debate: Should Practices Reconsider the Decision not to Fundhold?', *British Medical Journal* 306 (1993), 697.

3

Emergent Medical Models

The Growth of a 'Rights Perspective'

Much of the opposition to paternalism in medicine has focused on its denial of rights, particularly on the denial of the patient's moral and political agency when choice of treatment is pre-empted and more or less unquestioning trust expected. There has been far more concern that paternalistic medical practice undermines the patient's 'right to self-determination' than that it might be detrimental to patient welfare. A commitment to viewing individuals as ends in themselves, free to choose their own destiny, has of course featured very prominently in general ethical debate, if not in professional medical ethics. As Feinberg puts it, 'every person's moral right to govern himself surely outweighs the "right" of benevolent intermeddlers to manipulate him for his own advantage, whether that advantage be health, wealth, contentment, or freedom'.[1] Appeal to such sentiments can be especially powerful when invasive medical procedures are contemplated. The desire to protect and promote patients' 'rights' is both an understandable and a rhetorically compelling reaction against the traditional concern with their 'best interests'.

It is now commonly accepted that respect for personal dignity, and by implication for minority views, justifies putting a high value on patients exercising decision-making powers. The patient as the person who stands to be affected, it is argued, normally have the right (and, for that matter, the responsibility)[2] to decide whether or not to undergo any proposed treatment. It would seem to follow that patients should also have a right to such information

---

[1] J. Feinberg, *The Moral Limits of the Criminal Law: Harm to Self* (Oxford: Oxford University Press, 1986), 68.

[2] Except to the extent that it may be waived or subject to an informed decision to transfer the right to decide.

as would facilitate an informed decision, not only about what is proposed but also about other feasible options. Assuming that the patient is not to be deemed incompetent for reasons such as infancy or serious mental incapacity, and provided that a given decision does not entail unjustifiable harm to others, any reservations that the doctor might have about its medical appropriateness would prima facie be overridden by respect for individual choice as such.

Of course, giving effect to the choice might not be possible for extraneous reasons, such as limited resources. It is an unfortunate characteristic of the appeal to rights that it tends to suggest the existence of an absolute entitlement regardless of surrounding circumstances. Equally, the concept of 'patient competence' is not devoid of difficulty. The mere fact of being a patient usually involves some diminution of autonomy, whether due to the condition itself, the patient's deficient medical knowledge, or conventional expectations of passivity in the role. In addition, what counts as a 'competent' decision may be open to dispute in the light of competing moral values; the enduring controversy over the 'right to die' provides a familiar example. Nevertheless, our society can go to great lengths in upholding decisional autonomy. Even when a decision is commonly deemed irrational and difficult to reconcile with traditional medical ethics, it will normally be socially (and legally) condoned if it rests on some strongly held religious belief or cultural preference, the classic case being the refusal of a Jehovah's Witness to accept a life-saving blood transfusion.[3]

At the same time, openness to the notion that patients have rights which they are fully entitled to pursue has much to do with the declining belief in religion and supernatural forces associated with the rise of science. The major cultural shift whereby submissive resignation to divine providence gradually yielded to scientific explanations of natural phenomena was of great importance, both in encouraging people to believe that they had a right to decide whether or how they should be treated and in legitimating legal claims for personal injury and suffering. Considerations of cost and social deference, vital though they were, do not entirely

---

[3] For legal authority see, e.g. *R.* v. *Blaue* [1975] 1 WLR 1411; *Malette* v. *Shulman* (1990) 67 DLR (4th) 321.

explain the comparative rarity of medical negligence actions in the past. Only when people grew accustomed to thinking of human suffering as attributable to, and remediable by, human action did it become implausible to condemn as virtual blasphemers those who asserted individual rights by bringing a medical claim.[4]

That we have become more receptive, in the course of the twentieth century, to the notion of patients as bearers of rights owes a lot to the particular resonance of the issue for subjects of medical experimentation.[5] Much of the modern impetus for a rights perspective on experimental treatment is directly traceable to revelations of the atrocities committed by Nazi doctors during the Second World War. The various international guidelines (notably the Nuremburg Code and the Declaration of Helsinki), and national ethical codes which were drawn up as a result, gained in significance as rapid post-war advances in medical technology prompted forebodings of a Brave New World. More recently, biomedical innovation in reproductive technologies[6] has increased the demand for greater accountability and more lay control over the applications of such research.[7] The momentum for a rights-based approach to experimental medicine naturally served to draw attention to its potential role in therapeutic treatment.

New-found respect for patients' rights, as embodied in legislation and case law, is also at one level an offshoot of the growing commitment to civil rights generally in a number of countries over the last thirty years or so. A key influence was the emergence of the American Civil Rights Movement in the 1960s, with its focus on diverse underprivileged groups. The very process of highlighting social disadvantage and the denial of rights as experienced by racial minorities, women, the mentally ill, and prisoners, at times entailed political debate and prompted legal action over a

[4] Cf. K. De Ville, *Medical Malpractice in Nineteenth Century America: Origins and Legacy* (New York: New York University Press, 1990), ch. 5.

[5] 'Health care and the rights of patients are the latest entrants into the rights arena', a quotation from C. Faulder, *Whose Body Is It: The Troubling Issue of Informed Consent* (London: Virago Press, 1985), 17.

[6] See R. Hope, 'The Birth of Medical Law' (1991) 11 *Oxford Journal of Legal Studies* 247.

[7] See e.g. the Human Fertilisation and Embryology Authority, *Donated Ovarian Tissue in Embryo Research and Assisted Contraception* (London, HFEA, 1994); Justice M. Kirby, 'Legal Problems: Human Genome Project' (1993) 67 *Australian Law Journal* 894.

range of health care and medico-ethical issues, such as consent to treatment, access to information, and abortion. Here can be found the origins of the 'patient's rights movement' and the Patient's Bill of Rights (1973), a kind of non-legal charter which 'summarizes many of the deeply held convictions of both lay people and some physicians who are beginning to question their Hippocratic heritage'.[8]

Acknowledgment of 'patients' rights' in the United States was underlined by the introduction of Medicaid (in 1965), arguing a limited recognition of medical care as an entitlement. Growing expectations that patients might be more actively involved in their treatment were partially accommodated in landmark judicial decisions of the early 1970s on informed consent.[9] This was a time when judicial interpretation of the Constitution and enactments by state legislatures were noticeably sympathetic to the exercise of personal choice in matters of fundamental concern to the individual. A 'constitutional' right of privacy was invoked to permit a greater role for individual as opposed to state determination on contraception,[10] to justify access to abortion,[11] and as a means of reinforcing the ancient common law prohibition against 'unwanted infringements of bodily integrity'.[12] Over recent decades, there have been comparable developments in several commonwealth jurisdictions[13] and under the European Convention on Human Rights.[14]

Appeals to the intrinsic worth of individual autonomy and to a derivative 'right of privacy' can thus have important practical consequences in the medical sphere. In signifying the moral unacceptability of coercion, they stand as a corrective to any temptation for doctors, as well as experimental scientists, to ride

---

[8] R. Veatch, *A Theory of Medical Ethics* (New York: Basic Books, 1981), 47. Cf. T. Beauchamp, 'The Promise of the Beneficence Model for Medical Ethics' (1990) 6 *Journal of Contemporary Health Law and Policy* 145, 148.

[9] *Canterbury* v. *Spence*, 464 F 2d 772 (DC Cir., 1972); *Cobbs* v. *Grant* 502 P 2d 1 (1972); *Wilkinson* v. *Vesey*, 295 A 2d 676 (1972). See, further, ch. 6.

[10] *Griswold* v. *Connecticut*, 381 US 479 (1965).

[11] *Roe* v. *Wade*, 410 US 113 (1973).

[12] *Superintendent of Belchertown State School* v. *Saikewicz*, 373 Mass 728, 370 NE 2d 417 (1977), and cf. *Re Quinlan*, 70 NJ 10, 355 A 2d 647 (1976).

[13] e.g. under Canada's Charter of Rights and Freedoms.

[14] See I. Kennedy, 'Patients, Doctors and Human Rights' in R. Blackburn and J. Taylor (eds.), *Human Rights for the 1990s* (London: Mansell, 1991), ch. 9.

roughshod over patients; they also imply a model of medical relationships in which patients are entitled to such information as will enable them to decide for themselves how, if at all, they should be treated. By such means, patients become more open to the possibility of viewing the doctor as a source of information for decisions which, if they so wish, they may take entirely on their own.

A distinctive feature of the developments described above is that they have been facilitated, politically and legally, by abstract principles enshrined in foundational texts. Though logic dictates that without entrenchment 'enactment cannot change the weight of pre-existing rights',[15] in jurisdictions which have enacted fundamental rights, their reiteration in other instruments in respect of particular social groups[16] can be seen as a natural outgrowth of the constitutional structure with both a sensitizing and a legitimizing function. By taking such steps, legislative bodies can contribute to a change in social attitudes[17] whereby a given right is more readily invoked and accorded additional weight when a balance has to be struck in hard cases. The United States Constitution, in particular, is infused with a spirit of individualism and a commitment to self-determination wholly at odds with the pride of place given to professional judgement in traditional medical ethics.

In England, too, despite the absence of a written constitution or bill of rights[18] and notwithstanding the traditional inclination to presume the existence of individual liberty rather than acknowledge specific forms of entitlement, post-War developments involved a shift towards policies which identified and sought to protect particular rights as a matter of social obligation. Once it was accepted that basic welfare state provision should be available

[15] T. Allan, 'Constitutional Rights and Common Law' (1991) 11 *Oxford Journal of Legal Studies* 453, 456.

[16] e.g. legislation in several US jurisdictions requiring written informed consent for HIV antibody testing: see D. Pearl and A. Grubb, *Blood Testing, Aids and DNA Profiling* (Bristol: Family Law, 1990), 33–35.

[17] It is not fanciful to characterize in this way the achievements of the patients' rights movement in the United States, where the adoption by the American Hospital Association of a Patient's Bill of Rights in 1973 was soon to be followed by statutory equivalents in a number of states.

[18] The United Kingdom alone of the 28 parties to the European Convention on Human Rights has not incorporated it into its domestic law.

as of right in respect of health, education, housing, and general subsistence, it became easier to visualize citizens as rights-bearers in other spheres. For example, partly prompted by developments in the United States, legislation was introduced in the 1960s and 1970s to outlaw discrimination on grounds of race or sex and and state agencies were established, charged, *inter alia*, with the task of making people more attuned to seeing freedom from discrimination as a rights issue. More recent elaboration of this emphasis on the individual can be found in European ideas on fundamental rights and in emergent European law, as manifested in decisions of the European Commission and Court of Human Rights. Exposure to European legal analysis, with its strong attachment to the vindication of personal liberties, is beginning to have its effect on English legal thinking as, little by little, the legislature is required to implement and courts are asked to take account of specific provisions of the European Convention on Human Rights.[19] In regard to health care, a concrete example of this process at work is provided by the legislative history of data protection and its impact on access to medical records.[20]

In addition to external pressures to enunciate specific rights and make administrative discretion more justiciable, there is now new impetus for a 'rights perspective' in domestic law generally because of the more expansive system of judicial review which, as we have seen, could in principle have repercussions in the medical sphere. The provision under the NHS of comprehensive health care as a universal right may have tempered reluctance to sue when things went wrong, but it did not create an expectation of a

[19] See D. Feldman, *Civil Liberties and Human Rights in England and Wales* (Oxford: Clarendon Press, 1993), 60–9.

[20] See *Gaskin* v. *Liverpool City Council* [1980] 1 WLR 1549; *Gaskin* v. *The United Kingdom* [1990] 1 FLR 167. As Lee has observed, 'It was clear that the traditional line of refusing patient access to health records in general terms would have had difficulty surviving in the aftermath of the European Court judgment in *Gaskin*. Although the decision was limited in scope, the case paved the way for wider access to records, notes and reports': R. Lee, 'Confidentiality and Medical Records' in C. Dyer (ed.), *Doctors, Patients and the Law* (Oxford: Blackwell Scientific Publications, 1992), 39. See now Data Protection Act 1984, as modified by the Data Protection (Subject Access Modification) (Health) Order 1987 (SI 1987 No 1903). S. 29(1) of the 1984 Act provides in principle for the exemption of medical records, and the 1987 SI permits doctors to withhold data from medical records, *inter alia*, where they consider that disclosure is likely to cause serious harm to the patient's physical or mental health. See, also, Access to Medical Reports Act 1988; Access to Health Records Act 1990.

say in how doctors related to or treated their patients. It is only in the last ten years or so that we encounter legislative steps to promote sensitivity to patients' rights over health care delivery. The 1980s saw tentative moves in this direction, with the passage of the Hospital Complaints Procedure Act 1985, a largely anodyne enabling measure, and the beginnings of access to personal medical records, albeit in the latter case more directly as a response to European initiatives and requirements.

What seems different now is the extent to which individuals and their legal advisers see the assertion of rights as a viable option. The potential implications for English medical law of developing a rights perspective are easy to see. In most cases concerned with the propriety of medical treatment, the *Bolam* test reigns supreme. Whether the courts are being asked to pronounce on informed decision-making by competent patients or on the acceptability of sterilization for incompetent ones, almost everything is made to turn on whether or not a doctor's actual or proposed conduct constitutes a breach of duty according to a narrowly conceived medical criterion. If instead, judicial analysis of such issues seriously addressed the question of patients' rights, then considerations of concern to the patient and society at large, which are at present either ignored or merely hinted at, would help to shape the judgements.[21]

The Patient as Consumer

Though the Government's stance on the way health care should be provided cannot directly determine the nature of medical relationships, it does have a bearing on them and on how patients perceive medical care. At the present time, the official tone is set by the 'rights' and standards proclaimed in the Patient's Charter and by the recent organizational reforms to the NHS. Political appeal to individual rights has taken on a new form, as embodied in the 'Citizen's Charter'[22] and its various progeny, the expressed aim being to secure improved standards in public services. More

[21] See I. Kennedy, 'Patients, Doctors and Human Rights', n. 14 above, ch. 9.

[22] Cm. 1599, HMSO 1991. The Citizen's Charter is a White Paper accorded prominence by the Government. The Queen's Speech, 6 May 1992, intimated that it would give 'priority to improving public services through the Citizen's Charter, which will be at the centre of decision-making'.

specifically for our purposes, the Patient's Charter begins with the bold, if demonstrably false, claim that it 'sets out clearly for the first time your *rights* to care in the National Health Service'.[23] If one leaves to one side the occasional rhetorical flourish,[24] the Charter's stated objectives are worthy rather than inspirational. A familiar litany of standards and performance indicators over-shadows any intrinsic concern for human rights. In this respect the aims of the Government's Charters resemble those of many organizations dedicated to promoting the 'rights' of the individual in the guise of consumer. In stressing value for money and the achievement of set targets for delivery of services, the Citizen's Charter more or less equates *citizens'* rights with *consumers'* rights. In much the same way, the Patient's Charter confirms a policy shift away from the professional public service ideal traditionally associated with medicine towards a narrower concep-tion of medical relationships based on contractualism and customer service.[25] This approach is also a central feature of the reorganized NHS, as established under the 1990 Act. It was heralded by a White Paper entitled *Working for Patients*,[26] and a series of related official publications,[27] in which patients are redesignated 'customers' and where notions of 'consumer sovereignty' and 'consumer choice' resurface as 'patient sovereignty' and 'patient choice'. *Working for Patients* is shot through with expressions such as 'putting patients first', 'better service to the patient', 'a better deal for the public', and 'patients' choice of good quality service'.

At the rhetorical level, then, patient autonomy re-characterized as consumer sovereignty now looms large, it having been a much-vaunted governmental aim over a number of years 'to extend

[23] Department of Health, *The Patient's Charter* (London: HMSO, 1991), 6. Emphasis added.

[24] e.g. that the aim of the first National Charter Standard is 'respect for privacy, dignity, and religious and cultural beliefs': ibid. 12.

[25] D. Plamping and T. Delamothe, 'The Citizen's Charter and the NHS' (1991) 303 *British Medical Journal* 203. Cf. 'The relationship between state and citizen is implicitly conceptualised in the Citizen's Charter programme in terms of a contractual nexus': A. Barron and C. Scott, 'The Citizen's Charter Programme' (1992) 55 *Modern Law Review* 526, 543.

[26] Department of Health (London: HMSO, 1989), Cm 555.

[27] See generally, D. Hughes, 'The Reorganisation of the National Health Service: The Rhetoric and Reality of the Internal Market' (1991) 54 *Modern Law Review* 88.

patient choice'[28] by reorganizing the health care delivery system on more commercial lines. To be more than rhetoric even in its own limited terms, this disavowal of medical paternalism must ensure both a less passive role for patients in individual doctor–patient relationships and a greater say for them in determining priorities in health care provision. The language of commerce and marketization which pervades the Charters, the 1990 Act and related Department of Health publications seems designed to alter the very way we conceptualize the provision of public sector medical services. If it succeeds in doing so, it will facilitate a paradigm shift from public to private ordering in health care.

Medicine as Trade

Comparing American arrangements with those in the UK, Moran and Wood observe that 'the more competitive and commercialized character of US society has produced a more commercially-orientated system of professional organization. Doctors compete much more obviously for business; health care is much more consciously operated as an industry in which commercial rules of corporate rationality are to the fore.'[29] From the 1970s onwards, the complaint that codes of ethics were being invoked by professional associations as a means of fending off competition struck a sympathetic chord with the Federal Trade Commission[30] and the courts.[31] As a consequence, amendments were made to the American Medical Association's anti-competitive rules on advertising, price-fixing, accreditation, and boycotts of chiropractors. 'US doctors and their professional associations are now

---

[28] *Working for Patients*, 1989, n. 26 above, para. 13.5. Cf. Department of Health and Social Security, *Patients First* (London: HMSO, 1979) and Department of Health and Social Security, *The NHS Management Inquiry DA (83) 38* (London: DHSS, 1983).

[29] M. Moran and B. Wood, *States, Regulation and the Medical Profession* (Buckingham: Open University Press, 1993), 95. Cf. W. Wadlington, 'Legal Responses to Patient Injury: A Future Agenda for Research and Reform' (1991) 54(2) *Law and Contemporary Problems* 199, 210.

[30] J. Berlant, *Profession and Monopoly: A Study of Medicine in the United States and Great Britain* (Berkeley: University of California Press, 1975).

[31] *Goldfarb* v. *Virginia State Bar*, 421 US 773 (1975); *National Society of Professional Engineers* v. *US*, 435 US 679 (1978).

treated for many antitrust purposes as though they were engaged in normal business transactions'.[32]

It would be surprising if the introduction of competitive market values and corporate forms of practice into health care provision did not affect doctor–patient relationships. Brennan, for example, has described how in America the vigorous pursuit of cost-containment measures during the 1980s furthered the erosion of traditional medical ethics both by facilitating greater institutional control over medical decision-making and by encouraging all interested parties to approach medical transactions in a contractualist frame of mind. Thus he observes that 'as the virtues of the market place, including cost-benefit analysis, efficiency considerations and competition, are brought to medical care, then all actors—doctors, patients, and administrators—become more likely to utilize the language of rights and liberties, just as other people in a liberal state do'.[33] The net effect is to foster medical relationships 'in which rights rather than duties are the appropriate form of moral discourse'.[34] It is a climate in which both the doctor's overriding commitment to patient well-being and the patient's trust in that commitment are put to the test as a result of pressures exerted by government, hospital authorities, and insurance companies, to say nothing of the murkier depths of self-referral to physician-owned institutions.[35]

In England, the growth of private health care has been retarded by the widespread acceptance and use of the NHS, a pervasive feature of British life not solely rooted in considerations of cost. Deference by patients to GP decision-making authority on referrals further inhibits the effective exercise of consumer sovereignty via the private sector.[36] None the less, it has expanded significantly in recent years.[37] In large measure, this is due to

---

[32] *AMA* v. *FTC*, 638 F 2d 443 (1980); aff'd 452 US 960 (1982); cf. F. Miller, 'Competition Law and Anticompetitive Professional Behaviour Affecting Health Care' (1992) 55 *Modern Law Review* 453, 455.

[33] T. Brennan, *Just Doctoring: Medical Ethics in the Liberal State* (Berkeley: University of California Press, 1991), 61.   [34] Ibid. 58.

[35] See A. Relman ' "Self-Referral"—What's at Stake?' *New England Journal of Medicine* 327 (1992), 1522.

[36] See M. Calnan, S. Cant, and J. Gabe, *Going Private: Why People Pay for their Health Care* (Buckingham: Open University Press, 1993), 65–8.

[37] Ibid. ch. 1. Cf. 'the proportion of the population with (some) private medical insurance has grown in the 1980s from 5% in 1979 to 11.7% in 1990', *The Economist*, 12 Oct. 1991, 37.

employer run schemes,[38] tax incentives for health insurance, and more GP referral; but the private sector has also benefited from the relative inability of standard NHS provision to cater for certain individual preferences of patients. If one puts equity of access to one side, private medical practice is seemingly an ideal framework for the assertion of rights and the exercise of consumer choice. Better placed generally than the Health Service to respond to 'customer' demands, it can offer lengthier consultations and arrange for non-emergency operations and elective procedures to be performed with minimal delay, in congenial surroundings, by a surgeon selected by the patient. The appeal to patient choice is explicit, the commercial dimension undisguised.[39] Though many private facilities lack adequate specialized equipment and expertise in depth, private medicine continues to thrive.

As people get more accustomed to medical services being paid for privately, whether directly or, as is mostly the case, through insurance, they become less disposed to regard it as socially inappropriate. This shift in public perception owes much to a blurring of the lines between public and private provision which has been quite marked in the last few years. As well as the (limited) availability of private rooms for NHS patients prepared to pay, there is increasing use of Health Service facilities for private treatment. Since its inception the NHS has accepted the notion of 'pay-beds', but the latest reforms, in conjunction with the earlier Health and Medicines Act 1988,[40] which enabled health authorities to generate income for profit from the private sector, paved the way for much more extensive private practice in NHS institutions. Many NHS hospitals now have private units and some have established exclusively private-medicine buildings within their grounds. In 1989–90 private practice in the NHS expanded faster than in private hospitals for the first time since the 1970s. This trend seems set to continue, given the competitive structure of the new trust hospitals, the funding needs of NHS hospitals in

[38] Accounting for 54% of subscribers in 1987: OPCS, *General Household Survey 1987* (London: HMSO, 1989).

[39] S. Cant and M. Calnan, 'Using Private Health Insurance: A Study of Lay Decisions to Seek Professional Medical Help' *Sociology of Health and Illness*, 14 (1992), 39; see, also, P. Saunders and C. Harris, 'Privatisation and the Consumer', *Sociology* 24 (1990), 57.   [40] 1988 (c.49).

general, and the fact that many patients prefer to be treated in a private bed in the NHS than in private hospitals.

Complementary Therapies

The desire to exercise consumer choice is also a facet of the growing attachment to private medicine in the form of alternative or complementary therapies. In its most recent report on the subject, the BMA, noting that 'non-conventional and traditional forms of medicine are currently enjoying a renaissance throughout Europe', linked this increased popularity to the advent of 'alternative' life-styles in the 1960s.[41] However, pragmatic concerns are often uppermost in the minds of patients who avail themselves of such treatments—the relative ineffectiveness of conventional forms of treatment for back pain and similar disorders or, as with resort to orthodox private medicine, perceived deficiencies of provision within the NHS, notably lengthy waiting lists for certain chronic conditions, insufficient provision of physiotherapy, and the limited time available for individual attention. There are, too, elements of a rights-inspired challenge to paternalism in those health regimes which stress respect for the patient as a person and encourage patients to assume responsibility for their own health. Whatever risks may attach to the more extravagant alternative health care regimes, it would be presumptuous to deny patients for whom conventional medicine has been unavailing *any* right to exercise their 'consumer choice'. In fact, not only do many doctors transfer some aspects of patient care to non-medical therapists, but a small minority practise some form of non-conventional therapy themselves.[42] At the same time, precisely because holistic healing is apt to conjure up an image of selfless, dedicated practitioners, one should not understate the commercial basis of complementary medicine and the plain fact that, like private medical treatment generally, its viability depends on the ability to pay. Perhaps it is not overly cynical to point out that too much emphasis by therapists on the benefits of self-reliance could prompt questions about the need for

---

[41] British Medical Association, *Complementary Medicine: New Approaches to Good Practice* (Oxford: Oxford University Press, 1993), 9.
[42] Ibid. chs. 3 and 4. Estimates vary 'from about 2% to over 15%': ibid. 58.

their services. Nor should one understate the vulnerability, both economic and emotional, of patients who seek alternative therapy when they have life-threatening conditions untreatable by conventional means.

Illusory Rights

'Consumerism' is an elastic concept, which can embrace both vacuous public relations exercises and clearly defined rights of redress, with varying degrees of improved access to information and participation in between. Because of this imprecision, it is often difficult to know exactly what is envisaged when the language of consumerism is applied to health care provision. It may be little more than the shallow missionary zeal of some new-style Health Service managers: 'people will matter. Patients will be treated like customers and will be accorded the care, attention, courtesy, and understanding they would expect to receive in a top department store.'[43] Alternatively, it can take the form of legally enforceable rights. Though medical etiquette does have a part to play in the functioning of doctor–patient relationships, and professionalism in non-clinical aspects of medical care can properly be seen as integral to good health care provision, it remains important to distinguish form from substance. The niceties of nurses with name badges, for example, are not to be equated with a commitment to rights which finds concrete expression in the availability of effective remedies.

The Government's Charters are instructive in this respect, as their bold rhetoric and prescriptive tone tend to disguise both their paucity of content and general lack of legal enforceability. The Citizen's Charter, being only a White Paper, is devoid of legal force. The Patient's Charter is merely a document prepared by the Department of Health. But in using unqualified wording about 'Charter Rights,' it is at times seriously misleading about patients' actual rights, in matters as important as availability of free treatment, information disclosure, and access to health records.

---

[43] V. Williamson, 'Patients First—Reality or Rhetoric?' *Social Policy and Administration* 22 (1988), 245, 246; cf. 'the superficial "customer" or "charm-school-and-better-wallpaper" aspects of provision that have engaged managers in recent years': C. Williamson, *Whose Standards?* (Buckingham: Open University Press, 1992), 128.

For example, notwithstanding the case law qualifying the duty to provide treatment by reference to availability of resources,[44] we are informed that *'every* citizen' has a 'right' 'to receive health care on the basis of clinical need, regardless of ability to pay'.[45] We are also told that every citizen already has the 'right' 'to be given a clear explanation of any treatment proposed, including any risks and any alternatives before you [*sic*] decide whether you will agree to the treatment'. This claim is both unreal and legally unsustainable. Apart from implying the provision of what would often be an almost limitless amount of information, it fails to convey the degree of uncertainty and genuine controversy over the respective merits of various medical procedures and the risks associated with them. It also gives no inkling of how doctors themselves are liable to be misled by the often far from objective information to which they are routinely subjected on the relative efficacy of drug treatments.[46] Most importantly, the Charter's claim is plainly inconsistent with the clinical freedom embodied in the 'reasonable doctor' standard as laid down in *Bolam* and elaborated in *Sidaway*. The (separate) Welsh Charter, in similarly illiterate style, raises the patient's false hopes even further, in asserting that the patient may expect 'to help choose care and treatment appropriate to you'.[47]

Nor does the apparent commitment to a 'right to know', here and elsewhere in the Patient's Charter, sit easily with the Government's decision to talk out the Medicines Information Bill in early 1993.[48] This Bill would have created a right to precisely the kind of information about the safety of medicines[49] which would have assisted patients in assessing risks of treatment. In similar fashion we are told (and here the element of illiteracy becomes somewhat unnerving) that *'every* citizen' has the 'right' 'to have access to your health records', despite the legislative provisions which deny any access to some patients and provide for only modified access to certain others.[50] Any right of access is limited to

---

[44] See ch. 1, text at nn. 192–7.

[45] Patient's Charter, n. 23 above, 8. Emphasis in the original.

[46] J. Collier, 'Conflicts between Pharmaceutical Company Largesse and Patients' Rights' (1992) 60 *Medico-Legal Journal* 243.

[47] B. Stocking, 'Patient's Charter', *British Medical Journal* 303 (1991), 1148, 1149. [48] At the Commons Report Stage: 30 April 1993.

[49] Available in the USA, but denied in England by virtue of the Medicines Act 1968, s. 118. [50] See n. 23 above.

records made after October 1991, and the Charter makes no reference to the health authority's right to charge up to £10 for granting it.

Citizens who consider that they are being or are likely to be denied a National Charter Right are advised to write to the Chief Executive of the NHS. If such a right has been denied, 'he will take action to ensure that this is corrected'.[51] Not only is this puzzling in that some of these 'rights' do not exist, but it invites a degree of scepticism given the obscure legal status of the Patient's Charter. Promulgating it could be seen as incidental to the Secretary of State's duties, in exercising his statutory power to provide medical services.[52] It might then have a purely advisory status akin to that of the DHSS circular on contraceptive advice and treatment considered in *Gillick*.[53] If so, its provisions would not be subject to judicial review just because they were misleading. They could in principle be justiciable, assuming that the individual claimant were deemed to have the necessary standing to have the error corrected by way of a declaration, if they were held to be erroneous on a clear-cut point of law. It seems unlikely that a court would so construe such provisions. They might be regarded as considerations which a health authority must take into account as evidence of having reached its decision on reasonable grounds,[54] but considerations which could legitimately be overridden, for example, because of the limited resources available. Thus the 'consumer sovereignty' over choice and conditions of treatment conjured up by the Patient's Charter seems at best aspirational. The Charter is as misleading in the impression which it conveys of patients' rights, of the current law, and of its own legal status and efficacy as it is controversial in the image which it projects of operational reality in the delivery of health care.[55]

The National Health Service and Community Care Act 1990, passed with the avowed aim of promoting consumer choice,

---

[51] See n. 23 above, 19.   [52] National Health Service Act 1977, s. 2.
[53] Issued under the National Health Service Act 1977, s. 5(1)(b).
[54] See R. Lavery, 'What is the Patient's Charter?' (1992) 60 *Medico-Legal Journal* 201.
[55] 'a citizen's charter could ensure that the debate included consideration of entitlement, empowerment, and equity. These have been overshadowed by considerations of efficacy, efficiency, and economy in debates over the NHS, where the focus has narrowed to questions of cost at the expense of questions of purpose': Plamping and Delamothe, n. 25 above, 204.

exhibits a not dissimilar mismatch between form and substance. It has been aptly described as 'a new departure in the deployment of legislation as rhetoric'.[56] If it has the appearance of a 'consumer's charter', this is partly because it uses contractual terminology to describe what are in essence administrative procedures for the delivery of health care. The new NHS 'contract' is 'an arrangement under which one health service body ("the acquirer") arranges for the provision to it by another health service body ("the provider") of goods or services which it reasonably requires for the purposes of its functions'.[57] This statutory regime now applies to District Health Authorities purchasing services on behalf of patients from NHS hospitals outside their district or from self-governing NHS hospitals with 'Trust' status.[58] It also covers fund-holding general practices in their dealings with NHS hospitals. Yet the Act explicitly states that such arrangements 'shall not be regarded for any purpose as giving rise to contractual rights or remedies'.[59] In the event of a dispute, they are subject to conciliation and arbitration procedures, but with the Secretary of State granted extensive executive power to impose terms. This is scarcely a framework responsive to consumer choice.[60]

As regards hospital treatment, the scope for genuine consumer choice is almost bound to be slight, whatever the organizational framework, if only because for most patients the local general hospital is their only practical option.[61] In any event, the concept of an 'internal market' in health care seems misconceived. The belief that the importation of business attitudes and competition, however tightly controlled the market, will provide patients with improved quality of service is difficult to sustain, and doubly so

[56] D. Hughes, 'The Reorganisation of the National Health Service: The Rhetoric and Reality of the Internal Market': n. 27 above, 103.

[57] National Health Service and Community Care Act 1990, s. 4(1).

[58] Another, superficially comforting, misnomer. Each so-called Trust is a 'body corporate': 1990 Act, s. 5(5)(a).   [59] S. 4(3).

[60] Cf. 'the actual degree of contractual freedom of purchasers and providers is ultimately determined centrally by executive decision, not by the market. The true nature of the contract mechanism in the health service therefore is not an undertaking of any commercial risk but merely another stratagem for administrative planning': D. Longley, *Public Law and Health Service Accountability* (Buckingham: Open University Press, 1993), 48.

[61] 'In many areas the district hospital, whether self-governing or managed, may have a near monopoly of service provision. It is unlikely that DHAs and GP fund holders will place many contracts further afield': ibid. 91.

when the system is cash limited as in the case of the NHS. In relation to the provision of medical treatment, 'consumer choice' is a hollow enough slogan at the best of times. Judges declare themselves incompetent to choose between different schools of medical thought when they are well. Why should we expect people who are ill, and often in urgent need of treatment, to be capable of striking as good a bargain as they might when at their leisure and in good health they are shopping around for ordinary goods or services? Apart from the imbalance between doctor and patient as regards medical knowledge, it is virtually impossible for most patients to choose the medical staff who treat them in hospital, let alone assess the skills which they possess.

Hospital patients have rarely been the effective consumers of medical services in the past and, if anything, in the internal market their choice is likely overall to diminish. It is largely a 'proxy market', in which either the doctor or the District Health Authority acts as purchaser, belying the promise of individual choice in that much provision takes the form of prospective block arrangements, that is, 'contracts' managerially negotiated on a batch referral basis. The new, heavily bureaucratic, system threatens to restrict rather than enlarge the ambit of patient choice to the extent that fund-holding GPs or hospital doctors—themselves subject to managerial pressures and guidelines—feel unduly constrained in treatment decisions by considerations of cost. Hospital consultants are becoming more accountable, but to *management* and to fund-holding *GPs*, not to patients. As some Trust hospital providers seek to improve their financial situation by, for example, adopting a more selective approach to the provision of services, and as fund-holding GPs become more cost-conscious and exert their bargaining power with hospitals, the majority of patients can expect less choice and delayed treatment.

It is now clear that many hospitals have been operating a two-tier treatment system, bringing forward treatment for patients of fund-holding GPs originally due to be seen later in the year, because health authority purchasers had run out of money.[62]

---

[62] See e.g. L. Beecham, 'Royal Colleges Criticise Fundholding Distortions', *British Medical Journal* 307 (1993), 1092. Cf. Memorandum from Essex and Herts Health Services: 'It is therefore vital to the unit's financial situation that we identify and "fast track" GP fund-holder patients . . . as we know that the fund-holders have funds to support this activity': *Guardian*, 26 Jan. 1993.

There is inevitably a danger that in a number of institutions quality and choice of hospital treatment will be subordinated to through-put; just as there is a disincentive for cash-limited budget-holding practices to provide optimal treatment for, or take on, patients with expensive hospital or drug prescription needs.[63] Despite claims that the deployment of market mechanisms will extend consumer sovereignty, what seems to be taking place is the gradual erosion of the underlying NHS principle of equity of access and the emergence of 'a manager-driven consumerism rather than a patient-driven consumerism . . . substituting managerial bureaucracy for medical paternalism'.[64]

The clinical freedom which has traditionally been such a dominant force in medicine could hardly be unaffected by such developments. In fact, over the last twenty years or so, it has been put to the test by a number of changes in the management of health care delivery. In the hospital sector, the process began in 1974 with the relatively loose 'consensus' style of management associated with health care teams, which in the mid-1980s was to give way to the tighter control expected of the General Manager:

. . . in 1989–91 even more fundamentally the roles of purchaser of care and provider were separated. Within only 17 years, doctors' status had been reduced from playing a central role in a team determining the pattern of hospital services in a locality to part of a group of health-care workers within an organisation which had the task of providing care in accordance with contract specifications negotiated with a separate, purchasing health authority which was making hospitals compete with each other for contracts. During that period, not only General Managers . . . but also value-for-money accountants and auditors arrived on the scene, and the Audit Commission . . . began to publish reports which sharply impinged on the traditional clinical freedom of hospital doctors.

---

[63] Fund-holding GPs have explicit financial incentives *not* to refer patients for specialist care, insofar as funds earmarked for them but not spent can be invested in equipment, staff, and amenities for the practice to advance its competitive position: F. Miller, 'Informed Consent in English and American Law' (1992) 18 *American Journal of Law and Medicine* 37, 52–3.

[64] R. Downie and B. Charlton, *The Making of a Doctor* (Oxford: Oxford University Press, 1992), 177. Cf. R. Robinson and J. Le Grand, *Evaluating the NHS Reforms* (London: King's Fund Institute, 1994), who, though generally sceptical about what has been achieved so far, take a more positive view of GP fund holding and of the potential benefits of the restructuring. See also M. Whitehead, 'Who Cares about Equity in the NHS', *British Medical Journal*, 308 (1994), 1284.

In 1990, for example, the Commission criticized the failure of many surgeons to undertake what it considered to be a reasonable level of day surgery.[65]

However, deeply entrenched clinical freedom is not lightly abandoned. Writing shortly before the latest reforms were introduced, an American commentator making comparisons with the situation in the United States described the British doctor as 'still largely free and untrammelled in the practice of medicine. There are no regulations binding the doctor to treat a patient with a particular condition in a certain way, or need for written justification for the way in which the patient is treated'.[66] In fact, it would seem that in America, too, the overall impact of regulation has been less marked than might have been anticipated. Moran and Wood, in their comparative study of the UK, US, and German health care systems, conclude that in all three countries, 'self-regulation remains the norm, and state regulation is frequently fairly benign in its design, its implementation, or both. In essence, doctors have survived the introduction of large-scale governmental involvement in health care, and the contemporary debate about rising costs, if not unscathed then certainly in pretty good health'.[67] For present purposes, the crux of the matter is that such erosion of clinical freedom as may take place in the new NHS is not linked to any corresponding increase in patient choice.

If the proclaimed commitment to patient choice is to be achieved there must be effective mechanisms for allowing the patient's voice to be heard. These are singularly lacking in the recent restructuring, which perpetuates the tradition of pervasive discretionary decision-making and has done nothing to strengthen institutional sources of support for patients. In 1974, Community Health Councils (CHCs)[68] were established to represent the interests of the local community in the health service. However, limited resources have meant that their role is essentially reactive,

[65] Moran and Wood, *States, Regulation and the Medical Profession*, n. 29 above, 133. And see Audit Commission, *What Seems to be the Matter: Communication between Hospitals and Patients* (London: HMSO, 1993).

[66] G. Silver, 'Discordant Priorities', *Lancet* 1 (1987), 1195. J. Bunker, 'Can Professionalism Survive in the Marketplace?', *British Medical Journal*, 308 (1994), 1179. See generally E. Freidson, *Medical Work in America* (New Haven: Yale University Press, 1989).   [67] See n. 29 above, 122.

[68] See A. Simanowicz, 'Agencies' in M. Powers and N. Harris (eds.), *Medical Negligence* (London: Butterworths, 1990), ch 6.

and not primarily aimed at the concerns of individual patients. It has now been further diluted, in that the 1990 Act allows individual Trust hospitals to decide whether or not CHC representatives may attend their routine meetings. The White Paper which preceded the Act referred to CHCs as 'a channel for consumer views to health authorities and FPCs'[69] and assumed that health authorities would 'wish to monitor patient satisfaction'[70] as regards personal as well as clinical needs being met. But the scope for patients to have a real say, either directly or through representative bodies, on what most concerns them—the quality of care—is severely limited. In health, as elsewhere, there is a familiar pattern of diminished community and local authority representation, partially obscured by a panoply of performance indicators which conveniently omit any reference to quality of outcome. As Hughes concludes: 'it is clear that the 1990 Act is in no sense a charter for patients: it contains no specific safeguards for patient rights, and little to strengthen patient representation or involvement in service planning.'[71]

Rights as Subversive of 'Relationship'

In a climate where the impression is conveyed that decisions about clinical need are unduly driven by considerations of cost, patient trust may not be readily forthcoming. The risk that a trade model may lead to the erosion of trust is heightened by its tendency to encourage a minimalist 'patching up' mentality, and to play down the involvement and dialogue sought by many patients with medical conditions sufficiently serious to warrant hospitalization. In so far as the model implies a simple, straightforward purchase of services, it suggests a somewhat barren image, which fails to capture the sense of development over time implicit in the notion of a doctor–patient 'relationship'. 'Health care . . . is fundamentally a relationship of caring and is not fundamentally an object of production and exchange'.[72] By reinforcing the biomechanical

---

[69] Family Practitioner Committees. See *Working for Patients*, n. 26 above, para. 8.7.   [70] Ibid., para. 2.13.

[71] D. Hughes, *The Reorganisation of the National Health Service: The Rhetoric and Reality of the Internal Market*, n. 27 above, 97.

[72] D. Sulmasy, 'What's so Special about Medicine?' *Theoretical Medicine* 14 (1993), 27, 30.

emphasis of modern medicine, with its imagery of the doctor servicing the body/machine in one-off transactions, the trade model perpetuates the popular perception of illness as organic malfunctioning remediable by elective surgery and other acute treatment. Meticulous attention to the formal rights and duties which inhere in single transactions can too easily lead us to forget how often treatment and decision-making about it form part of a drawn-out process which ideally embraces longer-term aspects of the patient's well-being—'at crucial moments of choice most of the business of choosing is already over'.[73]

Moreover, the process will often not consist of the measured, dispassionate appraisal normally associated with abstract disquisitions on rights. Avowedly rational human beings, faced with the predicament of reaching a decision on medical treatment while inhabiting the role of patient may react in a far from rational way, betraying intense inner turmoil and vulnerability. One has only to think of the self-confessed irrationality and sense of powerlessness graphically portrayed in accounts by doctors of their own emotional reactions as patients.[74] In most transactions between a doctor and a patient, concern about the latter's rights, whether seen as intrinsic or bargained for, either does not feature at all or is very much in the background. The main focus of concern for both parties is cure or amelioration of the patient's condition, for which purpose the pursuit of mutual harmony is a better recipe than the assertion of rights. This is so even as regards issues which can legitimately be seen in terms of rights, not least because it is understandably difficult for doctors to relate to patients as bearers of rights. Research on how hospital consultants view their patients is relatively sparse, but a revealing small-scale study was recently conducted on their attitude to patients having access to GP records.[75] Though evenly split on whether or not access should be permitted, the consultants saw the issue preponderantly from a

---

[73] I. Murdoch, 'The Idea of Perfection' in *The Sovereignty of Good* (1970), 37, quoted by S. Jinnett-Sack, 'Autonomy in the Company of Others' in A. Grubb (ed.), *Choices and Decisions in Health Care* (Chichester: John Wiley & Sons, 1993), 105.

[74] e.g. O. Sacks, *A Leg to Stand on* (London: Pan Books, 1986). And see F. Inglefinger, 'Arrogance', *New England Journal of Medicine* 303 (1980), 1507.

[75] N. Britten, 'Hospital Consultants' Views of their Patients', *Sociology of Health and Illness* 13 (1991), 83, based on interviews conducted in 1988. Of the 24 consultants interviewed, 11 were against access, 10 for, and 3 ambivalent.

medical perspective, that is, from the standpoint of therapeutic values rather than rights. Broadly speaking, those opposed to access held to a biomedical model and did not consider that the patients wanted information. Those in favour of access held to a more psycho-social view.

Patients are normally all too aware that by staking out a position on the basis of rights, they risk transforming what may have been a caring and amicable relationship into an adversarial one, inimical both to constructive dialogue and their own future health. The appeal to intrinsic rights invites the assertion of counter-rights. The patient who insists on the 'right' to information is liable to be met by the doctor's claim to a 'counter-right' of non-disclosure based on therapeutic privilege. For if patients are autonomous beings, so too are doctors and their personal and professional values may dissuade them from following 'patients' orders'. The BMA, for example, while seeing 'significant benefits to advance directives within the framework of continuing doctor–patient dialogue', indicated in its 1992 statement on the issue that it was not in favour of them being legally binding,[76] observing that 'an individual patient's rights do not supersede the rights of other parties; doctors cannot be obliged to act contrary to conscience or the law'.[77] From a more extreme libertarian standpoint, Sade has argued that 'the concept of medical care as the patient's right is immoral because it denies the most fundamental of all rights, that of a man [i.e. the doctor] to his own life and the freedom of action to support it'.[78]

So, too, the 'metaphor of medicine as business',[79] with its hints of de-professionalisation and the growth of a culture of contractualism, threatens to undermine the commitment of doctors to their traditional ethical obligation to treat. At the institutional level this can take the form of abandoning or discouraging unprofitable treatment; among individual doctors, it can encourage the attitude that, just as patients are entitled to seek treatment,

---

[76] British Medical Association, *Statement on Advance Directives* (London: BMA, 1992), 10. See also British Medical Association, *Medical Ethics Today* (London: BMJ Publishing Group, 1993), 161–4.

[77] British Medical Association, *Statement on Advance Directives*, above, n. 76.

[78] R. Sade, 'Medical Care as a Right: A Refutation', *New England Journal of Medicine* 285 (1971), 1288, 1289.

[79] T. Brennan, *Just Doctoring*, see n. 33 above, 159.

doctors have a 'right' not to treat, a stance which a number of doctors (and dentists) now adopt towards AIDS patients, either in respect of specific procedures or by not accepting them on their list. In this particular context, it is too easy to denounce as self-serving protestations of inadequate expertise or arguments about the greater merits of treatment in specialized clinics. At the same time such protestations sit uncomfortably with conventional assumptions about the moral attributes of medical care, whether based on the principle of beneficence as traditionally understood or on a more objective view of how the interests of patients might best be served.[80]

An approach to medical relationships which is overwhelmingly concerned with the 'rights' of patients is open to the criticism that it is overly individualistic and artificially discounts the social dimensions of medical ethics. Rights discourse, with its essentialist overtones, often conveniently neglects not only the effects of an individual's decisions on other individuals but also broader consideration of how social benefits should be distributed.[81] Everyday decisions have to be made about the extent of an individual's 'right' to scarce and expensive treatment, which most of us would fight shy of taking even in the abstract. Equally, we cannot sensibly ignore the complex social dilemmas posed by biomedical advance. How far, for example, should we countenance genetic engineering to satisfy a 'right' to be born without avoidable defects? It seems unduly doctrinaire to try to resolve such questions without reference to their manifold social and economic implications. As Veatch has noted, 'the conflict over paternalism and autonomy that diverted our attention for a few years while this generation of medical ethics was in its infancy may provide a model for going on to the real work of building a more mature medical ethic that can handle social as well as individual ethical questions'.[82]

---

[80] In 1992 the BMA's Annual Representative Meeting adopted the resolution that 'it is unethical and unacceptable for a doctor to withhold treatment from a patient on the grounds that the patient's condition may pose a risk to the health of the doctor': see British Medical Association, *Medical Ethics Today*, n. 76 above, 355, n. 350.

[81] See, e.g. M. Glendon, *Rights Talk: The Impoverishment of Political Discourse* (New York: Free Press, 1991).

[82] R. Veatch, 'Autonomy's Temporary Triumph' (Oct. 1984) 14 *Hastings Center Report* 38, at 40.

A COLLABORATIVE APPROACH

As recently as the mid-1980s, the sharing of ideas in medical consultations could still be described in the literature as something of a novelty, 'a little-discussed aspect of these rather frequent occurrences'.[83] Communication, such as it was, had seldom been envisaged as a two-way process. Any inadequacies were largely explained away, as attributable to patients being unable to grasp or adjust to the information which the doctor imparted. The whole issue was and often still is trivialized, reduced to a discussion of 'bedside manners'; much in the same way as medical ethics is sometimes reduced to questions of professional etiquette. In 1986, acknowledging that all was not well in doctor–patient relationships, one British medical school created a post in communication and another instituted an annual prize for the best student communicator.[84] The publicity which these innovations attracted served only to highlight how pervasive was the problem. In 1992, a standard text by a noted obstetrician described inadequate communication as 'still the most common cause of complaint from patients or their relatives'.[85]

It has been suggested by Armstrong[86] that it is possible to trace three broad stages of development in patients' expectations of medical relationships: before the Second World War they seldom asked for anything more than competent treatment; after the War they also sought information but only in the last decade or so have they, in addition, begun to look for explanation, understanding and emotional support, from a doctor who listens and acknowledges the value of communication as a two-way, collaborative process. Too often, it would seem, they stand to be disappointed.

In leading medical journals, doctors continue to reflect not just on the difficulties of encouraging constructive dialogue, breaking bad news, and handling distress or uncertainty, but also on the

---

[83] D. Tuckett *et al.*, *Meetings Between Experts: An Approach to Sharing Ideas in Medical Consultations* (London: Tavistock, 1986), 3.

[84] Cambridge and Newcastle respectively.

[85] P. Myerscough, *Talking with Patients* (2nd edn.) (Oxford: Oxford University Press, 1992), 1. Cf. Audit Commission, *What Seems to be the Matter: Communication between Hospitals and Patients*, n. 65 above.

[86] D. Armstrong, 'What do Patients Want?' *British Medical Journal* 303 (1991), 261.

relative lack of attention paid to such matters in medical education. As noted earlier, for many years there has been a presumption that interviewing is a skill which any student can pick up through repeated unsupervised practice. In 1990, a medical authority on communication skills for doctors observed that, 'despite their relevance to clinical practice these skills are little taught in most medical schools at undergraduate or postgraduate level. Instead it is assumed that they are acquired through traditional training'.[87] In 1993 the *Lancet* was still bemoaning 'the reluctance of medical schools to devote much time to instructing students in this clinical skill'. 'Doctors are fearful of giving bad news', it concluded, 'and very few acquit themselves even passably in this area of their work.'[88] These criticisms were prompted by a survey of 150 bereaved parents, a third of whom 'thought that interviews had been badly or offensively handled', and that 'police officers (who generally receive more training than doctors in how to break bad news) were . . . more sympathetic than doctors or nurses'.[89]

The interview has been described as 'the cornerstone of medical practice'[90] and a great deal turns on how it is conducted. In what may be a fraught atmosphere, the doctor's style and choice of language acquire added significance. To take a rather stark example, recommending a procedure as 'substantially extending the lives of 70 per cent of the patients who select it' is quite different from describing it as 'potentially killing on the operating table 30 per cent of the patients who select it'.[91] Equally, there will be revealing non-verbal cues: 'tones of voice, facial expression, and failures to look the patient in the eye may communicate more to the patient about his condition than words could ever do.'[92] Being made to feel inadequate and foolish simply because of inability to remember details of childhood illnesses and previously

[87] P. Maguire, 'Can Communication Skills be Taught?' *British Journal of Hospital Medicine* 43 (1990), 215.

[88] Editorial, *Lancet* 341 (1993), 467.

[89] L. Fallowfield, 'Giving Sad and Bad news', *Lancet* 341 (1993), 476.

[90] J. Thompson, 'Communicating with Patients' in R. Fitzpatrick *et al.*, (ed.), *The Experience of Illness* (London: Tavistock Publications, 1984), 87.

[91] D. Brock and S. Wartman, 'When Competent Patients make Irrational choices', *New England Journal of Medicine* 322 (1990), 1595, 1598.

[92] J. Thompson, 'Communicating with Patients', n. 90 above, 88.

taken medications strikes a familiar chord with many patients.[93] Those who sense a lack of involvement or concern on the doctor's part are the less inclined to reveal what might be relevant information and additionally may be inhibited from doing so for reasons related to class and status. The cumulative effect of such inhibitions is most pronounced for patients in the hospital setting, attended to by doctors with whom they are likely to have had little, if any, contact or prior relationship.

As the recent Toronto consensus statement testifies, there is an array of research findings from numerous countries deploring the communication gap and confirming that an alarmingly high proportion of patients fail to understand or remember what they have been told about diagnosis and treatment.[94] Again, the problems are especially acute in the hospital setting, where often no single person assumes what is often a highly sensitive role. Armstrong's assessment of how the expectations of patients have grown are now routinely reflected in surveys eliciting their views and in the experience of organizations which seek to promote their interests. A recent Consumers' Association survey of outpatients seeing a specialist for the first time revealed substantial dissatisfaction with the amount of information provided and with failures of communication. It found that 'one in five . . . left the clinic without much of an understanding of their medical condition, or with no clear understanding at all'. 75 per cent of the outpatients wanted as much medical information as possible about their condition, as against 17 per cent who wanted to know only the broad facts and a mere 8 per cent who preferred to leave matters largely to the doctor. 30 per cent asked no questions, some two thirds of them assuming that they would be told all they needed to know and one third that their GP would tell them later. 35 per cent said that there did not seem to be time to ask questions, 32 per cent that the consultant seemed busy, and 22 per cent that they felt that they were keeping other patients waiting. 21 per cent were worried about what they would hear. 25 per cent had to ask to get any information.[95]

[93] I. Zola, 'Structural Constraints in the Doctor–Patient Relationship: The Case of Non Compliance' in L. Eisenberg and A. Kleinman (eds.), *The Relevance of Social Science for Medicine* (London: Reidel, 1981).

[94] M. Simpson *et al.*, 'Doctor–patient communication: The Toronto Consensus statement,' *British Medical Journal* 303 (1991), 1385.

[95] Consumers' Association, *Which?*, 7 Feb. 1991.

Patients naturally often do not have a clear or fully worked-out notion of what they want, or need, and would like to talk through various options. Typically lacking medical expertise themselves, they will expect the doctor to take the initiative in clarifying technical issues, but still value consultations which take the form of a common exploration and allow for open-ended questions.[96] Gradually doctors are becoming more responsive to this kind of approach and they may have additional reason to should the GMC implement proposals to extend its remit for disciplining incompetent doctors to cover repeated unsatisfactory performance in dealing with patients.[97] There is a greater readiness, more apparent in general practice than in hospitals, not merely to acknowledge the potential benefits of improved communication skills, but also the feasibility of students acquiring them[98] and putting them into practice without prolonged consultations. The force of the knee-jerk reaction that consultations which actively encourage patients to discuss their concerns are bound to be unduly time-consuming has been undermined by evidence to the contrary from consultant and general practice. One consultant has reported that encouraging patients to discuss their main concerns without interruption or premature closure produced a maximum duration of 2½ minutes and an average of ninety seconds.[99]

We have already noted some of the historical, psychological, and institutional factors which account for the dearth of initiatives on communication in the past, and for continued, if diminishing, resistance to a collaborative view of medical relationships at the present time. That there is now less resistance owes much to the persuasiveness of arguments akin to those enlisted to support patient autonomy. In other words, patients are more readily thought of as in some sense having a 'right' to be involved in their treatment. Naturally, many doctors still find it hard to adopt a mode of medical practice which incorporates active patient involvement, and the 'right to involvement' cannot escape some of

[96] Cf. C. Williamson, *Whose Standards?*, n. 43 above, 81; J. Jones, 'Telling the Right Patient', *British Medical Journal* 283 (1981), 291.

[97] See Ch. 7 below, text at n. 16.

[98] See e.g. P. Maguire and D. Rutter, 'Training Medical Students to Communicate' in A. Bennett (ed.), *Communication between Doctors and Patients* (London: Oxford University Press, 1976).

[99] J. Blau, 'Time to let the Patient Speak', *British Medical Journal* 298 (1989), 39.

the criticisms made earlier about any model grounded in 'patients rights'.[100] However, when contrasted with an unalloyed appeal to rights, 'collaborative autonomy'[101] emerges as a more generous conception of the doctor–patient relationship with distinctive *therapeutic* benefits.

A growing body of medical and social scientific research points to the therapeutic virtues of patients being actively involved in their treatment. The spoken language, it has been said, is 'the most important tool in medicine'.[102] Effective communication can help minimize diagnostic error (including failure even to notice medical problems), reduce levels of anxiety and depression, and facilitate better health outcomes.[103] The patient who is properly informed and fully involved prior to an operation is commonly less anxious, needs less anaesthetic, and is to that extent in better physiological condition prior to surgery. Psychologically prepared patients are likely to have a greater sense of personal control and thus to suffer less post-operative pain and stress. They are often able to leave hospital earlier, recover faster, and cope more effectively with post-operative symptoms, treatment, and future health care problems.[104] There is also some evidence that patients who do not seek more than minimal information prior to surgery in fact benefit from the provision of additional preparatory material.[105] Though it is common for surgical patients to experience high levels of anxiety long after discharge, lower levels of psychological distress have been found in those with serious illnesses when they feel that they have received adequate information.[106]

By analogy, similar therapeutic gains may be achieved through the encouragement, where appropriate, of self-administered medication within the hospital setting. This is not, as appears at

---

[100] See 115–6 above.   [101] See the Toronto Consensus, n. 94 above.

[102] E. Cassell, *Talking with Patients* (Cambridge, Mass.: MIT Press, 1985), 1.

[103] 'For many chronic illnesses communication is virtually the only form of treatment there is': D. Locker, 'Communication in Medical Practice' in D. Patrick and G. Scambler (eds.), *Sociology as Applied to Medicine* (2nd edn.), (London: Bailliere Tindall, 1986), 98.   [104] Ibid. 105–6.

[105] See L. Wallace, 'Informed Consent to Elective Surgery: The "Therapeutic" Value?' *Social Science and Medicine* 22 (1986), 29, 32, 33.

[106] Toronto Consensus, n. 94 above. And see J. Morris, M. Goddard, and D. Roger, 'The Benefits of Providing Information to Patients' (York: Centre for Health Economics, 1989), Discussion Paper 58.

first sight, an argument more compatible with a pure patient autonomy model. To the contrary, consistent with the nurses' Code of Professional Conduct,[107] it assumes a monitored regime, the benefits of which include 'more communication from nurse to patient; clearer understanding of the medication's purposes; [and] greater likelihood that patients will finish the course when they return home'.[108] Apart from its well-established use in childbirth, patient-controlled analgesia (PCA) is increasingly accepted by anaesthetists for controlling severe post-operative pain. It is of interest that their endorsement of PCA still meets with considerable professional opposition. This is based on an outmoded, and in some respects paternalistic, attitude towards pain relief, which has been openly condemned by the Royal College of Surgeons and the College of Anaesthetists. It is difficult to think of a medical problem more suited to a collaborative exploration by doctor and patient. Yet in their recent Report, the Colleges pointed to a number of erroneous beliefs commonly held by health professionals, such as 'that it is the doctor or nurse who is the authority on the patient's pain, not the patient; that the same causes of pain produce pain of the same severity, and that equal doses of analgesics produce equal pain control; that physical signs can be used to verify the existence of pain and its severity, independently of what the patient says; and that post-operative pain is unpreventable'.[109] Advocates of PCA point to a range of therapeutic benefits. First, it offers more effective pain relief; less analgesic can be used and there is less iatrogenic risk. In addition, patients generally establish a more effective relationship with nursing staff if they have a better understanding of their condition. The net result of all this is that both physical and psychological recovery can often be achieved more quickly.

The point, then, is not that once they are better informed patients will opt for total self-determination and dispense with the doctor's services; rather they will feel more equipped to engage in fruitful dialogue. The same holds true for much of the research which emphasizes the value generally of providing patients with

[107] *Code of Professional Conduct for the Nurse, Midwife and Health Visitor* (London: UKCC 1984), cls. 1 and 2.

[108] C. Williamson, *Whose Standards?*, n. 43 above, 90.

[109] Royal College of Surgeons of England and College of Anaesthetists, *Pain after Surgery* (London: RCSE/CoA, 1990), 3; C. Williamson, ibid. 90–2.

information. Though stress may be laid on the 'provision' of information, much of it in leaflet form (and increasingly on cassette), and though there is evidence that patients welcome written information which can be read and re-read in private,[110] the explanation for this preference is that 'questions can then be formulated and items discussed with the family doctor or specialist'. Patients who are encouraged to take an active role in the medical exchange often experience a greater sense of well-being which, in turn, can assist their recovery. By the same token, when the patient understands, appreciates, and is involved in what is being done, a collaborative approach can enhance the doctor's job satisfaction, not least by alleviating the burden of decision-making.

Subjective, 'non-medical' dimensions of ill health and well-being can be vital to an assessment of what constitutes good medical treatment in a particular case. Only the patient can be fully aware of the impact that an illness is having on his or her life, and any number of environmental, cultural, and personal considerations may influence the way different people react to the 'same' illness. Thus most people only consult a doctor when their symptoms interfere with their social functioning, rather than when they first appear. This suggests that in trying to determine what is the most appropriate medical approach in a given case there may be personal values, circumstances, or priorities which need to be explored. The optimum choice of treatment is not necessarily that which is conventionally deemed medically best, even when such a judgement can confidently be made. The preferred course of action may, for example, reflect family considerations, which could involve financial and other work-related concerns, or particular interests of patients and facets of their life-style, including how risk-averse they are.[111] None of this is meant to suggest that a collaborative framework rules out the voicing of disagreement between doctor and patient. That the doctor may ultimately accede to what patients want or appear to want does not preclude putting, forcefully if need be, a contrary point of view. Equally, their respective views may be modified in the process.

[110] Editorial, 'Write for your Patient', *Lancet* 1 (1989), 1175.
[111] In these respects, as Lee has noted, 'The truth is that, valuable though health is, we trade it quite regularly for other pleasures, opportunities and activities': R. Lee, 'Doctors as Allocators—The Bald Facts' in S. McVeigh and S. Wheeler (eds.), *Law, Health and Medical Regulation* (Aldershot: Dartmouth, 1992), 172.

What is central is that the overall venture should be a co-operative one which allows for mutual influence to be exerted.

Barriers to Collaboration

The Toronto consensus statement begins by recognizing that effective communication is a central clinical function that cannot be delegated. The doctor's inter-personal skills, aided by patient participation, are seen as largely determining patient satisfaction and compliance, and as positively influencing health outcomes. Yet the relative importance which a patient attaches to, say, mental alertness as against diminution of pain, physical appearance as against relief of suffering, or quality as against length of life, are matters about which surgeons, in particular, may in practice never become adequately informed. They routinely delegate the process of obtaining consent to a junior doctor or nurse[112] and may themselves be temperamentally ill-suited to exploring patients' attitudes to risk, however skilled they are in operating on them. However, the optimum outcome is not necessarily to be equated with the technically successful result of a given operation or course of therapy. It will often involve a prognosis of the likely medical and psychological condition of patients and of their general ability to function. There is more to the debate over 'informed consent' than simply assessing willingness to undergo a particular procedure, even when, as it should be, obtaining consent is conceived of as a process throughout rather than a one-off assent and signature. Properly understood, informed consent embraces prospective ability to cope.

To its detractors, the collaborative ideal is at best a noble

---

[112] The information deemed relevant to patient consent is commonly provided by 'the most junior and inexperienced doctor, who will not perform the operation and who knows nothing of the likely complications': *The Times*, 27 Feb. 1985, correspondence col. Cf. D. Byrne, A. Napier, and A. Cuschieri, 'How Informed is Signed Consent?' *British Medical Journal* 296 (1988), 839, describing the ward procedure in an academic surgical unit and noting that after the consultant round on the day before an operation, a junior member of staff—house surgeon or senior house officer—would obtain the signed consent from the patient. Cf. 'its contractual language is alien both to the clinical priorities of the surgeon and the practical interests of patients. Consequently the routine violation of conditions of signing by service providers, and of its spirit by patients is likely to continue': P. Meredith, 'Patient Participation in Decision-making and Consent to Treatment: The Case of General Surgery', *Sociology of Health and Illness* 15 (1993), 315, 329.

dream, an exercise in 'naïve utopianism'.[113] Doctors and patients, they claim, have essentially irreconcilable perspectives on treatment, different agendas, and different priorities. To the limited extent that there is common ground between them, the attempt to forge a therapeutic alliance is beset with obstacles. Even when doctors are in principle committed to collaboration and see themselves as engaging in it, they are deluded. The enterprise is, or so the argument goes, doomed from the start, because the doctor's frame of reference differs so markedly from that of the patient. Where the doctor is intent on following rational diagnostic procedures as a guide to appropriate treatment, patients are preoccupied with how they feel and with their desire for cure or relief. Often determined to establish the 'cause' of their illness, they are apt to see connections which have no medical basis. This tendency may in itself be a source of conflict, if the doctor is unable to account for what has happened in a way which is satisfying to the patient. Doctors are no different from members of other social groups in having only a limited and variable capacity for empathy.

They also, of course, have only a limited amount of time to devote to each patient, whereas[114] some patients may have unlimited time to discuss their own symptoms. Alternatively, they may need more time than is readily available to assimilate information, for reasons such as anxiety, reluctance to ask questions, or limited capacity to understand. Also it can often be difficult in practice for a doctor to assess how much a particular patient actually wants to know. In the hospital setting, even where in principle the policy is that only the doctor in charge should discuss treatment and prognosis, one cannot discount the possibility of multiple communicators who may have varying viewpoints, or of doctors and nurses succumbing to the perils of routinization, offering stock responses deemed appropriate for the 'average patient'. It is much easier to stress the virtues of communicative competence than to ensure that it is displayed.

One reason the quality of communicative competence is so elusive is the ease with which people can persuade themselves,

---

[113] P. Maseide, 'Possibly Abusive, Often Benign, and Always Necessary: On Power and Domination in Medical Practice' *Sociology of Health and Illness* 13 (1991), 545, 558.   [114] *Pace* Blau's findings, see n. 99 above.

often against the evidence, that they possess it. The dissonance between doctors' assumptions about how they communicate and the reality has been explored in Miyaji's thought-provoking study of truth-telling in the care of dying patients.[115] From interviews with thirty-two doctors at an American teaching hospital, Miyaji detected three styles of informing terminally ill patients about their disease: 'telling what patients want to know', 'telling what patients need to know', and 'translating information into terms that patients can take'. Five guiding principles were commonly invoked by these doctors: respect for the truth and for patients' rights, a duty to inform and to preserve hope, and respect for the individual nature of the 'contract' between patient and doctor, in the sense that communication about illness should primarily be confined to exchanges between them. Taken at face value, the use of these styles and principles as described by the doctors suggested a belief on their part that they were adhering to patient-centred medical ethics based on informed consent and on patient control over the information received. But closer examination of their detailed narratives shows how, by selective use of the styles and flexible interpretation of the principles, especially as regards prognosis, they would retain and exercise the power of control over the information-giving process, to serve both their own needs and the needs they imputed to patients.

Since so much depends on the doctor's assessment of what patients want and need, 'the patient's apparent level of willingness to know can often become just a reflection of the physician's willingness to impart information'.[116] As noted earlier, much will turn on how information is conveyed—locution, tone, and body language. Just as any lecturer knows that it is *how* you tell the class that they can always ask questions that is crucial, so, too, with the doctor. Similarly, a doctor can provide the same information in ways that have a strikingly different impact on patients untutored in probability reasoning.[117] Particularly when it comes to

[115] N. Miyaji, 'The Power of Compassion: Truth-Telling among American Doctors in the Care of Dying Patients', *Social Science and Medicine* 36 (1993), 249.

[116] Ibid. 252.

[117] Myerscough cites the example of an epileptic woman taking two or more anticonvulsant drugs. Told that she has a three times greater than normal risk of having an abnormal baby, she may react much more negatively than if the message is that '94 out of 100 babies will be normal and unaffected': P. Myerscough, *Talking with Patients*, n. 85 above, 87.

prognosis, there is much leeway for casuistry. Miyaji's most interesting finding was the extent to which doctors gave less and vaguer information about *prognosis* than about *treatment*. Where it is not intrinsically uncertain, a prognosis may be open to variation depending, amongst other things, on the natural course of a disease, the results of diagnostic tests, treatment options and the possibility, however remote, of some medical breakthrough. Thus the principle of truth-telling can be 'saved'—and reconciled with preserving hope—by over-emphasizing the irreducible elements of uncertainty.

Mirroring Katz's analysis in *The Silent World of Doctor and Patient*, the doctors' accounts described by Miyaji reveal how, beyond the principle of 'preserving hope', lurk rationalizations of the doctors' own emotional needs for coping with the demands of clinical practice. These include the need to retain power and control, to instil confidence, and to preserve the image and self-image of being compassionate and caring. Accordingly, he concludes, 'doctors can hold power over patients even if they accept the idea of sharing information with patients'.[118]

There are strong indications in all of this that the ideal of shared decision-making can be very difficult to achieve. Sweeping claims about informed consent must be treated with caution. The subject is intrinsically difficult to research and findings have, in the main, been based on small-scale studies of particular medical conditions.[119] They rarely reveal the precise content or manner of doctor–patient exchanges. Nor is it always clear in what sense imparted information has been understood. However, there is mounting empirical evidence that doctors underestimate the desire of patients for information and discussion, if not always their desire to take the ultimate decision.[120] None of the obstacles to 'collaborative autonomy' would seem to justify not making the attempt to achieve it, if its capacity to produce desirable decisions

[118] Miyaji, n. 115 above, 260.

[119] A. Meisel and L. Roth, 'What We Do and Do Not Know about Informed Consent', *Journal of the American Medical Association* 246 (1981), 2473.

[120] R. Faden *et al.*, 'Disclosure of Information to Patients in Medical Care', *Medical Care* 19 (1981), 718; H. Waitzkin, 'Doctor–Patient Communication' *Journal of the American Medical Association* 252 (1984), 2441; R. Strull *et al.*, 'Do Patients Want to Participate in Medical Decision Making?', *Journal of the American Medical Association*; 252 (1984), 2990; A. Fraser, 'Do Patients Want to be Informed?' *British Heart Journal* 52 (1984), 468. See also n. 95 above.

on treatment and better outcomes is granted. Several of the objections are commonly exaggerated, particularly as regards the constraints of time and technical complexity. It does not require inordinate time or elaborate explanation to indicate that a particular procedure carries a given percentage risk of paralysis. Nor should it generally be too exacting a task to provide a reasonably succinct and intelligible account of the risks and options attaching to treatment. On the other hand, much time may be wasted by repeat visits of ill-informed patients who have not experienced the kind of guidance and involvement that could assist them to cope with their condition both before and after treatment.

CONCLUSION

The overall picture then is of a situation in which much medical practice still reflects the notion of the patient as passive recipient of medical care, whether from choice, apathy, or deferential submission. At the same time, however, this state of affairs has been a source of mounting discontent. The discontent has begun to find expression in other approaches, which, though united in their rejection of the dominant tradition, differ considerably as to the proper basis and goals of doctor–patient relationships. In one way or another, all of these latter approaches emphasize the importance of the patient's voice. But it is contended that, in practice, only the collaborative model is compatible with genuine communication. We must now examine in more detail the legal implications of these approaches, always bearing in mind that it is in the hospital, the arena of primary legal interest, that the intrinsic difficulties of ensuring effective communication in medical relationships are normally most pronounced.

PART THREE

The Choice of Legal Category

4

Patients' Rights

BATTERY

A doctor-centred conception of health care is beginning to lose ground in part because of growing sympathy for the view that patients are entitled to decide what is done to them. In its insistence that individuals be viewed as ends in themselves, a model of patient autonomy seems to offer an appealing contrast to the Hippocratic emphasis on presumed best interests. It also translates naturally into legal form in any system of law which puts a high value on the 'right' to self-determination and to bodily inviolability. Like the crime of assault, the tort of battery has been said to hinge on 'the fundamental principle, plain and incontestable . . . that every person's body is inviolate'.[1] As Lord Donaldson was to put it, 'in the absence of consent all, or almost all, medical treatment and all surgical treatment of an adult is unlawful however beneficial such treatment might be. This is incontestable.'[2] At first sight, then, the availability of the action for battery suggests the clearest possible repudiation of paternalism and a vindication of patient choice. In Judge Cardozo's well-known formulation; 'every human being of adult years and sound mind has a right to determine what shall be done with his own body; and a surgeon who performs an operation without his patient's consent commits an assault for which he is liable in damages'.[3] Modern American decisions on informed consent routinely cite this statement as definitive of the law's commitment

---

[1] *Collins* v. *Wilcock* [1984] 1 WLR 1172, 1177, *per* Goff LJ.

[2] *F* v. *West Berkshire Health Authority* [1989] 2 WLR 1025, 1034: i.e. apart from necessary treatment for the unconscious, for the mentally disordered under the Mental Health Act 1983, and arguably in other very exceptional circumstances: see *Re T (Adult: Refusal of Treatment)* [1992] 3 WLR 782; *Re S (Adult: Refusal of Treatment)* [1992] 3 WLR 806, and 152–8 below.

[3] *Schloendorff* v. *Society of New York Hospital*, 211 NY 125, 105 NE 92, 93 (1914).

to the rights of patients. In fact there had been earlier, even more assertive, dicta holding out the promise of rigorously observed protection. In one case it was stated that 'no right is held more sacred, or is more carefully guarded by the common law, than the right of every individual to the possession and control of his own person, free from all restraint or interference of others'.[4] In another there is a reference to 'the free citizen's first and greatest right, which underlies all the others—the right to the inviolability of his person, in other words, his right to himself'.[5] However, on closer examination it becomes clear that in law a patient's inviolability and 'right to the self' are far from absolute.

Competent Adult Patients

The above principles afford rather less protection for patients than might be supposed because of the ways in which legal rights are circumscribed, both by the definitional limitations of legal categories and by judicial interpretation. The tort of battery entails active physical interference with bodily security, in the absence of consent. In the medical context, as elsewhere, the focus of the law is, of course, on whether or not battery has technically been committed, not on whether there has been a failure to respect the plaintiff's rights; it is not concerned with patient autonomy or choice as such. By definition, therefore, battery does not extend to non-invasive procedures, as where a patient suffers from having taken prescribed drugs,[6] nor does it cover harm due to a doctor's decision not to treat, both significant sources of damage.

The scope for battery actions is further diminished by the courts' narrowly formalistic stance on what counts as consent. Thus, despite the basic legal tenet that consent is ineffective unless freely given, there is still some authority for the view that consent granted under economic duress and in the mistaken belief that it was obligatory is valid, and that it is to be deemed involuntary only when given through fear of violence.[7] Though courts are more disposed nowadays to accept that other forms of constraint might

---

[4] *Union Pacific Ry.* v. *Botsford*, 141 US 250, 251 (1891).
[5] *Pratt* v. *Davis*, 118 Ill. App. 161, 79 NE 562 (1905).
[6] *Malloy* v. *Shanahan*, 421 A 2d 803 (1980).
[7] *Latter* v. *Braddell* (1881) 50 LJQB 448.

be equally inimical to genuine consent,[8] this is not always so. In *Freeman* v. *Home Office (No. 2)*, for example, it was held that being a prisoner did not of itself invalidate the plaintiff's consent to treatment by a prison medical officer, though it was acknowledged that voluntariness might require particular scrutiny in such circumstances. At first instance, the court also concluded that the plaintiff bore the onus of disproving consent instead of the doctor having to prove it,[9] as is arguably more appropriate given the confidential nature of medical relationships.[10] The combination of a minimalist view of what counts as voluntary conduct with a burden on the plaintiff to prove absence of consent is regrettable, and not only because of the general vulnerability of patients and their desire not to damage their relationship with the doctor. As Somerville perceptively comments, 'coercive factors may be at their most subtle and difficult to detect, and freedom of choice most threatened, in a situation in which the more powerful party believes he is acting for the benefit of the other'.[11]

Similarly, one might have thought that true consent, sufficient to negate battery, was lacking if material risks of invasive treatment had not been disclosed. Such a view is consistent with the general requirement in tort law that the defence of assumption of risk, or *volenti*, is only available where the plaintiff has full knowledge of the extent of a risk as well as its nature.[12] It also corresponds with our common understanding of what should count as consent, in that it is artificial to speak of someone making an autonomous decision when unaware of important relevant

---

[8] See e.g. *Norberg* v. *Wynrib* (1992) 92 DLR (4th) 449 (Canadian Supreme Court), where sexual relations between a drug addict and her doctor were deemed to have resulted from 'power dependency', and three of the judges made a finding of battery on the basis that the equitable doctrine of unconscionable transactions negated the defence of consent.

[9] [1984] 2 WLR 130. The issue was not addressed on appeal: [1984] 2 WLR 802.

[10] Cf. *Collins* v. *Wilcock* [1984] 1 WLR 1172, 1177, and *T* v. *T* [1988] 2 WLR 189, 203. Cf. F. Trindade, 'Intentional Torts: Some Thoughts on Assault and Battery' (1982) 2 *Oxford Journal of Legal Studies* 211, 228–9. Cf. S. Blay, 'Onus of Proof of Consent in an Action for Trespass to the Person' (1987) 61 *Australian Law Journal* 25. The issue remains unresolved: See M. Jones, *Medical Negligence* (London: Sweet & Maxwell, 1991), 206–7.

[11] M. Somerville, *Consent to Medical Care* (Ottawa: Law Reform Commission of Canada, 1980), 47–8.

[12] *Morris* v. *Murray* [1991] 2 WLR 195; *Barrett* v. *Ministry of Defence*, *Independent*, 3 June 1993.

information.[13] By the same token, one might be tempted to question whether consent to a proposed procedure can be meaningfully construed as evincing autonomous choice when the patient has not been informed of possible alternatives.

On these issues, too, English law has opted for a formal, minimalist approach to the consent requirement, ruling out battery where the patient has been informed 'in broad terms' about the nature of a proposed procedure.[14] Only if the procedure actually carried out was totally different from what had been agreed, or if consent was obtained through fraud or misrepresentation could the action succeed. It is submitted that consent to medical procedures which is 'uninformed', in the sense of being given in ignorance of risks attaching to them, should not be deemed valid for the purpose of negating trespass. To insist that patients have 'consented' to procedures when they do not really know what they entail is at best over-literal and artificial, even if it is perhaps no more incongruous than labelling well-intentioned medical treatment 'battery'. No doubt reluctance to characterize the behaviour of doctors in this way helps to explain why the criteria of liability are so limited.[15]

It has been observed that what constitutes consent or the lack of it can quite properly vary according to context. Whereas a minimum of pressure exerted on a worker by an employer may be deemed incompatible with 'freely given' consent in the context of a negligence claim, more latitude might reasonably be thought in order before doctors recommending treatment are held liable for battery.[16] That said, to rule out liability on the strength of a narrowly construed 'consent' to the 'nature' of the act seems unduly restrictive in a sphere where well-founded trust is so crucial, especially if seriously invasive treatment is in issue. Yet, however questionable the distinction between the *nature* of a medical procedure and serious *risks* associated with it,[17] it is firmly

---

[13] See R. Crisp, 'Medical Negligence, Assault, Informed Consent, and Autonomy' (1990) 17 *Journal of Law and Society* 77; K. Tan, 'Failure of Medical Advice: Trespass or Negligence' (1987) 7 *Legal Studies* 149.

[14] *Chatterton* v. *Gerson* [1981] QB 432.

[15] Cf. J. Fleming, *The Law of Torts* (8th edn.) (Sydney: The Law Book Company, 1992), 81: 'one is loath to equate a healing physician to a violent ruffian'.

[16] P. Skegg, *Law, Ethics, and Medicine* (Oxford: Clarendon Press, 1984), 95–6.

[17] See Tan, n. 13 above. Cf. M. Somerville, 'Structuring the Issues in Informed Consent' (1981) 26 *McGill Law Journal* 740, 742–52.

established that one can legally consent to an operation even when oblivious of such risks.[18] This dubious differentiation between substance and attributes has affinities with the 'trust the doctors' mind-set that underpins the *Bolam* test. It undermines the claim that an action in battery provides patients with a 'right to self-determination'.

Such an undemanding and vague criterion of consent, reinforced by judicial distaste for stigmatizing doctors,[19] greatly diminishes the effectiveness of the battery action as a means of impugning inadequate disclosure. The issue has aroused renewed interest because of controversy over testing for HIV. When a patient consents to a blood sample being taken for 'tests', does this entitle the doctor to test the sample for HIV without obtaining consent explicitly for this purpose?[20] Can it be said that such a patient has been informed 'in broad terms' of the nature of the procedure? In 1987, the BMA passed a motion which said that 'testing for HIV antibodies should be at the discretion of the patient's doctor, and should not necessarily require the consent of the patient'. After obtaining counsel's opinion that testing for HIV could not be deemed a 'routine' procedure, the BMA decided not to implement the resolution.[21] However, it was argued in a second counsel's opinion[22] that there would be no battery as there would have been broad consent to the 'nature' of the procedure.[23] If this

---

[18] *Sidaway* v. *Governors of Bethlem Royal Hospital* [1985] AC 871; *Reibl* v. *Hughes* (1980) 114 DLR (3d) 1 (Canadian Supreme Court).

[19] See e.g. *Hills* v. *Potter* [1984] 1 WLR 641, 653; *Sidaway* v. *Governors of Bethlem Royal Hospital* [1985] AC 871, 883, *per* Lord Scarman.

[20] I. Kennedy and A. Grubb, 'Testing for HIV Infection: the Legal Framework', *Law Society's Gazette*, 15 Feb. and 1 Mar. 1989; J. Keown, 'The Ashes of AIDS and the Phoenix of Informed Consent' (1989) 52 *Modern Law Review* 790; A. Grubb and D. Pearl, *Blood Testing, AIDS and DNA Profiling* (Bristol: Family Law, 1990), ch. 1; P. Wilson, 'Testing the Boundaries of Consent' (1994) 144 *New Law Journal* 574.

[21] Opinion of M. Sherrard, QC, and I. Gatt, 'Human Immunodeficiency Virus (HIV) Antibody Testing', *British Medical Journal* 295 (1987), 911. Ibid. 940. Cf. I. Kennedy and A. Grubb, n. 20 above, arguing that it is battery because consent to testing generally does not include consent to touchings which are *prima facie* contrary to public policy and because the 'procedure' is not merely the obtaining of a sample, but obtaining it for an HIV test.

[22] *Advice Re: HIV Testing*, HMSC 13 (1988): Opinion of L. Charles, QC, for the Central Committee for Hospital Medical Services.

[23] Viz. the 'needle in the arm': Opinion of G. Langley, QC, A. Hochhauser, and M. Griffiths, *AIDS: Medico-Legal Advice* (London: Medical Defence Union, 1988), 4–5.

is correct, it would almost certainly preclude *any* action for non-disclosure in such circumstances. A claim based on negligence would be very likely to fall foul of the *Bolam* test, since many, if not most, doctors would not disclose the specific purpose until they had the result.[24] Moreover, as would be required in an action based on negligence, patients might find it hard to prove compensatable harm or, for that matter, causation, that is, that they would not have agreed to testing had they been aware of the undisclosed purpose.

To the non-lawyer it must seem strange that liability in such a matter could depend on the level of generality at which we construe 'the nature of the procedure', or on whether any physical contact occurs that is specifically referable to testing for HIV, or whether non-disclosure is accepted medical practice, rather than by directly addressing the legitimate extent of the patient's right to know. Though, from an ethical standpoint, an informed consent approach might seem preferable,[25] in English law it would seem that the 'reasonable doctor' test prevails and, in 1988, the BMA passed another motion on the subject which reaffirmed the primacy of clinical judgement.[26] Ultimately the example of HIV testing is no more than a particularly graphic illustration of the general point that, in matters of disclosure, the law is *not* fundamentally concerned to ask 'what must be done in order to safeguard, to the fullest extent possible, the right of the patient as an autonomous person to choose between courses of action affecting him or her?'[27] Its focus is on whether the doctor's conduct satisfies the constituent elements of the tort of battery (or negligence, as the case may be). The accent is squarely on the extent of the doctor's technical legal duty, not on the patient's rights.

[24] See Keown, n. 20 above, 799.

[25] It is required by the relevant legislation in several states in the USA, e.g. New York Public Health Code, s. 2781, art. 27. See Grubb and Pearl, *Blood Testing, AIDS and DNA Profiling*, n. 20 above, 33–5.

[26] Though in *Medical Ethics Today* it is stated that 'some diagnostic procedures, particularly HIV-testing, have such profound implications for the patient that specific patient consent is deemed indispensable': British Medical Association (London: British Medical Association, 1993), 23, para. 1:5.1. The GMC has expressed a similar view: GMC Statement, 25 May 1988, paras. 12–13.

[27] D. Feldman, *Civil Liberties and Human Rights in England and Wales* (Oxford: Clarendon Press, 1993), 142.

In practice, then, treatment is rarely deemed to be battery and hardly ever for want of disclosure. Judges hesitate to label dedicated surgeons 'negligent'. They positively recoil from equating medically justifiable, skilfully performed, and beneficial surgery with trespass, let alone violent criminality, solely because it has not been preceded by appropriate communication. Furthermore, irrespective of the level of disclosure, if, as has been held,[28] battery requires physical contact which is in some sense 'hostile', there would appear to be hardly any scope for such liability at all in the medical context. Though the better view is that the touching need not be hostile,[29] unwanted invasive treatment remains a serious matter even in the absence of hostile intent. It is the more serious if we accept that the doctor–patient relationship should reflect trust. On this view, patients are morally entitled to expect such disclosure as would make the act of consenting a meaningful exercise; anything less is tantamount to paternalism. However, concerned about the rising incidence of medical claims, judges are averse to extended disclosure requirements, even within the ambit of negligence. They would be more loath still to incorporate them in the tort of battery, for several reasons. Battery, unlike negligence, permits recovery for all direct damage (not only for that which was reasonably foreseeable), and does not require plaintiffs to prove harm, or proximate cause—that they would not have consented to the procedure had they been adequately informed of the risks. Nor does it normally permit the doctor a defence of professional judgement or 'therapeutic privilege' not to disclose in the interests of patient welfare. As we have seen, such considerations have led to an unduly narrow view of vitiated consent.

Incompetent Patients

Sterilisation of Mentally Incompetent Adults

Though doctors may have little reason to be concerned about the law of battery when they treat mentally competent adults, one might have expected it to be fairly demanding in respect of

---

[28] *Wilson* v. *Pringle* [1987] QB 237.
[29] *Re F (Mental Patient: Sterilization)* [1990] 2 AC 1, 73, *per* Lord Goff; *T* v. *T* [1988] 1 All ER 613, 625, *per* Wood J.

patients who lack the capacity to consent. Yet this is not the case. There is, in fact, something of a gap in this area.[30] The law does provide for parental or court authorization of treatment in the case of children, and for non-consensual psychiatric treatment of mentally disordered patients detained under the Mental Health Act 1983, but it has had remarkably little to say about the position of health care professionals regarding ordinary medical treatment for the mentally handicapped adult. As Brazier observes, presumably in the past 'they just went ahead on the paternalistic theory that "doctor knows best" '.[31] By the late 1980s the climate of opinion had changed, and when several instances of proposed abortion and sterilization for mentally handicapped women attracted public attention, there were calls for a more explicit statement of patients' rights and doctors' duties, which ensuing litigation sought to provide.

Since involuntary sterilization will almost invariably 'deprive the woman concerned of what is widely . . . regarded as one of the fundamental rights of a woman',[32] the care with which the legal criteria permitting such a drastic step are formulated is a good indicator of how far the tort of battery in practice protects the integrity of the individual. Against this yardstick, the leading House of Lords authority, *Re F*,[33] can scarcely be judged a success. The Court of Appeal did at least recognize that, in determining whether such an operation was necessary, or in the *best* interests of a patient unable to consent, it would not suffice merely to show that it would not amount to negligence as construed under the *Bolam* test. According to Lord Donaldson MR, what needs to be ascertained is the course of action 'best calculated to promote [the] *true* welfare and interests' of the

[30] The Law Commission is currently reviewing the law relating to medical treatment of mentally handicapped patients: The Law Commission, *Mentally Incapacitated Adults and Decision-Making: An Overview* (London: HMSO, 1991), Consultation Paper No 119; *Mentally Incapacitated Adults and Decision-Making: A New Jurisdiction* (London: HMSO, 1993), Consultation Paper No 128; *Mentally Incapacitated Adults and Decision-Making: Medical Treatment and Research* (London: HMSO, 1993), Consultation Paper No 129.

[31] M. Brazier, *Medicine, Patients and the Law* (2nd edn.), (Harmondsworth: Penguin Books, 1992), 97.

[32] *Re F (Mental Patient: Sterilization)* [1990] 2 AC 1, 56, *per* Lord Brandon; cf. 'the deprivation of a basic human right': *Re D (A Minor) (Wardship: Sterilization)* [1976] 2 WLR 279, 286, *per* Heilbron J.　　　　[33] Ibid.

patient,[34] for which 'consultation with other doctors and with those in other caring disciplines may be necessary'.[35] 'Greater caution', he said, 'would be needed before deciding to treat than in the case of the ordinary adult patient'. Lord Justice Neil defined 'necessary' treatment in this context as what 'the general body of medical opinion in the particular speciality would consider to be in the best interests of the patient in order to maintain the health and to secure the well-being of the patient'.[36]

In addition, the Court of Appeal took the view that where the court sanctioned procedures of this kind, a more explicit form of endorsement than a mere declaration of lawfulness was needed. Lord Donaldson said that 'in the context of the most sensitive and potentially controversial forms of treatment the public interest requires that the courts should give express approval before the treatment is carried out and thereby provide an independent and broad based "third opinion" '.[37] But in the absence of clearly articulated criteria, it is not apparent how stringent the Court of Appeal's approach to 'best interests' would have proved to be in practice. Certainly, the primacy accorded to medical opinion[38] in itself argues a largely cosmetic supervisory role for this 'third opinion' providing 'outside scrutiny',[39] 'final approval',[40] and 'an assurance to the public that the facts have been fully investigated in a court of law'.[41] In the event, as we have seen, the House of Lords by relying on the *Bolam* test and not requiring a mandatory declaration was content to exercise a largely symbolic role.[42]

The Law Lords took a broad view of what legally constitutes 'necessary' treatment and a narrowly medical approach to the 'best interests' of the incompetent patient. By applying the *Bolam* test, they effectively treated the matter as one for clinical decision alone. Their expansive view of 'necessity' is most apparent in Lord

---

[34] *Re F (Mental Patient: Sterilization)* [1989] 2 WLR 1025, 1040.
[35] Ibid. [36] Ibid. 1053. [37] Ibid. 1042.
[38] Especially by Butler-Sloss LJ: 'The criteria for making that medical decision are matters for the medical profession': ibid., 1062.
[39] Ibid. 1053, *per* Neil LJ. [40] Ibid. 1062, *per* Butler-Sloss LJ.
[41] Ibid. 1054, *per* Neil LJ.
[42] Cf. 'if the question whether the operation is in the best interests of the woman is left to be decided without the involvement of the court, there may be a greater risk of it being decided wrongly, *or at least of it being thought to have been decided wrongly*': *Re F (Mental Patient: Sterilization)* [1990] 2 AC 1, 56, *per* Lord Brandon. Emphasis added.

Brandon's formulation, which sanctions treatment 'to ensure improvement or prevent deterioration in . . . physical or mental health'.[43] Lord Bridge, too, considered it 'axiomatic' that treatment 'necessary to preserve the . . . well-being of the patient may lawfully be given without consent'.[44] The House was much influenced by the argument that a strict test of 'necessary' treatment for the non-consenting incompetent adult would rule out a great deal of mundane but beneficial treatment,[45] leaving carers vulnerable to a claim for battery if they did administer treatment and a claim for negligence if they did not. Certainly the myriad daily intrusions deemed necessary by those who care for severely handicapped and institutionalized patients[46] require lawful justification. However, to accommodate most of them within the notion of 'physical contact which is generally acceptable in the ordinary conduct of everyday life', would be no more artificial than the Law Lords' interpretation of 'necessity'.

As regards more serious interventions, the incompetent patient should arguably share the 'right' of the competent to forego medical treatment that is not in the normal sense of the word 'necessary'. There is naturally a temptation for doctors to persuade themselves that treatment which they regard as medically desirable is in fact necessary. It is well illustrated in cases where procedures additional to those consented to are undertaken in the course of surgery.[47] In a recent instance of an unauthorized hysterectomy, a senior consultant was reported as saying 'these allegations are outrageous. She was an elderly lady with a large degree of prolapse. She was told she needed surgery and agreed. She stipulated she would rather keep her uterus. It would have been possible to do the repair operation, but the doctor decided it would give a less satisfactory repair, so she did a hysterectomy,' The surgeon, he added, had made a proper medical judgement.[48]

---

[43] [1990] 2 AC 1, 55.   [44] Ibid. 52.

[45] Ibid. 56, *per* Lord Brandon.

[46] 'Such humdrum matters as routine medical or dental treatment, even simple care such as dressing and undressing and putting to bed': ibid. 76, *per* Lord Goff.

[47] See *Marshall* v. *Curry* (1933) 3 DLR 260 and *Murray* v. *McMurchy* (1949) 2 DLR 442.

[48] *Observer*, 11 July 1993. Actions for unwanted surgery are not that uncommon. See D. Brahams, 'Unwanted Hysterectomies', *Lancet* 342 (1993), 361.

Partly because of this kind of reaction and because doctors' decisions are routinely made with the best of intentions, there is a good case for greater caution and for a stronger consensus than is required by the *Bolam* test to sanction even some non-essential procedures for those who cannot say no. *A fortiori*, the argument applies to controversial, highly invasive treatment.

In *Re F* and in cases like it,[49] the courts treated the issues at stake as if they were almost exclusively referable to doctors' views of 'best interests' and 'welfare'. The House of Lords seemed to be signalling that legal protection for incompetent patients' rights is secondary to facilitating whatever treatment doctors deem appropriate. As one commentator put it, 'the decision-making process appears to be almost entirely in the hands of the medical profession—who are protected against legal sanction by the doctrines of necessity, best interests and an internally defined notion of professional competence'.[50] Consistent with their reliance on *Bolam*, the Law Lords showed little inclination to elaborate on the human rights dimension of involuntary sterilization or to establish any concrete guidelines. The extent of their reliance on medical opinion seems almost cavalier when compared with approaches in a number of other jurisdictions.[51] In particular, it stands in stark contrast to the comprehensive analysis and scrupulous attention to relevant research findings of the Canadian Supreme Court in *Re Eve*, as evidenced in its unanimous judgment delivered by La Forest J, who said:

The grave intrusion on a person's rights and the certain physical damage that ensues from non-therapeutic sterilization without consent, when compared to the highly questionable advantages that can result from it, have persuaded me that it can never safely be determined that such a procedure is for the benefit of that person.[52]

---

[49] Cf. *T* v. *T* [1988] 2 WLR 189, 199, *per* Wood J.

[50] J. Shaw, 'Regulating Sexuality: A Legislative Framework for Non-Consensual Sterilisation' in S. McVeigh and S. Wheeler (eds.) *Law, Health and Medical Regulation* (Aldershot: Dartmouth, 1992), 101.

[51] See e.g. *Re Guardianship of Hayes*, 608 P 2d 635 (Wash. SC, 1980); *In Re Grady*, 426 A 2d 467 (1981); *In Re Jane*, 85 ALR 409 (1988) (United States); *Department of Health and Community Services (NT)* v. *JWB and SMB* (1992) 66 ALJR 300—court approval necessary (High Court of Australia); and the emphasis on choice where possible, in line with constitutionally guaranteed human rights, in German law's interpretation of 'best interests': Shaw, above, n. 50.

[52] (1987) 31 DLR (4d) 1, 32.

For our purposes it is not the conclusion as such which is in point, but rather the preparedness to tackle the case as one which raises an issue of fundamental rights and the readiness to draw a distinction between therapeutic and non-therapeutic sterilization.[53] The Official Solicitor's Practice Note on sterilization[54] does show some sensitivity to the potential enormity of such operations and stresses the need to be sure that no less intrusive solution is practicable. Citing *Re F*, it also states that 'sterilization of . . . a mentally incompetent adult . . . will *in virtually all cases require* the prior sanction of a High Court judge'.[55] But since such sanction is not legally mandated and the Note itself is only non-binding guidance on procedure, the use of the term 'require' is at most indicative of common practice. As regards legal protection of patients' rights, the Note's provisions do not compensate for the paucity of safeguards in the English system; they are merely another manifestation of largely symbolic judicial oversight. Essentially they reiterate the strong advice to doctors in *Re F* that, as a matter of good practice, they should seek a declaration confirming that sterilization is in the woman's interests and in conformity with responsible medical opinion. In fact, court sanction has been deemed neither necessary nor desirable when the procedure is 'medically indicated' or 'therapeutic',[56] or when abortion is proposed for a mentally handicapped woman patient.[57] In addition, in 1990 the Practice Note was amended so that 'straightforward' cases 'may be disposed of at the hearing for directions without oral evidence'.[58]

It is partly because many judges tend to assume that decisions involving doctors are almost by definition medical decisions and nothing else, that they are reluctant to accept that clinical

---

[53] Cf. the mandatory court authorization requirement established in *Department of Health and Community Services (NT)* v. *JWB and SMB*, see n. 51 above.

[54] Last revised in May 1993: see [1993] 2 FLR 222. For previous versions see [1989] 2 FLR 447 and [1990] 2 FLR 530.

[55] Emphasis added.

[56] *F* v. *F* (1992) 7 BMLR 135 and *Re GF (Medical Treatment)* [1992] 1 FLR 293, both cases of sterility resulting from therapeutic hysterectomy. It should be noted that the therapeutic/non-therapeutic distinction had been expressly rejected by the House of Lords in *Re B (A Minor) (Wardship: Sterilization)* [1988] AC 199.

[57] *Re SG (Adult Mental Patient: Abortion)* [1991] 2 FLR 527.

[58] *Practice Note. Official Solicitor: Sterilization* [1990] 2 FLR 530, para. 6, following Thorpe J's decision in *J* v. *C (Practice Note) (Mental Patient: Sterilization)* [1990] 1 WLR 1248.

judgement should carry less weight in respect of non-therapeutic procedures or those not performed exclusively for medical reasons.[59] Under the guise of giving effect to presumed 'best interests,' they are authorizing doctors to make choices which may reflect the interests of people other than the patient as well as controversial individual and social values. These interests and values may differ from those of the patients and the choices may be contrary to their expressed views.[60] None of this means, of course, that recommendations by doctors of non-consensual sterilisation which the judiciary authorize are commonly unwise or indefensible.[61] Frequently they will be based on compelling considerations, following extensive consultation and deliberation, as seems to have been the case with F herself.[62] But to the extent that the law of battery could be deployed either to ensure some attenuated form of patient choice or some informed and articulated conception of 'best interests', English courts have shown little sign of seeking them.[63]

Advance Directives

The same point emerges when one considers the relatively undeveloped state of English law concerning advance directives. A society seriously committed to the principle of self-determination for patients might be expected, within limits, to give legal effect to preferences which they have expressed about treatment in anticipation of mental incapacity or terminal illness. Invasive procedures which contravened an advance declaration of this kind would then constitute battery. Such a prior arrangement can take

---

[59] e.g. in *Re B (A Minor) (Wardship: Sterilization)* [1988] AC 199, Lord Hailsham said that the distinction between 'therapeutic' and 'non-therapeutic' was 'totally meaningless' (203–4) and Lord Bridge that it was 'an area of arid semantic debate' (205). Cf. *Gold* v. *Haringey Health Authority* [1988] QB 481, 488–90, *per* Lloyd LJ. But cf. *Re D (A Minor) (Wardship: Sterilization)* [1976] 2 WLR 279, 286, *per* Heilbron J and *Gold* v. *Haringey Health Authority* [1987] 1 FLR 125, 139–40, *per* Schiemann J. Cf 'The shift from *Re D* to *Re B* shows how easily "best medical interests" have become "best interests" with the obliteration of the therapeutic/ non-therapeutic distinction': M. Freeman, 'Sterilising the Mentally Handicapped' in M. Freeman (ed.), *Medicine, Ethics and Law* (London: Stevens, 1988), 55, 78.

[60] J. Shaw, n. 50 above, 104–6.

[61] M. Brazier, *Medicine, Patients and the Law*, n. 31 above, 109.

[62] *The Times*, correspondence col., 7 Dec. 1988.

[63] See especially Freeman, n. 59 above.

the form of a 'living will', a written statement for use when patients can no longer communicate their wishes about medical care,[64] or the appointment of a proxy decision-maker through an enduring power of attorney. In the United States and many other jurisdictions there has been extensive debate culminating in statutory recognition of advance directives for patients with a terminal medical condition.[65] By contrast, in England, apart from whatever weight doctors happen to attach in any given case to 'living wills', there is no clear authority on the matter, though important recent dicta suggest that they could be valid at common law. Subject to caveats about their genuinely autonomous character and relevance to the situation in hand, Lord Donaldson endorsed advance declarations in *Re T*, and without apparently confining his remarks to cases of terminal illness.[66] His view was cited with approval in *Bland* by Lord Goff, who said that the principle of self-determination applies:

where the patient's refusal to give his consent has been expressed at an earlier date, before he became unconscious or otherwise incapable of communicating it; though in such circumstances especial care may be necessary to ensure that the prior refusal of consent is still properly to be regarded as applicable in the circumstances which have subsequently occurred.[67]

[64] By 1993, at least 60,000 people in Britain already had such documents, according to the Voluntary Euthanasia Society: *The Times*, 25 Feb. 1993. See K. Stern, 'Advance Directives' (1994) 2 *Medical Law Review* 57.

[65] 'International comparisons reveal an extensive involvement of the law in sanctioning advance directives, particularly in common law jurisdictions. In the United States, statutes regulate advance directives in 48 out of 50 states': C. Brennan, 'The Right to Die' [1993] *New Law Journal* 1041. After the United States Supreme Court decided in the case of Nancy Cruzan (a PVS patient) that states could require 'clear and convincing evidence' before action could be taken on the patient's supposed wishes: *Cruzan* v. *Director, Missouri Department of Health*, 110 S Ct 2841 (1990), the Patient Self-Determination Act 1990 was passed, requiring institutions in receipt of federal funding (which constitute the majority of health care facilities) to inform patients of their right to make an advance directive and to respect the patient's wishes. The Act demonstrates the strength of commitment to the principle of people controlling their own destiny. Enabling legislation along similar lines exists in several Commonwealth and European jurisdictions. See also *Malette* v. *Shulman* (1990) 67 DLR (4th) 321 (Ontario, CA): validity of Jehovah Witnesses' card refusing blood transfusion upheld.

[66] 'An anticipatory choice . . . if clearly established and applicable in the circumstances—two major 'ifs'—would bind the practitioner': [1992] 3 WLR 782, 787.

[67] *Airedale NHS Trust* v. *Bland* [1993] AC 789, 864. See also *Report of the House of Lords Select Committee on Medical Ethics* (London: HMSO, 1994).

In the Court of Appeal decision in the same case, Lord Bingham MR said that had Bland:

given instructions that he should not be artificially fed or treated with antibiotics if he should become a P.V.S. patient, his doctors would not act unlawfully in complying with those instructions but would act unlawfully if they did not comply, even though the patient's death would inevitably follow.[68]

The case for legislation to validate advance directives is cogent; the case for clarification of their legal status seems unanswerable. If nothing else, they can provide some concrete indication of what patients' views once were, and under a system of mandatory renewal at regular intervals, there would often be little or no reason to suppose that the views expressed would have changed. That is not to say that courts will easily be persuaded that such directives should continue to prevail when serious illness occurs.[69] Consequently, patients have no guarantee that their wishes will be respected, while doctors and other third parties could find themselves in an invidious position. In *R* v. *Smith*,[70] for example, a devoted husband was charged with manslaughter for abiding by his wife's unequivocal and long-maintained refusal to receive medical attention.

Past diffidence about legislating in this area is readily explicable: 'death, perhaps, is too important, too awe-inspiring to be pronounced upon in advance'.[71] Certainly it would be deeply disturbing if, like consent forms, 'living wills' ever came to be regarded as a mechanical bureaucratic substitute for authenticity. But as life expectancy continues to grow and medical advances make it possible, by artificial means, to prolong both existence and

---

[68] [1993] 2 WLR 316, 335. Cf. Hoffman LJ, 'The right of self-determination entails that such wishes should be respected': ibid. 353.

[69] Though see *Re C (Adult: Refusal of Treatment)* [1994] 1 WLR 290 where a mental patient obtained an injunction upholding his adamant oral refusal to consent, at the time or prospectively, to amputation of a gangrenous foot. The order was made despite an estimated 85% risk of resultant death and despite the virtual inevitability, given his condition, that the refusal would become irrevocable with the deterioration of his mental state. See R. Gordon and C. Barlow, 'Competence and the Right to Die' [1993] *New Law Journal* 1719.

[70] [1979] Criminal Law Review 251. On the particular facts there was no advance directive in written form.

[71] A. McCall Smith, 'Ending Life', in C. Dyer (ed.), *Doctors, Patients and the Law* (Oxford: Blackwell Scientific Publications, 1992), 116.

the process of dying, the arguments in favour of people being able to exercise this kind of control over their destiny become stronger; they are all the more urgent as a response to the spread of AIDS.[72] The absence of legislation and the fact that the case law is only now tentatively addressing the issue is a further illustration of the gap between long-standing rhetorical endorsement of self-determination and concrete legal provision for it.

Children

The strength of the law's commitment to the autonomy principle has also been called into doubt by recent decisions on treatment for young people[73] which seem difficult to reconcile with both the letter and spirit of related statutory and common law developments.[74] The Family Law Reform Act 1969[75] made it possible for 16- and 17-year-olds to give effective consent to 'surgical, medical, or dental treatment'. A parallel judicial trend towards enhanced autonomy for children reached its high point in 1985, when *Gillick*, by a bare majority in the House of Lords, extended the right to consent to children under 16 with sufficient understanding of what the proposed treatment was about, that is, with the intellectual and emotional maturity to appreciate its implications and consequences. Respecting the views of children capable of making their own decisions is also a key feature of the Children Act 1989. Under several of its provisions relating to child assessment, they may refuse to submit even to a court-ordered medical, psychiatric or other examination if they have 'sufficient understanding to make an informed decision'.[76]

Gillick was unquestionably seen as a landmark decision in advancing children's rights over their medical treatment, and in

---

[72] See King's College Centre of Medical Law and Ethics, *Advance Directives and AIDS* (London: KCCMLE, 1992).

[73] See J. Montgomery, 'Consent to Health Care for Children' (1993) 5 *Journal of Child Law* 117.

[74] A. Grubb, 'Treatment Decisions: Keeping it in the Family' in A. Grubb (ed.), *Choices and Decisions in Health Care* (Chichester: John Wiley & Sons, 1993), 37.

[75] S. 8(1).

[76] A formula plainly influenced by the House of Lords' approach in *Gillick*. See ss. 38(6), 43(8), 44(7) and paras. 4(4)(a) and 5(5)(a) of Sched. 3. But note *South Glamorgan County Council* v. *W & B* [1993] 1 FLR 574: inherent jurisdiction of the High Court subsequently invoked to override such refusal.

signalling a corresponding diminution of that 'dwindling right' which we call parental authority.[77] In fact, by acknowledging the need for a sensitive and thorough dialogue such that the mature child's voice could be heard and respected, the decision could be seen as vindicating the very doctrine of 'informed consent' which the House of Lords had firmly rejected in relation to adults only months earlier in *Sidaway*.[78] But although, or perhaps because, it symbolized the demise of Victorian-style *parental* paternalism, it was not generally appreciated how far the decision was from signifying the end of *medical* paternalism. For it is the child's voice as mediated through the clinical judgement of the doctor which ultimately counts under *Gillick*, and that judgement will often be highly influential, if not dispositive. This is explicitly the case for medical or health-related decisions made in accordance with Lord Fraser's formulation, rooted as it is in the doctor's perception of the 'best interests' or welfare of the child. It is implicit in the analysis of Lord Scarman, who, in addressing the specific issue before the court, said that the doctor would have to 'satisfy himself' that the girl understood the nature and implications of contraceptive advice and treatment. 'The truth may well be', he concluded, 'that the rights of parents and children in this sensitive area are better protected by the professional standards of the medical profession than by a priori legal lines of division between capacity and lack of capacity to consent'.[79]

Though the analysis in *Gillick* was confined to the effect of a child's consent to treatment, it is widely accepted that it was also intended to apply to refusal of treatment. In Lord Scarman's words:

. . . parental right yields to the child's right to make his own decisions when he reaches a sufficient understanding and intelligence to be capable of making up his own mind on the matter requiring decision.[80]

And again:

. . . as a matter of law the parental right to determine *whether or not* their minor child below the age of 16 will have medical treatment terminates if and when the child achieves a sufficient understanding and intelligence to enable him or her to understand fully what is proposed.[81]

---

[77] *Hewer* v. *Bryant* [1970] 1 QB 357, 369, *per* Lord Denning.
[78] Cf. S. Cretney [1985] *All ER Ann Rev* 173.
[79] *Gillick* v. *West Norfolk and Wisbech AHA* [1986] AC 112, 191.
[80] Ibid. 186.   [81] Ibid. 188–9. Emphasis added.

If the last few years have seen something of a retreat from the degree of autonomy originally envisaged for competent under-age patients in *Gillick*, this would seem to have at least as much to do with judicial anxiety about the position of the medical profession as with any conscious attempt to restore an outmoded model of parental control. Certainly the restrictive interpretation of the case later advanced by Lord Donaldson owed a great deal to his concern about its legal implications for doctors. The objections to his much-criticized view that *Gillick* covers only *consent* to treatment, and does not give a competent child an effective right to *refuse* treatment consented to by a parent (or someone with parental rights, or the court, as the case may be),[82] have been exhaustively addressed elsewhere.[83] What is of most interest for present purposes is the extent to which he was prompted by concern that doctors should be able to treat unwilling children without subsequently being held liable for trespass to the person. Thus in *Re R* Lord Donaldson spoke of the 'intolerable dilemma' doctors would face if *Gillick*-competence entailed a complete transfer of the right of consent from parent to child. If this were so, he argued, doctors could end up being sued for battery or even charged with criminal assault if, with parental consent, they treated non-consenting children whom they had wrongly assessed as lacking *Gillick*-competence. True though this claim may be in theory, it is hard to see why in practice it should constitute a serious threat to a doctor who has reached a responsible decision about such an inherently nebulous legal concept. It should also be remembered that, as was indicated in *Re R* and *Re W*, and emphatically reaffirmed by the Court of Appeal in *Re J (A Minor) (Child in Care: Medical Treatment)*,[84] not even courts, let alone patients or parents, can *require* doctors to undertake any treatment which in their bona fide clinical judgement is not in the

---

[82] *Re R (Wardship)(Consent to Treatment)* [1991] 3 WLR 592; *Re W (A Minor) (Medical Treatment)* [1992] 3 WLR 758. In *Re R*, his remarks were plainly *obiter* because the child was not deemed to be '*Gillick*-competent'. Equally, neither case involved an actual parent. In *Re R*, the Court was exercising its inherent wardship jurisdiction; in *Re W*, the Court was exercising its inherent jurisdiction on the application of the local authority.

[83] See e.g. A. Grubb, 'Treatment Decisions' in A. Grubb (ed.), *Choices and Decisions in Health Care*, above, n. 74, 54–68, who calls it 'a remarkably narrow reading of the *Gillick* decision'. But see also N. Lowe and S. Juss, 'Medical Treatment—Pragmatism and the Search for Principle' (1993) 56 *Modern Law Review* 865.   [84] [1992] 3 WLR 507.

patient's best interests. What Lord Donaldson's view does reveal is a value judgement in which protecting doctors against a relatively remote risk is more highly prized than the autonomy interest of competent patients in not having to submit to invasive treatment.

Lord Donaldson returned to the 'doctor's dilemma' in *Re W*, where he described consent as having 'two purposes, the one clinical and the other legal.'[85] It was a legal 'flak jacket', 'which protects the doctor from claims by the litigious',[86] and clinically valuable because 'in many instances the co-operation of the patient and the patient's faith or at least confidence in the efficiency of the treatment is a major factor contributing to the treatment's success'. 'Failure to obtain such consent', he added, 'will usually make it much more difficult to administer the treatment'.[87] Noticeably absent from this heavily instrumental characterization of consent is any reference to a possible third purpose, namely, the endorsement of patients' rights.[88]

Several commentators have taken exception to Lord Donaldson's approach for its perceived hostility towards adolescent autonomy. Grubb, for example, says that arguably in *Re R* 'the court's philosophy is out of step with the post-*Gillick* era, which turns its face against parental paternalism'.[89] In 'controversial cases', he observes, 'where doctors, parents, and others concerned about the child's welfare instinctively feel the child is making the wrong decision . . . the state interest in preserving life seems, according to *Re W*, to trump the individual interests of the competent child (although not of the competent adult)'.[90] To like effect, Edwards concludes that '*Re J*[91] . . . although clearly a difficult and sensitive case on its own facts, can be seen as a considerable setback to the autonomy of 16-year-olds in England.

---

[85] *Re W*, n. 82 above, 765.   [86] Ibid. 767.   [87] Ibid. 765.
[88] Cf. 'the new analogy [legal "flak jacket"] indicates that, somewhat in the tradition of Lord Denning, Lord Donaldson was concerned, in the main, with the interests of the medical profession. Consent was to be regarded as an aid to therapy and a protection for the doctor rather than as an expression of the patient's autonomy': J. Mason, 'Master of the Balancers; Non-Voluntary Therapy under the Mantle of Lord Donaldson' [1993] *Juridical Review* 115, 126.
[89] 'Treatment Decisions', n. 74 above, 68.
[90] Ibid. 75.
[91] i.e. *Re W, sub nom. Re J*.

They are unequivocally subject to the paternalistic supervision of the courts.'[92]

However, in several of these cases there remains a respectable argument for paternalism, given the objective gravity of the medical circumstances. When the paternalistic instincts of Lord Donaldson and other judges are most evident, in denying or doubting competence and in overriding refusal of treatment, they are almost invariably responding to strong medical recommendations about children with life-threatening or very serious medical conditions. They are not merely acquiescing in parental preferences. In *Re E*,[93] for example, a 15-year-old Jehovah's Witness suffered from leukaemia and was supported by his parents in refusing a blood transfusion which the judge later authorized as in his best interests, after he had been made a ward of court. In *Re R* it was the consultant who sought, and was refused, permission from the local authority to administer the antipsychotic medication which the court ultimately authorized, also under its wardship jurisdiction.

According to the medical evidence, R, who was 15 years old, was becoming increasingly psychotic and was at times a serious suicidal risk. Without the medication which she was refusing to take during lucid intervals, she was likely to lapse into such a state again. In *Re W*, W was a 16-year-old[94] who suffered from anorexia nervosa, a clinical feature of which is a firm desire not to be cured other than in a manner and at a time of the sufferer's own choosing. When her case came before the Court of Appeal, she had refused solid food for nine days and was existing on twelve cups of tea per day. Her condition had so deteriorated that the 'agreed medical opinion' was that, if she continued in her then state, 'within a week her capacity to have children in later life would be seriously at risk and a little later her life might be in danger'.[95] Her wishes, said Lord Donaldson, were 'completely

---

[92] L. Edwards, 'The Right to Consent and the Right to Refuse: More Problems with Minors and Medical Consent' [1993] *Juridical Review* 52, 72.

[93] *Re E (A Minor) (Wardship: Medical Treatment)* [1993] 1 FLR 386 (case decided 1990).

[94] The Court of Appeal rejected the argument that the Family Law Reform Act 1969, s. 8 conferred on 16- and 17-year-olds an absolute right to *refuse* medical treatment.

[95] [1992] 3 WLR 758, 768, *per* Lord Donaldson MR.

outweighed by the threat of irreparable damage to her health and risk to her life'.[96]

It is submitted that Lord Donaldson's understandable concern that vulnerable adolescents should not forgo treatment through what, on a longer term view, would seem ill-considered or inappropriate decision-making can be met without denying the applicability of *Gillick* to refusal of consent. For it is not simply a case of saying that a child who is mature enough to accept treatment is *ipso facto* mature enough to reject it. The determination of whether or not a child has sufficient understanding and intelligence to make a decision about medical treatment must depend on the circumstances of each case. A higher level of maturity is often needed to grasp the implications of a refusal and for it to constitute a considered commitment to what may be a catastrophic outcome. Refusal of treatment is more prone to reflect the turbulent and/or transient emotional states associated with adolescence than is its acceptance. Lord Scarman himself acknowledged that a basic understanding of the options is one thing, the ability to evaluate their implications another. Equally, it will be recalled that among Lord Fraser's prerequisites were the 'best interests' of the child and 'a judgement of what is best for the welfare of a particular child'.[97] Most importantly, the case, while conceding that there could be long-term issues to be resolved, does not really address the difficulty of making the imaginative leap needed to arrive at what the child might retrospectively have wanted. As Eekelaar points out, the autonomy interests of children may conflict with their 'developmental' interest in having their potential realized, and relatively few adults would retrospectively applaud a policy of giving the autonomy interest primacy in such circumstances.[98]. It is, of course, true that many adults will lack mature understanding when it comes to medical decision-making, but as a matter of practicality a line has to be drawn somewhere.

[96] For a contrary view see J. Masson, 'Re W: Appealing from the Golden Cage' (1993) 5 *Journal of Child Law* 37, 39.

[97] *Gillick* v. *West Norfolk and Wisbech AHA* [1986] AC 112, 173.

[98] See J. Eekelaar, 'The Emergence of Children's Rights' (1986) 6 *Oxford Journal of Legal Studies* 161, 181. Cf. Balcombe LJ's endorsement of Ward J's comment in *Re E*, that the court 'should be very slow to allow an infant to martyr himself': *Re W (A Minor) (Medical Treatment)* [1992] 3 WLR 758, 776. Cf. Nolan LJ, 'it is the duty of the court to ensure so far as it can that children survive to attain that age [18]': ibid., 781.

Even if *Gillick* did not contemplate unrestricted self-determination for mature minors in the medical sphere, or purport to
address autonomy as an abstract proposition, the case still
inevitably came to be seen as a symbolic milestone in the
enfranchisement of children. But we may nevertheless wish to
question the wisdom of allowing full rein to an ethic of self-
assertion in medical decision-making by minors. It is one thing to
approve the approach in *Gillick* to the particular issue of children
obtaining contraceptive advice and treatment without parental
consent;[99] it is quite another matter to espouse an absolutist stance
on adolescent rights. One might reasonably feel less than sanguine
about condoning an adolescent's refusal of treatment for a life-
threatening condition. Where there is a possibility of death or
serious, irreversible damage to health, the problematic nature of
what might count as 'sufficient understanding' or competence even
in a relatively mature child should give one pause about jettisoning
paternalistic welfare considerations.

Overriding the Refusal of Adults to Consent

That the courts are reluctant to take the legal implications of
patient autonomy to their logical conclusion, even as regards adult
patients who are not deemed incompetent, was graphically
demonstrated in *Re S.*[100] S was a 'born again' Christian mother of
two, whose third pregnancy was beyond full term. In labour, with
her unborn child in a position of 'transverse lie', she had refused,
on religious grounds, to undergo a caesarean section. The surgeon
gave evidence, which the judge unreservedly accepted, that the
life of the mother and her unborn child could be saved only if the
operation were performed, and only if it were carried out within
minutes rather than hours. There was no English precedent
directly in point, though Lord Donaldson had anticipated such a
problem, without hazarding an answer.[101] In these circumstances,
the judge felt impelled to override the woman's 'rights' over her
body and authorized the operation.

---

[99] Though even here a measure of scepticism is in order as to how often the
level of understanding envisaged by Lord Scarman about the various medical,
moral, and family-related dimensions of the decision will be required.

[100] *Re S (Adult: Refusal of Treatment)* [1992] 3 WLR 806.

[101] *Re T (Adult: Refusal of Treatment)* [1992] 3 WLR 782, 786.

In so doing, he invoked an American authority, *Re AC*.[102] In that case the court had initially authorized a forced caesarean for a terminally ill mother who was not expected to survive for more than a day or two, when she was in the twenty-sixth week of pregnancy and there was an outside chance of saving the unborn child.[103] However, this decision was reversed at a re-hearing before a full court,[104] in a judgment which in fact was to influence American doctors and courts to *reject* intervention in such cases. The court said, 'We hold that in virtually all cases the question of what is to be done is to be decided by the patient . . . on behalf of herself and the foetus.' And again, 'we do not quite foreclose the possibility that a conflicting State interest may be so compelling that the patient's wishes must yield, but we anticipate that such cases will be extremely rare and truly exceptional. This is not such a case [and] it would be an extraordinary case indeed'.[105] It is however of interest that, without expressing approval or dis-approval, the court contrasted the facts of an earlier American decision which had authorized a caesarean where there was strong evidence that it would benefit both mother and child, the baby being at full term and the mother having been in labour for two days.[106] In other words, *Re AC* did leave open the possibility that intervention was lawful on facts very similar to those in *Re S*.

The hearing in *Re S* lasted a mere twenty minutes and S herself was not legally represented.[107] Though the judge accepted the medical evidence that the only possible means of saving the un-born child and the life of the mother was for her to have the operation, it is not at all clear what criteria he was applying in authorizing it or precisely what influences were at work. It seems prima facie implausible, even allowing for the pressure of time, that he would have considered saving the mother's life a sufficient reason in itself; such a justification had been ruled out in the strongest possible terms in the very passage in *Re T* where Lord Donaldson had contemplated the situation which arose in *Re S*:

An adult patient who . . . suffers from no mental incapacity has an absolute right to . . . refuse [medical treatment] . . . The only possible

---

[102] *Re AC*, 573 A 2d 1235 (1990).
[103] *Re AC*, 533 A 2d 611 (District of Columbia Court of Appeals, 1988).
[104] See n. 102 above.   [105] Ibid. 1252.
[106] *Re Madyun*, 114 Daily Wash L Rpt 2233 (DC Super Ct, 1986).
[107] Though there was an *amicus curiae* for the Official Solicitor.

qualification is a case in which the choice may lead to the death of a viable foetus . . . when . . . the courts will be faced with a novel problem of considerable legal and ethical complexity . . . This right of choice is not limited to decisions which others might regard as sensible. It exists notwithstanding that the reasons for making the choice are rational, irrational, unknown or even non-existent[108]

It would therefore appear that in *Re S* the judge must have seen the interests of the unborn child as determinative. Some support for this view can be derived from the tenor of the judgment in dealing with the medical evidence. After referring to the surgeon's evidence that the operation was 'the only means of saving [the mother's] life', the judge continued, 'and also *I emphasise* the life of her unborn child . . . The surgeon is emphatic. He says it is absolutely the case that the baby cannot be born alive if a Caesarean operation is not carried out.'[109] Moreover, the terms of the declaration authorizing the operation referred to it as being 'in the vital interests of the patient *and the unborn child she is carrying*'.[110] The powerful objection has been raised that to justify the decision in this way is to confer on the foetus a juridical status which it has not normally been accorded in English law.[111] Indeed, only a few months earlier, in a case of alleged negligence during an attempted forceps delivery and Caesarean section, the Court of Appeal had reaffirmed 'the general proposition that a foetus enjoys, while still a foetus, no independent legal personality'.[112] It is true that Lord Donaldson does not offer any authority for his assertion that avoiding 'the death of a viable foetus' may justify overriding patient autonomy, but if it be sustainable, there could not be a more compelling example than the case of a foetus beyond full-term,[113] when birth by Caesarean section could not in any way diminish the mother's prospects of recovery.[114] Patient

---

[108] *Re T*, n. 101 above, 786.

[109] *Re S*, n. 100 above, 807. Emphasis added.   [110] Emphasis added.

[111] *Re F (in utero)* [1988] Fam 123; *C* v. *S* [1988] QB 135; and *Paton* v. *BPAS* [1979] QB 276.

[112] *De Martell* v. *Merton Health Authority*. See *Burton* v. *Islington Health Authority* and *De Martell* v. *Merton Health Authority* [1992] 3 WLR 637, 654, *per* Dillon LJ. Cf. *R* v. *Tait* [1990] 1 QB 290—foetus not 'a third person' within the meaning of s. 16 of the Offences Against the Person Act 1861, not being 'another person' distinct from its mother.

[113] Cf. the significant degree of protection accorded to the viable foetus under the Infant Life Preservation Act 1929.

[114] On the facts of *Re S* it could only have enhanced them.

autonomy may be highly desirable, but at this very late stage there was a legitimate countervailing interest in a successful birth.

Thus the dynamics of the situation in *Re S* go a long way towards explaining why the court took the admittedly grave step of overriding S's autonomy. By contrast, where, for example, a 5-year-old child suffering from leukaemia would die unless its mother agreed to donate her bone marrow, it is quite clear that the law would not contemplate authorizing compulsory treatment.[115] Despite the fact that the focus of attention in such a situation would be a live human being rather than a foetus, the inappropriateness of compulsion is arguably more apparent than in the circumstances of *Re S*. For though she did not consent to the Caesarean, S was already actively engaged in the process of giving birth. In *Re Madyun*, the court cryptically observed that 'all that stood between the Madyun fetus and its independent existence . . . was, put simply, a doctor's scalpel'. Whatever one's stance on the medicalization of childbirth, once the medical staff had the task of coping with the transverse lie, it seems artificial to distinguish S's situation from that of a patient undergoing a medical procedure. It would also seem inappropriate to equate her with someone forced to become a donor, to consent, as it were, to invasive treatment from cold. To say, as in the leukaemia example, that no one should be compelled actively to endure self-harm in order to prevent the death of another does not mean that we must condone a course of conduct which inexorably leads to the 'death' or non-survival of another. If, whatever the technical position in law, it is considered appropriate to regard a foetus beyond full term as akin to a live human being, S's insistence that the natural labour process should continue would make her appear more actively and directly responsible for causing 'death'.

It may be that *Re S* is best understood simply as a one-off instance of a judge responding to the natural human desire to try and save the life of the mother and the unborn child. In a highly charged situation, with literally only minutes to reach a decision, this would have been an all-too-human response. However in its repudiation of the consent requirement, *Re S* does raise serious

[115] In *Re AC*, n. 102 above, the majority opinion noted that courts in the United States have uniformly refused to require people to donate organs or undergo other types of 'significant intrusion' for the benefit of others.

questions about the strength of the law's commitment to patient autonomy. The case provoked severe criticism from some commentators who saw it as paving the way for substantial state regulation of pregnant women's behaviour.[116] The lack of a clearly delineated approach, however understandable, could in theory facilitate coerced medical treatment in less drastic circumstances. It is important to appreciate the potentially far-reaching implications of the decision, not least in the sheer mechanics of its practical implementation. How far, if at all, as a matter of human rights, should a society authorize medical staff to deal with recalcitrant patients by forcible injection or by dragging them kicking and screaming to the operating theatre?[117] Might such a decision result in some women becoming unduly fearful of hospital delivery? Unless strictly confined to its own special facts, *Re S* could foreshadow serious dilution of the principle that patients have a right to decide what should be done with their own bodies.

However, in practice there is more scope for derogation from the autonomy principle as a result of the Court of Appeal's approach in *Re T*.[118] T had been brought up by her mother, a 'fervent Jehovah's Witness'. Though T herself was not a practising Jehovah's Witness, she was an ex-member, who still maintained some beliefs. At the age of 20, when thirty-four weeks pregnant, she was injured in a car accident and admitted to hospital. After private conversations with her mother, she indicated that she did not want a blood transfusion and, following an emergency Caesarian operation, her baby was stillborn. T's condition deteriorated and she was put under sedation. The consultant anaesthetist, who felt inhibited about administering a transfusion, did so only after a judge, at an initial hearing of the matter, had declared that it was necessary in the emergency which had arisen and was thus 'in her best interests'. Reiterating this view at a subsequent full hearing, the judge found that though T's earlier decision had been voluntary, having been made when she was mentally competent and capable of balanced judgement, the evidence did not point to

---

[116] See K. Stern, 'Court-Ordered Caesarian Sections: In Whose Interests?' (1993) 56 *Modern Law Review* 238. Cf. B. Hewson, 'When "no" means "yes" ' *Law Society's Gazette*, 9 Dec. 1992, 2.

[117] See A. McCall Smith, 'Law, Liberty and Maternity', *The Times*, 15 Oct. 1992, pointing to the implications for attitudes towards abortion.

[118] [1992] 3 WLR 782.

'a settled intention on her part to persist in that refusal even if [it would be] injurious to her health'. An appeal was dismissed on the basis that T's will had been overborne by the undue influence of her mother and that she was, in any event, probably in no fit state to reach a decision.

The main point of interest is Lord Donaldson's analysis of the justification for overriding a seemingly competent adult's refusal of treatment. In a manner reminiscent of his judgment in *Sidaway*, he proceeded from a ringing endorsement of patient autonomy to a position which in practice affords doctors substantial opportunity to discount the genuineness of patients' decisions and to be the arbiters of their 'true wishes'.[119] He begins, as noted above, by saying that 'an adult patient who, like Miss T, suffers from no mental incapacity has an absolute right to . . . refuse' medical treatment (except, perhaps, where there is a viable foetus), however irrational the decision may appear to be.[120] Later in the judgment he describes the case as presenting a conflict of principle:

This situation gives rise to a conflict between two interests, that of the patient and that of the society in which he lives. The patient's interest consists of his right to self-determination—his right to live his own life how he wishes, even if it will damage his health or lead to his premature death. Society's interest is in upholding the concept that all human life is sacred and that it should be preserved if at all possible. It is well-established that in the ultimate the right of the individual is paramount. But this merely shifts the problem where the conflict occurs and calls for a very careful examination of whether, and if so the way in which, the individual is exercising that right. In case of doubt, that doubt falls to be resolved in favour of the preservation of life for if the individual is to override the public interest, he must do so in clear terms.[121]

It might be objected that society's interests are too narrowly conceived in this passage and inappropriately represented as exclusively the polar opposite of those of the patient. For society, too, has an interest in promoting patient autonomy, and the extent of the public interest in the preservation of life as such is increasingly a matter of dispute. When there is a desire to preserve life at almost all costs, genuine refusals of treatment can too

[119] Cf. *Sidaway* [1984] 2 WLR 778, 791.
[120] *Re T*, n. 101 above, 786.   [121] Ibid. 796.

readily be misconstrued as evidencing incapacity sufficient to negate competence.[122]

Nonetheless, determining whether a given consent or refusal is genuine can pose very real difficulties, as the facts of *Re T* itself demonstrate. If concepts such as 'capacity' and 'competence', being inherently elusive, are malleable, the leeway which they afford has its positive aspects. If courts, and doctors, find it difficult to suppress paternalistic instincts when the fate of desperately ill patients is in the balance,[123] on the particular facts of some cases at least they are understandably influenced by the sheer enormity of the consequences that would flow from unfettered patient choice. Consider again *Re S*. S was a 'born again' Christian. Though her sincerity was not doubted by the court, she had not articulated her religious objections and the procedure proposed for her was not contrary to the tenets of evangelism. The only chance for her and the full-term unborn child to survive was a Caesarian. In the event the operation did save her life, though not the unborn child. S also had two young children, a further element in the moral equation which might make us ponder the wisdom and virtue of a legal principle that would favour almost unbridled individualism. In eschewing the remorseless logic of self-determination, *Re S* can still be seen as embodying a compassionate, if unfashionable, moral vision. If nothing else, it is a salutary reminder that judicial rhetoric has at times exaggerated the extent of the law's commitment to patients' rights.[124]

CONCLUSION

The availability of a battery action may still, in principle, act as a valuable deterrent against doctors taking decisions on question-

---

[122] Cf. G. Williams, *Textbook of Criminal Law* (2nd edn.) (London: Sweet & Maxwell, 1983), 613, commenting on *R.* v. *Smith* [1979] Criminal Law Review 251.

[123] See, e.g. M. Wright, 'Medical Treatment: The Right to Refuse' [1993] *Journal of Social Welfare and Family Law* 204.

[124] It is of interest that at the 1993 Bar Conference, responding to suggestions that *Re S* had been wrongly decided, Stephen Brown J reportedly said that 'it should not be taken as laying down any general rule about taking the course of caesarean section. It was decided entirely on its own, very extreme facts' [1993] *New Law Journal* 1394. See also C. Wells, 'Patients, Consent and Criminal Law' (1994) *Journal of Social Welfare and Family Law* 65.

able or spurious grounds. It can help counter any temptation for doctors to engage in major procedures of uncertain benefit to the patient. It can also help minimize the risk that they will be carried out to alleviate inconvenience or hardship to carers, or in order to conserve resources. However, in practice, the courts are reluctant to find that there has been a battery, except in the most blatant of circumstances, and doubly so where the patient is suffering from a life-threatening or very serious condition. Generally speaking, judicial distaste for 'medical battery' is well founded. There are sound reasons for not regretting its demise, which go beyond any judicial concern to keep litigation in check or any desire to respect doctors' sensitivities. Its accompanying rhetoric offers the worst of all worlds, exaggerating the virtues of full patient self-determination, and creating false expectations about the law's capacity or willingness to ensure it.

Trespass is a legal category which displays transparent conceptual limitations in the medical sphere. In remaining true to its historical roots as a mechanism for protecting people from unwanted, typically hostile, physical contact it is, for the most part, out of place in medicine. Its credentials as an obstacle to unwanted treatment are undermined by an artificially narrow conception of consent and by the propensity of judges to re-characterize 'irrational' decisions as evidence of incompetence sufficient to permit a welfare-based 'best [medical] interests' test to prevail. The well-intentioned paternalism apparent in a controversial case such as *Re S* is difficult to square with a principled commitment to patient autonomy, and at times the courts have seemed more preoccupied with medical autonomy. Nevertheless, the moral complexity of some of the decisions which have been most heavily criticized suggests that it is possible to espouse too absolutist a view of patients' rights.

CONTRACT

Apart from the action for battery, in early English common law the civil liability of doctors derived from their status and was rooted in failure to exercise the skill and diligence expected in their calling. There was, in other words, from the outset a perceived public interest in their standard of performance. But in some respects medical transactions seem to fall more naturally within the realms of private ordering and, though delictual in origin, the liability of doctors also came to be seen as contractual when contract emerged as a distinct legal category.[125] Over many centuries, the bulk of professional medical practice was explicitly commercial, in the form of fee-for-service, private transactions.[126] Well into the twentieth century, by which time negligence was emerging as an independent tort and had become the effective basis of most medical malpractice actions,[127] judgments were still apt to use the language of contract for transactions in which patients had not strictly speaking provided consideration for the doctor's services.[128] A significant, if dwindling, number of cases continued to be resolved within a contractual framework, albeit one largely conditioned by the implied professional obligation to use care and skill. In private medicine today, this implied obligation is perceived as an instance of the duty of care in negligence and cannot be excluded.[129]

The standard of performance required of a doctor technically liable in contract, then, is almost invariably the same as that for NHS treatment, namely reasonable care as defined in the tort of negligence. The patient may sue under either head, the implied duty to exercise reasonable care in a professional contractual relationship existing concurrently with the duty of care in tort.[130] Though it is, of course, possible for the express or implied terms of a contract to impose a higher duty on the doctor, this happens infrequently in practice, as doctors are not disposed to guarantee a particular outcome and the courts do not readily infer that they

---

[125] Sir W. Holdsworth, *History of English Law* (3rd edn.) (London: Methuen, 1923) iii. 448; *Everard* v. *Hopkins* (1615) 2 Bulst 332, 80 ER 1164; *Slater* v. *Baker* (1767) 2 Wils 359, 95 ER 860.

[126] Cf. 'nineteenth-century lawyers would surely have seen the relationship as primarily contractual': P. Atiyah, 'Medical Malpractice and the Contract/Tort Boundary' (1986) 49(2) *Law and Contemporary Problems* 287, 292.

[127] See D. Giesen, *International Medical Malpractice Law* (Tübingen: J. C. B. Mohr; Dordrecht: Martinus Nijhoff Publishers, 1988), 6–7.

[128] e.g. *Banbury* v. *Bank of Montreal* [1918] AC 626, 657; *Everett* v. *Griffiths* [1920] 3 KB 163, 193, *per* Scrutton LJ.

[129] Unfair Contract Terms Act 1977, s. 2.

[130] 'The classic example of this situation is the relationship between doctor and patient': *Forsikringsaktieselskapet Vesta* v. *Butcher* [1988] 3 WLR 565, 571, *per* O'Connor LJ.

have done so.[131] Significantly, in a modern Canadian case involving plastic surgery, where such an inference was drawn, the judge observed that a cosmetic surgeon was in a different position from an ordinary physician, being someone selling a special service who was more akin to a businessman.[132]

Ordinary physicians may be more readily perceived as 'selling' services when they are actually supplying work and materials, as when giving patients drugs, medical devices, injections, or blood transfusions. Though the courts have generally been averse to characterizing such transactions as sales, where they are based on contract an implied term as to reasonable fitness for purpose may lead to liability despite the absence of negligence. This was the outcome at common law in two situations closely analogous to medical practice, involving ill-fitting dentures and a defective serum injected into cattle by a veterinary surgeon.[133] Now, under the Supply of Goods and Services Act 1982, there is statutory authority for such an approach where medical materials supplied[134] or administered by a doctor under contract are not merchantable or fit for their purpose.[135] Such liability cannot be excluded in respect of consumer transactions,[136] though the 1982 Act affords the doctor some opportunity for escaping liability by disclosing to the patient the limitations of proposed treatment. The interest of patients in specifying their requirements and that of doctors in minimizing their potential liability could result in more fully articulated arrangements which, in theory at least, might help to promote the autonomy of patients in precisely the ways envisaged by the proponents of a contractual framework for doctor–patient relationships.[137]

The 1982 Act has the built-in limitation of applying only to contractual relationships, which it is generally accepted do not

---

[131] *Thake* v. *Maurice* [1986] QB 644; *Eyre* v. *Measday* [1986] 1 All ER 488, 495, *per* Slade LJ.

[132] *La Fleur* v. *Cornelis* (1979) 28 NBR (2d) 569.

[133] *Samuels* v. *Davis* [1943] KB 526 and *Dodd* v. *Wilson* [1946] 2 All ER 691, respectively.

[134] Even temporarily.

[135] Supply of Goods and Services Act 1982, s. 4 (where goods are transferred) and s. 9 (where they are hired). See, further, A. Bell, 'The Doctor and the Supply of Goods and Services Act 1982' (1984) 4 *Legal Studies* 175.

[136] Unfair Contract Terms Act 1977, s. 6.

[137] See A. Bell, n. 135 above, 184.

exist in respect of treatment provided under the NHS.[138] However, in some common law jurisdictions, legislation designed to enhance consumer protection generally may provide patients with remedies not otherwise available to them at common law or available only in a more restricted form. Thus, in countries where medical services are routinely rendered in return for fees, medical transactions would often appear to be covered by the wording of fair trading statutes. For example, in a recent Australian case concerning blood contaminated with HIV, a public hospital in New South Wales described by the court as engaged in 'trading activities' comprising patients' fees and other 'business activities'[139] was deemed to be a 'trading corporation' within the meaning of the Commonwealth Trade Practices Act 1974.[140] Its fee-paying patients were regarded as 'consumers' for the same purpose. 'The "trade" of a hospital', said the judge, 'is the provision of services to patients. That is its business. I see no reason to doubt that its contract with the applicant was made "in the course of a business" '.[141] The invocation of fair trading statutes could be of particular importance in claims based on non-disclosure or inadequate disclosure of information which are liable to fail in tort because the patient cannot prove negligence or causation. Since statutory liability for misleading the consumer tends to be strict rather than fault-based, in the medical context it would typically depend on the fact or likelihood of the patient having been misled

---

[138] There is a somewhat tenuous argument to the effect that patients have a contract with their GP because inclusion of their names on a GP's list augments the doctor's remuneration: see R. Jackson and J. Powell, *Professional Negligence* (3rd edn.) (London: Sweet & Maxwell, 1992), 448. However, it must be doubtful whether this is the case, as there is no direct payment by the patient and the capitation fee is merely one facet of the statutory scheme under which doctors are *required* to provide their services. Cf. *Pfizer Corp.* v. *Ministry of Health* [1965] AC 512, 535–6: statutory entitlement to drugs under the NHS precludes a contract between patient and pharmacist, notwithstanding the prescription charge. Following *Roy* v. *Kensington and Chelsea and Westminster Family Practitioner Committee* [1992] 1 AC 624, it is not even clear that a GP has a contract with the Family Health Services Authority. In any event, no such contract could determine the full scope of the doctor's obligations in respect of particular treatment.

[139] Albeit in amounts 'dwarfed by its State Government subsidy'.

[140] S. 4. See *E* v.*Australian Red Cross Society* [1991] 2 Med LR 303.

[141] Ibid. 327. Cf. Though in *R* v. *Crayden* [1978] 1 WLR 604, 609, it was held that an NHS hospital is not a 'business', it is unclear whether the same view would be taken today of trust hospitals, in view of their enhanced managerial and financial freedom, which includes the power to borrow, to buy and sell assets, and accumulate surpluses.

rather than on whether he or she would have undergone the treatment if properly informed.[142]

Though, in England, most individual patients will not derive any benefit from fair trading legislation, in view of the market orientation of the restructured NHS, statutory provisions designed to promote competition in the economy generally may acquire a new significance for health care delivery and indirectly affect the nature of doctor–patient relationships. It is a measure of the profession's success in resisting the identification of medicine with trade that, in the past, restrictive practices in the provision of its services barely featured as an issue in English law.[143] The Restrictive Trade Practices Act 1976 expressly exempts medical services from the requirement that restrictive agreements or arrangements must be registered to determine whether or not they are contrary to the public interest.[144] Until very recently, the Director General of Fair Trading showed little inclination to investigate the health sector for anti-competitive conduct,[145] but in the run up to implementation of the recent NHS reforms, he made a reference (at the Government's request) to the Monopolies and Mergers Commission about restrictions on the advertising of doctors' services. Following the Commission's finding that they were contrary to the public interest,[146] the restrictions were duly relaxed, without any of the soul-searching about the ethical propriety of such a change which the GMC's traditional strictures against advertising might have led one to expect.[147] In 1994, the Commission found that BMA guidance on consultants' charges for medical and surgical procedures operated as a tariff, producing a 'complex monopoly' in private health which kept fees artificially

---

[142] See e.g. the Western Australian Fair Trading Act 1987: S. Laufer, 'Aggrieved Patients Who Claim They were not Told' (1990) 20 *University of Western Australian Law Review* 489.

[143] See F. Miller, 'Competition Law and Anticompetitive Professional Behaviour Affecting Health Care' (1992) 55 *Modern Law Review* 453.

[144] Sched. 1 para. 2.

[145] As provided for under the Competition Act 1980, s. 3, and the Fair Trading Act 1973, ss. 6,7.

[146] *Services of Medical Practitioners: A Report on the Supply of the Services of Registered Medical Practitioners in Relation to Restrictions on Advertising* (London: HMSO, 1989), Cm 582.

[147] GMC, *Professional Conduct and Discipline: Fitness to Practise* (London: General Medical Council, 1991), 15.

high.[148] The impetus for regulation of anti-competitive behaviour under EC law seems bound to exert additional pressures for legislative reform, which, like the volte-face on advertising, will further redefine the limits of acceptable professional behaviour. One predictable consequence is that patients will become more attuned to the notion of the doctor as entrepreneur.

Could such developments foreshadow the introduction of a contractual regime for the disposition of individual medical claims generally? The fact that they have for many years been overwhelmingly determined by tort principles cannot preclude such a possibility. Since medical relationships are capable of being conceptualized in terms of tort or contract, social and economic considerations may determine which category is in the ascendant at any given time. As Partlett puts it, 'their relative strengths have depended upon social moods and predominant ideas'.[149] Erosion of welfarist principles in the new climate of contractualism, combined with official encouragement of patient choice, could presage much more growth in private sector health care than has occurred so far, within Health Service facilities as well as outside. In the long run, a more fundamental shift in the nature of the system, and hence in its legal framework, cannot be ruled out. One significant step in this direction was taken in 1992, when the two main dental associations[150] voted against accepting new NHS patients on their lists, thus formalizing what is already to all intents and purposes a two-tier system of dental services. The legal, as well as social, implications of a contractual model are no longer mainly of theoretical interest.

In certain respects the relationship between doctor and patient does have more affinity with contract than with tort, an affinity which tends to be obscured because we naturally associate personal injury claims with tort. To begin with, it is a *relationship*. Medical encounters differ from stock situations in tort in that the parties are seldom total strangers to one another prior to the event precipitating litigation. There is, in principle, scope for negotiation

---

[148] Monopolies and Mergers Commission, *Private Medical Services* (London: HMSO, 1994).

[149] D. Partlett, *Professional Negligence* (Sydney: Law Book Company, 1985), 27.

[150] The British Dental Association and the General Dental Practitioners' Association.

about the terms of the arrangements which they make; the doctor is paid for having undertaken to provide professional services to the patient.[151]

Partly because NHS treatment is so pervasive, courts have felt it invidious to distinguish between the standard of care owed to different patients receiving identical treatment (possibly from the same doctor) under different financial regimes.[152] But as the public service ethic of the NHS progressively gives way to a more commercial one, health care is more readily perceived as a commodity and its provision as a matter of private ordering. The more this altered perception takes root, the stronger might appear to be the case for a contractual framework, with terms designed by the parties, in place of externally imposed criteria, largely shaped by the medical profession via the *Bolam* 'one club' approach.[153] If the doctor–patient relationship is truly envisaged as consensual and especially if patient autonomy is to be taken seriously, what could be more natural, mutually acceptable, and effective than for the parties to frame the terms of engagement to suit individual circumstances? Indeed, there is something rather odd about insisting on public ordering in health care when we are prepared, in the name of autonomy, to take the notion of its private ordering to the ultimate lengths of condoning the refusal of life-saving treatment.

Under a conception of medicine as trade, all patients would be entitled to negotiate for a higher standard of treatment than that required under tort law—as is already in principle possible with

[151] Cf. C. Havighurst, 'Altering the Applicable Standard of Care' in (1986) 49(2) *Law and Contemporary Problems* 265–6, arguing that, in such circumstances, tort rules as to their rights and duties 'can be seen as terms of an implied contract by which the law allocates risk according to a combination of factors, including the probable preferences and interests of the parties and the public's interest in spreading losses and deterring injuries'.

[152] See *Hotson* v. *East Berkshire Area Health Authority* [1987] 2 WLR 287, 294, *per* Lord Donaldson MR; cf. *Naylor* v. *Preston Area Health Authority* [1987] 1 WLR 958, 967, *per* Lord Donaldson MR; *Gold* v. *Essex County Council* [1942] 2 KB 293, 297, *per* Lord Greene MR.

[153] Cf. in the American context, 'tort law must recede from a dogmatic regulatory role in which it alone specifies rights arising out of the provider/patient relationship and should recognise that private agreements altering its prescriptions may benefit everyone appropriately concerned': C. Havighurst, 'Private Reform of Tort-Law Dogma: Market Opportunities and Legal Obstacles' (1986) 49(2) *Law and Contemporary Problems* 143.

private medicine—or indeed to opt for a lower one, through a waiver of tort rights and the dismantling of statutory protections.[154] By the same token, one could in theory construct a legal regime under which bargains could be struck on particular facets of the medical transaction, such as the extent to which risks and alternative procedures are to be disclosed, the preferred mode of dispute resolution, categories of recoverable loss, and the parameters of monetary awards.[155] In short, so the argument goes, there should be freedom for the parties to construct what *they* consider to be an optimal arrangement.

A contractual regime can thus be portrayed as providing a framework which, while preserving the professional independence of the doctor, respects the personal autonomy of patients and, if the terms of the contract are properly articulated, facilitates their understanding of any proposed treatment. It would seem to be an appropriate mechanism for expressing their individual rights and concerns and for modifying the imbalance in medical relationships which tends to perpetuate the dominance of the health care provider. As we have seen, the structural changes introduced under the 1990 Act have been justified as an attempt to pave the way for a not dissimilar outcome at the institutional level. Thus the 'NHS contract' exemplifies the greater power which budget-holding practices, as purchasers, now have to strike advantageous deals with hospitals on behalf of their patients, and the correspondingly diminished power of the institutional provider.

Calls for publically imposed tort principles to be replaced by an essentially private contractual regime have featured quite prominently in recent American legal literature. The basic legal framework for medical malpractice liability in the United States is akin to that for private treatment in England. Though there is a contract between doctor and patient, the implied duty to provide a reasonable standard of care is governed by tort principles and cases are routinely decided in tort. In the mid-1970s, the intensity

---

[154] Such as obtain under the Unfair Contract Terms Act 1977 and the Supply of Goods and Services Act 1982.

[155] Cf. the recent Government proposals for arbitration of civil claims for medical negligence, aimed at minimizing costs and avoiding the more unsatisfactory features of adversarial proceedings: Department of Health, *Arbitration for Medical Negligence in the National Health Service* (London: Department of Health, 1991).

of the debate over the 'medical malpractice crisis' reinforced growing scepticism about the claims made for the tort-based system as an effective deterrent and an appropriate compensatory mechanism. It was suggested, most notably by Epstein, that a preferable system would be one in which patients could waive all or some of their tort rights and negotiate the terms of liability through individualized contracts.[156] Reform along these lines has since attracted much academic attention in the United States,[157] amid talk of a second 'medical malpractice crisis', following the very limited success of state legislatures in reducing the frequency and severity of claims by such measures as modifying the informed consent doctrine and/or capping awards and attorneys' fees.[158]

The courts have so far held the line on familiar public policy grounds. Maintenance of high standards in health care is seen as an overriding need, not to be jeopardized by allowing providers to exercise their bargaining power to the detriment of relatively vulnerable and inadequately informed patients. Such a change of regime could, it is argued, easily lead to a widespread diminution of standards, contrary to the interests of patients and difficult to reconcile with the ethical obligations of doctors. Attempts by doctors and hospitals in the late 1950s and early 1960s to enforce contractual waivers of patients' tort rights were struck down as contrary to public policy, the courts firmly resisting the imposition of standard form contracts in a matter as vital as health care. In *Tunkl* v. *Regents of the University of California*,[159] for example, reference was made to the essentially fiduciary role of the health care provider. The objection that the decided cases happen to

---

[156] R. Epstein, 'Medical Malpractice: The Case for Contract' (1976) 76 *American Bar Foundation Research Journal* 87.

[157] See R. Bovbjerg and C. Havighurst (eds.), 'Medical Malpractice: Can the Private Sector Find Relief?' (1986) 49(2) *Law and Contemporary Problems*; R. Bovbjerg and T. Metzloff (eds.), 'Medical Malpractice: Lessons for Reform' (1991) 54 (1 & 2) *Law and Contemporary Problems*, and P. Danzon, *Medical Malpractice: Theory, Evidence, and Public Policy* (Cambridge, Mass.: Harvard University Press, 1985).

[158] Cf. D. Partlett, in the Australian context, in P. Finn (ed.), *Essays on Tort* (Sydney: Law Book Company, 1990), 99: 'private ordering, that is contracting, should be permitted a greater place in modifying the common law rules . . . voluntary arrangements which may alter the standard of care, limit damages, or put in place alternative dispute resolution'.

[159] 383 P 2d 441 (Cal, 1963).

have been almost exclusively concerned with standardized form contracts, containing terms which purported to exclude *any* liability, merely highlights the risk that such adhesive contracts would become commonplace.[160]

According to advocates of contractualism, the public policy objections are too abstract and assume too readily a world of 'powerless patients and all-powerful providers'.[161] They point out that though most medical relationships entail some imbalance of power, by no means all medical encounters conform to this stereotype. We are perhaps too prone to think in terms of emergency treatment requiring instantaneous decision-making and to overlook the fact that much medical provision is in principle amenable to private ordering, often in the form of prior negotiation. Instinctive resistance to the notion of medicine as trade can be tinged with elements of mystification and romanticism, which are perhaps more deeply embedded in the English context because the structure of NHS health care delivery largely obscures its commercial dimensions. Yet for all that, the contractualists tend to understate the vulnerability of any patient suffering from a serious medical condition. They also gloss over the dangers of creating an atmosphere in which doctors come to think of contractual provisions as defining the outer limits of their professional obligations. Both the retention of a tort-based regime for medical liability in England, never wholly displaced over centuries of contractual classification, and the stance of the judiciary in the much more overtly commercial American system testify to the endurance of the belief that standards of medical practice and the criteria for resolving medical disputes should ultimately be the subject of public ordering.[162]

It is submitted that this belief is soundly based. Contract, as the natural legal expression of a commercial model, merely serves to compound its more undesirable features. This is especially, though not exclusively, the case for patients with serious medical

---

[160] Cf. C. Newdick, 'Rights to NHS Resources after the 1990 Act' (1993) 1 *Medical Law Review* 53, 68, on the risk of similar lowering of standards under NHS 'contracts'.

[161] W. Ginsburg *et al.*, 'Contractual Revisions to Medical Malpractice Liability' (1986) 49(2) *Law and Contemporary Problems* 253, 255.

[162] See *Banbury* v. *Bank of Montreal* [1918] AC 626, 657, *per* Lord Finlay LC.

conditions for whom hospitalization and long-term treatment are envisaged.[163] As we have seen, in addition to the vulnerability which stems from the illness itself, they are beset by a whole range of problems relating to imperfect consumer information which cannot be adequately overcome except in a tiny minority of cases. Freedom of contract is of little avail if the doctor nearly always has a better understanding of the medical indications and knows more about the nature and quality of proposed treatment and available alternatives. Furthermore, unlike health care providers, very few patients appreciate the sheer statistical risks of hospitalization.[164] As the American cases indicate, an unconstrained contractual regime would make it too tempting for both parties to enter into an unconscionable arrangement, in which the patient forgoes tort rights in return for cheaper and inferior services.[165]

If the absence of an arm's-length relationship should make us question private contractual ordering even for fully competent adult patients, it would, as Atiyah has pointed out, seem wholly misconceived for the innumerable treatment decisions that have to be made for the very young, the geriatric, and the mentally disturbed.[166] Decision-making on their behalf, by adding a further layer of complication to what is already a 'proxy market', increases the risk of patients' interests being subordinated to those of other persons or institutions. Leaving to one side its limited current applicability to medical actions in England, contract is a legal category which, like trespass, displays transparent conceptual limitations in the medical sphere. It, too, is a model primarily geared to the assertion of formal rights which it cannot adequately safeguard in practice. It, too, is more effective as an instrument for establishing the rights and duties which arise from single transactions than the obligations inherent in what are ideally relationships built up over time.

---

[163] See e.g. *Yepremian* v. *Scarborough General Hospital* (1980) 13 CCLT 105, 174, *per* Blair JA.

[164] See, generally, C. Vincent, M. Ennis, R. Audley (eds.) *Medical Accidents* (Oxford: Oxford University Press, 1993).

[165] See P. Weiler, *Medical Malpractice on Trial* (Cambridge, Mass.: Harvard University Press, 1991).

[166] P. Atiyah, 'Medical Malpractice and the Contract/Tort Boundary', n. 126 above, especially 295.

CONCLUSION

Extensive patient autonomy, whether under a contractual or tort-based regime, is a largely undesired goal and, in certain important respects, an undesirable one. It is a recipe for confrontation in doctor–patient relationships and for unsuccessful medical outcomes. Any surface appeal, and indeed any therapeutic value, which it might have for patients must take account of these very real dangers and also of possible obstacles to legal redress should litigation ensue. The price in practice of a formal but illusory equality can be a substantial shift in legal responsibility. The greater the stress on patients as autonomous agents or independent contracting parties, the more vulnerable they become, as plaintiffs, to onerous contractual terms and to defences based on consent to risks.

The problem is well illustrated by demands for better information for patients. As we have noted, it is unusual for patients to seek information in order to override the doctor's judgement, or to dispense with the doctor's services. Typically their objective is to have a fuller dialogue, a more fruitful and collaborative consultation, rather than to assert an abstract 'right to know' and then act independently. The Government's avowed aim of 'working for patients' cannot be achieved simply by bombarding them with leaflets. The provision of information to patients can, under the guise of enhanced communication, result in doctors becoming less involved and minimizing their legal responsibilities in the name of patient choice. In the long term, the trend towards various modes of self-diagnosis and medical self-help, encouraged by such developments as health screening; franchises to test cholesterol, blood pressure, and glucose; and the marketing of nicotine patches could create similar pitfalls for patients.[167]

For some doctors and medical administrators the formalism of contract holds similar attractions to the apparent certitudes of the consent form. Obtaining signatures on elaborate forms can

---

[167] It is of interest that implementation of the EC Directive on Product Liability, aimed at imposing a strict liability regime on producers for injuries caused by defective products, led to a widespread policy within the pharmaceutical industry of introducing patient package leaflets for products, a practice that has been made mandatory: Council Directive 89/341, Art. 3, 1989 OJ L142/12.

become a mechanical substitute for dialogue, valued to the extent
that what is at best rebuttable evidence of consent is believed to
afford protection against liability.[168] The letter of the contract is
akin to the terms of the consent form. The desired meeting of
minds between doctor and patient is no more to be divined from
assent to the wording of a contract than is true consent to be
identified by the signature on a form.[169] In the context of hospital
treatment, contractualism easily degenerates into an impersonal
substitute for genuine communication, subverting rather than
inspiring the patient's trust and confidence. In a health service
characterized by managerial dominance and batch referrals,
'medicine can become preoccupied with the characteristics of
groups, and become distracted from the assessment of, and
response to, the needs of the individual. Strong contracts enfeeble
professionalism.'[170]

Courts and the medical profession alike have recognized that to
reduce doctor–patient relationships to straightforward commercial
exchanges is as demeaning and dangerous for doctors as it is
unacceptable to patients. Even in mid-nineteenth century
America, at the height of the 'golden age of contract' and of
Jacksonian democracy's disdain for relationships based on status,
when most states had rejected medical licensure laws as élitist
regulatory devices inimical to 'free trade in doctoring',[171] and

---

[168] Cf. Ormrod LJ, 'A Lawyer Looks at Medical Ethics' [1977] 18 *Medico-Legal
Journal*, 31: 'It is just another piece of paper in the case notes, which is put there by
the administrators at the behest of their lawyers, and when the crunch comes the
court will say, "Well, what's the good of this?" ' In one American study of five
surgical consent forms, it was found that four of them would have been understood
by less than 4.5% of the adult population: T. Grunder, 'On the Readability of
Surgical Consent Forms' *New England Journal of Medicine* 302 (1980), 900. As
Somerville points out, the formality of a written consent form may act as a coercive
influence on patients not to change their minds: M. Somerville, *Consent to Medical
Care* (Ottawa: Law Reform Commission of Canada, 1980), 45, so that consent
could become 'a cover for coercion or duress, rather than guaranteeing their
absence': ibid. 33.

[169] Cf. Lord Donaldson MR on standard forms of refusal to accept a blood
transfusion: 'It is clear that such forms are designed primarily to protect the
hospital from legal action. They will be wholly ineffective for this purpose if . . .
there is no good evidence (apart from the patient's signature) that he . . . fully
appreciated the significance of signing it': *Re T (Adult: Refusal of Treatment)* [1992]
3 WLR 782, 798.

[170] Dr M. Marinker, reported in *The Times*, 6 July 1992.

[171] See K. De Ville, *Medical Malpractice in Nineteenth Century America: Origins
and Legacy* (New York: New York University Press, 1990), chs. 3 and 7.

when the language of contract and of market relations increasingly infiltrated the case law, the courts drew back from a repudiation of medical law's doctrinal roots. If some doctors were attracted by a trade model, and in particular by the scope for waiver of liability afforded by contract theory, many others and their professional bodies had long appreciated that the equation with commerce posed a threat to their moral standing and public image that could destroy the ethical underpinnings of their calling.

A few academic analysts may have toyed with the notion that obstetricians should be permitted to avoid or minimize tort liability for deformed infants for a contractual quid pro quo.[172] If this view has had less of an airing in England than in the United States, it is to be hoped that this is not only because there is not a comparable dearth of provision in particular localities and because basic medical and social care for such infants is free. Whatever role malpractice suits and rising insurance premiums may have had in helping to bring about such a state of affairs in parts of the United States, to follow this pattern here would be morally offensive and socially retrogade. Furthermore, it suggests an alarming insensitivity to the symbolic nature of the doctor's role and to the psychological dynamics of medical relationships. In its own way, a commercial model—in common with both patient autonomy and medical paternalism—runs the risk of weakening doctor–patient relationships and of minimising patient involvement at the expense of patient welfare.

---

[172] e.g. G. Robinson, 'Rethinking the Allocation of Medical Malpractice Risks between Patients and Providers' (1986) 49(2) *Law and Contemporary Problems* 173, 199 and C. Havighurst, 'Private Reform of Tort-Law Dogma: Market Opportunities and Legal Obstacles', 169; R. Epstein, 'Market and Regulatory Approaches to Medical Malpractice: The Virginia Obstetrical No-Fault Statute' (1988) 74 *Virginia Law Review* 1451.

5

Patient Welfare

Reasonable Care and Skill

Nowadays it would not seem unnatural to think of doctors' duties towards their patients as deriving from the rights that patients have against their doctors. Such a view is compelling as a matter of abstract reasoning and accords with modern attitudes towards the status of individual rights. But recognition of the individual's rights is a relatively modern notion. As Feinberg has observed, until about forty years ago moral philosophy was overwhelmingly concerned with duties. Duties were seen as foundational and moral rights as a kind of afterthought: 'rights were merely an alternative way of speaking of other people's duties'. 'This', he said, was 'especially puzzling when one remembers that statements of rights are often logically connected to statements of duties.' 'The right-holder's right often provides the whole grounding for the other party's duty'. And again, there is '. . . considerable plausibility in the view that your rights have a moral priority over my duties, in the sense that the duties are derived from them rather than the other way around'. 'It is because I have a claim-right not to be punched in the nose by you, for example, that you have a duty not to punch me in the nose . . . My claim and your duty both derive from the interest that I have in the physical integrity of my nose.'[1]

This is a telling example of a moral right endorsed by the law of trespass from early times. It accords with the theory underlying the tort of battery as applicable, *inter alia*, to medical procedures. It is because I have a claim-right not to have my bodily integrity infringed that the doctor has a duty not to operate on me without

---

[1] J. Feinberg, 'In Defence of Moral Rights' (1992) 12 *Oxford Journal of Legal Studies* 149, 154–6.

my consent. Contract theory, too, is responsive to the patient's rights, in so far as freedom of contract in principle permits patients to negotiate an arrangement that respects their rights. But as we have seen, these forms of classification, contract in particular, have a relatively minor role in English medical law. In the crucial category of negligence, the doctor's duties are foundational and the patient's rights at best a moral afterthought.[2]

Liability for medical negligence has its roots in the duty of a professional person to exercise reasonable care and skill in undertaking the activity professed.[3] If only forty years ago it was still almost taken for granted that duties rather than rights should be the focus of attention in moral philosophy, it ought not to occasion surprise if medieval common law displayed the same sense of priorities. Medicine was a 'common calling'. Its practitioners assumed 'the general obligation of those exercising a public or "common" business to practise their art on demand, and show skill in it'.[4] There was, in other words, a clearly acknowledged public dimension to their calling and a presumption that they were reasonably competent in it. In Fitzherbert's words, 'it is the duty of every artificer to exercise his art rightly and truly as he ought'.[5] Thus the legal duty arose from an implied undertaking or holding out derived from status; it was not conceptualized by reference to the patient's rights and existed independently of any express agreement with the patient.[6] Liability reflected the defendant's shortcomings as a craftsman and member of a learned profession,

---

[2] Cf. 'The law of negligence historically starts from the idea of failure in the performance of a determinable provable legal duty': T. Street, *The Foundations of Legal Liability* (Northport, NY: Thompson, 1906), i. 195.

[3] Ultimately traceable to the Lex Aquilia, 287 BC Digest 9.2.1. The earliest actions against healers in English law were probably heard in local courts and went unrecorded. For the earliest recorded action see A. Kiralfy, *A Source Book of English Law* (London: Sweet & Maxwell, 1957), 184 (Nottingham Eyre 1329).

[4] O. Holmes, *The Common Law* (Boston: Little Brown & Co., 1881), 184.

[5] Sir A. Fitzherbert, *Natura Brevia* (1534). See also A. Sandor, 'The History of Professional Liability Suits in the United States' *Journal of the American Medical Association* 163 (1957), 459; *Sidaway* v. *Board of Governors of the Bethlem Royal Hospital* [1985] AC 871, 892, *per* Lord Diplock; *Gold* v. *Haringey Health Authority* [1988] QB 481, 489, *per* Lloyd LJ.

[6] See Sir W. Holdsworth, *A History of English Law* (London: Methuen, 1923), iii. 385–6, 428–32, 448–50. Cf. 'The public profession of an art is a representation and undertaking to all the world that the professor possesses the requisite ability and skill. An express promise or express representation in the particular case is not necessary': *Harmer* v. *Cornelius* (1858) 5 CB (NS) 236, 246, *per* Willes J.

but in a form which made allowance for fallibility. By the mid- to late-fourteenth century some conception of what we would now describe as negligence was already in evidence, as appears from *The Surgeon's Case*,[7] where an analogy is drawn with a horse-doctor who escapes liability 'if he does all he can and applies himself with all due diligence to the cure'.[8]

In much the same way as would now be true of a claim in negligence, a medieval action against someone who pursued a common calling—an 'action on the case'—centred on discharging one's duty in the context of the surrounding circumstances. The defendant was obliged to exhibit the care that would have been shown by a reasonable person, and reasonableness was referable to the surrounding circumstances, or the situation in which the task was undertaken. One such circumstance was special expertise, and doctors like anyone else were bound to behave as would a reasonable person who possessed it: 'the doctrine of common callings merely reflected a first conception of "duty" and "circumstance", as those words bear on today's notions of negligence. The medieval physician was liable under the rule of common callings and medieval medical malpractice cases were thus based on negligence and little else'.[9]

There is no rational justification for regarding medical negligence as somehow conceptually distinct from negligence in general. There is no sufficient reason for singling out one particular group in the workforce and making its own customary practices or self-proclaimed standards the yardstick of liability. If medical practice can be said to have acquired a unique status in this respect, part of the explanation would seem to lie in judicial readiness to interpret loose expressions in the case law in ways which reflected, some would say pandered to, the prestige and mystique associated with medicine. If anything, this process

---

[7] *Stratton v. Swanlond*, Y B Hill. 48 Edw III, f. 6, pl. 11 (1374).

[8] C. Fifoot, *History and Sources of the Common Law: Tort and Contract* (London: Stevens & Sons, 1949). *The Surgeon's Case* was probably the first significant malpractice case in English law. See also M. Cosman, 'Medieval Medical Malpractice: The Dicta and the Dockets', *Bulletin of the New York Academy of Medicine* 49 (1973), 22.

[9] T. Silver, 'One Hundred Years of Harmful Error: The Historical Jurisprudence of Medical Malpractice' [1992] *Wisconsin Law Review* 1193, 1205. See, further, W. Prosser, 'The Borderland of Tort and Contract' in *Selected Topics on the Law of Torts* (Ann Arbor: University of Michigan, 1953), 380, 382; Lord Nathan, *Medical Negligence* (London: Butterworths, 1957), ch. 2.

became more marked with the progressive professionalization and entrenchment of medical practice from the latter part of the nineteenth century onwards, culminating in the *Bolam* test as narrowly understood.

At common law, physicians, like barristers in their capacity as advocates, were apparently considered entitled only to an honorarium. The history of the matter remains somewhat obscure, but it seems that, largely as a measure of their status and public or community service role, physicians, unlike people engaged in ordinary commercial transactions, or for that matter surgeons and apothecaries, were not entitled to compensation but only to what was voluntarily given to them.[10] Any private arrangements between the parties were subordinate to the obligations of public service.

Down the centuries, the case law continued to identify the required standard of performance with the public nature of the activity. Hence the consistent judicial assertion that medical liability arose independently of any notion of contract. In 1765, Blackstone declared that '*mala praxis* is a great misdemeanour and offence at common law, whether it be for curiosity and experiment, or by neglect'. Confirming that it was actionable on the case, he defined it to include damage to a person's 'vigour or constitution' due to 'the neglect or unskilful management of [a] physician, surgeon, or apothecary'.[11] Some twenty-five years later, Lord Loughborough said that 'if a man gratuitously undertakes to do a thing to the best of his skill, where his situation or profession is such as to imply skill, an omission of that skill is imputable to him as gross negligence'.[12] '. . . The surgeon', said Heath J, 'would also be liable for such negligence, if he undertook gratis to attend a sick person, because his situation implies skill in surgery'.[13] For the same reason, he would be held equally liable to

[10] Cf. *Turner* v. *Philipps* (1792) Peake N.P. 166, 170 ER, 116: Lord Kenyon refers to the general opinion of the profession that 'the fees of barristers and physicians were as a present by the client, and not a payment or hire for their labour'. See also P. Starr, *The Social Transformation of American Medicine* (New York: Basic Books, 1982), 61–2.

[11] Sir W. Blackstone, *Commentaries on the Laws of England* (19th edn.) (London: Sweet & Maxwell, 1836), iii. 121–2.

[12] *Shiells and Thorne, etc.* v. *Blackburne* (1789) 1 H. Bl. 158, 161.

[13] Ibid.

the patient if remuneration was by means of a contract made with a third party.[14]

However, though the courts were clearly of the view that medical transactions involved an element of public ordering, what became increasingly unclear was how independent that element was of customary medical practice, or of appropriate medical practice as medically conceived. When courts referred to a requirement of reasonable care and skill, to what extent was the criterion one of actual professional practice, or of professionally accepted standards, rather than a supposed form of societal judgement, fashioned by judicial guidance to juries? In so far as we can talk of a required community standard, it was undoubtedly shaped by professional considerations, but just how determinative of liability were professional practices or professional standards? In this respect, many of the pre-twentieth century cases incorporated an ambiguity and tension that was to resurface with a vengeance in *Bolam* and which continues to bedevil analysis of medical liability to the present day.

In an illuminating historical examination of this issue, Silver[15] has shown that in the United States, up to around the middle of the nineteenth century, a number of cases revealed 'a fairly clear distinction between the physician's supposed duties to possess such skill as is normally possessed by others of his calling and to exercise "ordinary care", a phrase those decisions initially did not relate to customary practice within the profession'.[16] In other words, until well into the nineteenth century, the United States had no special rule for medical cases. For example, in *Leighton* v. *Sargent*[17] it was said that, 'different things may require different care . . . Such differences must exist among the cases requiring medical attention. But the common rule still applies, which requires such care and diligence as men in general, of common prudence and ordinary attention, usually apply in similar cases.'[18] And again, 'like the medieval common law that preceded it, early nineteenth century law held the physician to the standard that was destined to become the foundation of negligence. The courts of that day did not consider that it should be otherwise, nor was there

---

[14] *Everard* v. *Hopkins* 2 Bulst. 332; 80 ER 1164 (1650). Cf. *Everett* v. *Griffiths* [1920] 3 KB 163, 213, *per* Atkin LJ.

[15] T. Silver, 'One Hundred Years of Harmful Error: The Historical Jurisprudence of Medical Malpractice', n. 9 above. [16] Ibid. 1208.

[17] 27 NH (7 Foster) 460 (1853). [18] See Silver, n. 9 above, 1210.

any reason they should have.'[19] But in the latter half of the nineteenth century, Silver argues, the concept of reasonable care came to be so identified with customary medical practice as often to be equated with it. The common law then 'purported to provide that a physician's duty is not measured by the ordinary rule of reasonableness, but rather by professional custom. The doctor is bound to do no more than follow ordinary practice within the profession.'[20] In consequence, 'the medical community is answerable not for want of care but for want of conformity . . . [it] has the curious advantage of establishing, on its own, the standard of care to which it is legally obliged'.[21]

Silver sees this shift as having arisen 'through conceptual confusion, compounded by the law's propensity toward "lazy repetition" '.[22] The *early* nineteenth century American cases typically described the duty owed by doctors in terms of a 'two-tier entity'.[23] First, their calling required them to possess the customary *skill* of the competent and qualified physician; secondly, in actually treating patients, they were obliged to use 'ordinary care' in the sense of the care and prudence to be expected of the reasonable person in like circumstances. But later cases 'began blindly to blend the two very different concepts to form one misguided idea: that the physician's duty was that of ordinary skill and care which meant the skill and care that would be manifest generally within the profession . . . these same courts further misled themselves by misreading the articulated rule that rendered custom *relevant* to the matter of ordinary care as one that made custom *equivalent* to ordinary care'.[24]

The interplay of community and professional standards is apparent in numerous passages in the leading English authorities of the same period, though often in too oblique a form for it to be discernible precisely where the courts stood on the issue. What is clear is that allusions to reasonable (or ordinary) care *and* skill do not relate to customary or professional standards. There is, in fact,

---

[19] See Silver, n. 9 above, 1211.   [20] Ibid. 1212.   [21] Ibid. 1213.
[22] Ibid. 1219.   [23] Ibid. 1220.
[24] Ibid. 1222. Cf. P. Zepos and P. Christodoulou, 'Professional Liability' in *Torts*, xi. *International Encyclopedia of Comparative Law* (Tübingen: J. C. B. Mohr (Paul Siebeck), 1978), 12: 'The principle which seems to emerge is that it is care, not skill, which is owed to the patient. That means that negligence does not consist in the lack of skill, but in undertaking the work without the necessary skill.'

relatively little direct reference to customary practice and a lack of explicit assertion that it was dispositive. As in spheres other than medicine, such evidence was admissible without being conclusive, and this remained the orthodox position at least until *Bolam* was decided.[25] In the famous eighteenth century case of *Slater* v. *Baker and Stapleton*, where it was noted that according to the 'usage and law of surgeons' the defendant should not have proceeded without consent and that it was 'ignorance and unskilfulness' so to act 'contrary to the rule of the profession', the court continued, 'and indeed it is *reasonable* that a patient should be told what is about to be done to him'.[26] In *Seare* v. *Prentice*, after telling the jury that 'the gist of the action was negligence; of which direct evidence might be given', the judge continued, 'or it *might* be inferred by the jury if the defendant had proceeded without any regard to the common ordinary rules of his profession'.[27]

The very fact that juries decided such cases would have prevented them from being automatically determined by reference to customary medical practice, but there are also clear intimations that the jury was not simply expected to rubber-stamp such practice. In *Lanphier* v. *Phipos*, a key decision of the period, Tindal CJ directed the jury as follows: 'what you will have to say is this, whether you are satisfied that the injury sustained is attributable to the want of a reasonable and proper degree of care and skill in the defendant's treatment. Every person who enters into a learned profession undertakes to bring to the exercise of it a reasonable degree of care and skill . . . he undertakes to bring a

---

[25] A few early twentieth century English and Commonwealth cases toyed with the notion that adherence to common practice *cannot* be negligence, especially in a technical or specialized field such as medicine. See *Vancouver General Hospital* v. *McDaniel* (1934) 152 LT 56; *Marshall* v. *Lindsey County Council* [1935] 1 KB 516; *Whiteford* v. *Hunter* [1950] WN 553. But they did so in dicta which were qualified and subsequently much-criticized. Thus in *Marshall*, though Maugham LJ said that he did not doubt 'the general truth of the observation [in *Vancouver General Hospital*] that a defendant charged with negligence can clear himself if he shows that he has acted in accord with general and approved practice', he also felt constrained to declare that the particular custom relied on was 'founded on good sense' [1935] 1 KB 516, 542. See, further, A. Linden, 'Custom in Negligence Law' (1968) 11 *Canadian Bar Journal* 151, 156. Linden points out that where compliance with customary practices appears to have been deemed conclusive evidence of due care, 'the practices in question were found to have been reasonable or, alternatively, their reasonableness was not challenged by expert evidence': ibid. 159.   [26] (1767) 95 ER 860, 862. Emphasis added.
[27] 103 ER 376, 377 (1807). Emphasis added.

fair, reasonable, and competent degree of skill.'[28] Far from
suggesting that customary medical practice could be dispositive, he
does not even expressly refer to it. The same is true of the
summing up in *Rich* v. *Pierpoint*, where the emphasis on the jury's
evaluative role could not have been clearer: 'it was an action
charging [the defendant] with a breach of his legal duty, by reason
of inattention and negligence and want of proper care and skill;
and if they [the jury] were of opinion that there had been a
culpable want of attention and care, he would be liable. *A medical
man . . . was bound to have that degree of skill which could not be
defined, but which, in the opinion of the jury, was a competent
degree of skill and knowledge. What that was the jury were to
judge.*'[29] Similar formulations were being used well into the
twentieth century. The doctor, it was said, 'owes a duty to the
patient to use diligence, care, knowledge, skill and caution in
administering the treatment . . . It is for the Judge to direct the
jury what standard to apply and for the jury to say whether that
standard has been reached. . . . The law requires a fair and
reasonable standard of care and competence.'[30]

The Ambiguity of Bolam

Today we might be tempted to say that the law should require 'a
fair and reasonable standard of care and competence' because
patients have a right to expect it. At all events, Lord Chief Justice
Hewart's formulation clearly suggests that what is required is a
legally authenticated medical norm, and not merely legally rubber-
stamped medical practice. This, we might think, is as it should be.
It is no disrespect, and certainly no disservice, to the medical or
any other profession if in the quest for acceptable standards we are
wary of placing exclusive trust in a combination of common
practice and the testimony of fellow professionals.[31] We have

---

[28] *Lanphier* v. *Phipos* (1838) 8 C & P 475, 479. Cf. 'the question is, whether you
think the injury which the plaintiff has sustained is attributable to a want of proper
skill': *Hancke* v. *Hooper* (1835) 173 ER 37, 38, *per* Tindal CJ.

[29] (1862) 176 ER 16, 18–19, *per* Erle CJ. Emphasis added.

[30] *R* v. *Bateman* (1927) 19 Cr App R 8, 12, *per* Hewart CJ. Cf. '[the surgeon]
must use reasonable care . . . he must use that degree of care which is reasonable in
the circumstances': *Mahon* v. *Osborne* [1939] 2 KB 14, 47, *per* Goddard LJ.

[31] As King CJ was to observe in the Australian case of *F* v. *R*, 'in many cases an
approved professional practice as to disclosure will be decisive. But professions
may adopt unreasonable practices' (1982) 33 SASR 189, 194.

argued that historically our medical case law for the most part acknowledged the appropriateness of external evaluation. However, the seminal direction to the jury in *Bolam* contains some passages which seem to envisage effective immunity from legal sanction for medical practices that have gained minimal professional support.

In situations involving special skill or competence, the test of whether or not there has been negligence is, according to McNair J, '*the standard of the ordinary skilled man exercising and professing to have that special skill* . . . it is sufficient if he exercises the *ordinary* skill of an *ordinary competent* man exercising that particular art'. In the context of medicine, 'negligence', he says, 'means failure to act in accordance with the standards of *reasonably competent* medical men at the time', adding that '*A doctor is not guilty of negligence if he has acted in accordance with a practice accepted as proper by a responsible body of medical men skilled in that particular art.*'[32]

It is unlikely that McNair J would have regarded mere conformity with what a number of other doctors happened to do as *ipso facto* incompatible with negligence. He specified that 'proper standards' had to be adhered to and that there had to be 'reasonable grounds' for using a particular technique. But the precise nature of the test he was propounding, and the mechanics of determining whether or not it had been satisfied, remain elusive. His direction notoriously blurred the line between the normative and the descriptive senses of standard or accepted practice[33] and he did not elucidate the evaluative role, if any, of the court in respect of expert medical evidence.

Expressions such as 'the standard of the ordinary skilled man' and 'a practice accepted as proper by a responsible body of medical men', even if intended to be prescriptive, might be taken to mean little more than what is done by a number of doctors in practice. The same ambiguity is discernible in a contemporaneous address to the Medico-Legal Society, in which McNair J also proposed several different formulations of the test:

---

[32] *Bolam* v. *Friern Hospital Management Committee* [1957] 1 WLR 582, 586, 587. Emphasis added.

[33] See J. Montrose, 'Is Negligence an Ethical or a Sociological Concept?' (1958) 21 *Modern Law Review* 259.

[The test is to be based] on the proper standard of behaviour of a person having that professional skill and competence. The surgeon and physician must exercise such skill and competence as accords with the general and approved standard in the profession for a person carrying out those functions . . .

. . . The question must always be whether the particular act or omission in the circumstances was or was not negligence tested by the standard of the ordinary practitioner in a similar position. . .

. . . a professional man must be judged by the standard of knowledge and approved practice at the date of the alleged negligence.

. . . Was the technique in fact adopted one commonly adopted by competent practitioners or in a case against a specialist, by competent specialist practitioners at the material time?

. . . the practitioner whether newly qualified or not must show the skill of the reasonably competent person.[34]

Taken as a whole, the above passages suggest that McNair J did in fact subscribe to an objective, normative test for medical negligence, but was perhaps subconsciously too ready to identify common practice with acceptable practice. The same would seem to be true of his direction to the jury in *Bolam*. Doctors, he said, must exercise the degree of care and skill to be expected of a 'reasonably competent' practitioner. Their conduct must be acceptable to a reasonable and competent body of professional opinion. Thus, in principle, mere conformity with ordinary practice would not necessarily suffice, any more than it does in the field of negligence generally. That this is the more plausible interpretation is apparent from his repeated use of normative terminology: '*proper* standards', 'a practice accepted as *proper* by a *responsible* body of medical men *skilled* in [the] particular art'.[35] And again, 'a *proper* standard of *competent* professional opinion'.[36]

---

[34] 'Medical Responsibility in Hospitals' [1957] *Medico-Legal Journal* 129, 131–3.
[35] [1957] 1 WLR 582, 587. Emphasis added.
[36] Ibid. 590. Emphasis added. Cf. in *Greaves & Co (Contractors) Ltd* v. *Baynham Meikle and Partners* [1975] 3 All ER 99, 104–5, Lord Denning states that the standard of care expected of a professional man is 'reasonable care and skill in the course of his employment' because that was the test laid down by McNair J in *Bolam*.

The Authority to Decide

As regards who is to determine whether or not the doctor has fallen below the requisite standard of care, courts have found themselves torn between the natural impulse to assert their own authority and reluctance to impugn practices which have received a stamp of approval from medical experts. It does not seem credible that, uniquely in the medical sphere, McNair J could have intended courts to relinquish entirely their quintessential function of weighing evidence. For example, in saying that conformity with 'a practice accepted as proper by a *responsible* body of medical men' would suffice (emphasis added), he must presumably have meant to reserve to the court the right to determine whether or not the body of opinion relied upon could properly be described as 'responsible'.

Lord Diplock drew attention to this judicial role in *Sidaway*:

[the court] has to rely upon *and evaluate* expert evidence, remembering that it is no part of its task of evaluation to give effect to any preference it may have for one responsible body of professional opinion over another, *provided it is satisfied by the expert evidence that both qualify as responsible bodies of medical opinion.*[37]

In similar vein, Hirst J said in *Hills* v. *Potter*:

I do not accept [the] argument that by adopting the *Bolam* principle, the court in effect abdicates its power of decision to the doctors. In every case the court must be satisfied that the standard contended for on their behalf accords with that upheld by a substantial body of medical opinion, and that this body of medical opinion is both respectable and responsible, and experienced in this particular field of medicine.[38]

The ultimate authority of the court was also vigorously asserted by Sachs LJ in *Hucks* v. *Cole*: 'the fact that other practitioners would have done the same thing . . . is not . . . conclusive', he said,[39] and he was not swayed by the evidence of the four defence experts to the effect that 'they and other responsible members of the medical

---

[37] *Sidaway* v. *Board of Governors of the Bethlem Royal Hospital* [1985] AC 871, 895. Emphasis added.
[38] [1984] 1 WLR 641, 653. For an excellent discussion of these issues, see M. Jones, *Medical Negligence* (London: Sweet & Maxwell, 1991), ch. 3.
[39] [1993] 4 Med LR 393, 397 (case decided 1968).

profession would have taken the same risk in the same circumstances.' On the particular facts, he considered that failure to use
penicillin was 'not merely wrong but clearly unreasonable. The
reasons given by the four experts do not to my mind stand up to
analysis.'[40] There are several recent instances of judges analysing
the reasoning behind expert medical evidence, with a view to
rejecting it if they deem it to be flawed.[41] In some cases at least,
perhaps another way of putting the argument is that where on the
court's assessment of the evidence a given practice was plainly
unreasonable, it could not be regarded as the conduct of a
'responsible' body of medical opinion.

It is, none the less, interesting that it should be in a medical
context that the leading authority on the standard of care for
professional negligence seems to contain a normative test of
reasonable competence juxtaposed, if not conflated, with a
descriptive one. For there had been previous statements in the
House of Lords in *non*-medical cases to the effect that generally in
negligence the test is normative and that common practice is not
determinative,[42] a position which the House was to reiterate
shortly after the decision in *Bolam*.[43] McNair J's use of the term
'ordinary man' as effectively synonymous with 'reasonable man',[44]
with the corollary that the 'ordinary doctor' is the 'reasonable
doctor', is a further indication of his predisposition to elide the
distinction between 'is' and 'ought' in the medical context. He is
not alone in this respect. In *Maynard*, for example, prior to saying
that 'in the realm of diagnosis and treatment' negligence entails
'failure to exercise the *ordinary* skill of the doctor', Lord Scarman
states that a decision to operate is not negligent if a competent
body of professional opinion 'supports the decision as *reasonable*

[40] [1993] 4 Med LR 398.

[41] e.g. 'it is not enough for a defendant to call a number of doctors to say that
what he had done or not done was in accord with accepted clinical practice. It is
necessary for the judge to consider that evidence and decide whether that clinical
practice puts the patient unnecessarily at risk': *Bolitho* v. *City and Hackney Health
Authority* [1993] 4 Med LR 381, 386, *per* Farquharson LJ. Cf *Defreitas* v. *O'Brien*
[1993] 4 Med LR 281, 287–8.

[42] e.g. *Bank of Montreal* v. *Dominion Gresham Guarantee and Casualty Co.*
[1930] AC 659, 666, *per* Lord Tomlin; *Lloyds Bank* v. *E. B. Savory & Co.* [1933]
AC 201, 233, *per* Lord Wright.

[43] *Cavanagh* v. *Ulster Weaving Co. Ltd* [1960] AC 145.

[44] 'The man at the top of the Clapham omnibus. He is the ordinary man': *Bolam*
[1957] 1 WLR 582, 586.

in the circumstances', and again, if it is *'reasonable* in the sense that a responsible body of medical opinion would have accepted it as proper'.[45]

Until the demise of the civil jury any such tendency to equate the 'reasonable' with the 'ordinary' would, as in *Bolam* itself, have been subjected to the additional filter of lay notions about acceptable medical practice. But the leeway afforded by *Bolam* and by its subsequent interpretation[46] has reinforced judicial disinclination to challenge medical credentials. Adherence either to common practice or to medical procedures which enjoy only a modicum of acceptance within the profession, even if not technically dispositive, all but ensure that the doctor will not be held liable. In an early comment on the 'responsible body of medical opinion' test, Fleming said that it 'does not, of course, imply that conformity is necessarily conclusive, but suggests that it will be accepted as such, unless the practice is demonstrably fraught with obvious hazards'.[47] If this is so, it has added significance when one remembers how broadly most judges construe the doctor's remit.

In fact Fleming's prediction has been amply borne out by the case law, and it is easy to see how this has come about. The most egregious examples of malpractice are routinely settled. As for cases where doctors are advised to defend, in a field which judges are quick to point out is far from being an 'exact science'[48] it is not surprising if evidence is usually forthcoming that the defendant's conduct was acceptable at least to a minority of medical opinion.[49] It is all the less surprising given the degree of judicial respect accorded to anyone designated a medical expert, notwithstanding the often perfunctory nature of the inquiry as to his or her

---

[45] *Maynard* v. *West Midlands Regional Health Authority* [1984] 1 WLR 634, 638.

[46] Especially in *Maynard*, but also in *Sidaway* and its progeny. See 212–217 below.

[47] J. Fleming, 'Developments in the English Law of Medical Liability' (1959) 12 *Vanderbilt Law Review* 633, 642.

[48] e.g. *Sidaway* v. *Board of Governors of Bethlem Royal Hospital* [1984] 2 WLR 778, 782, *per* Lord Donaldson MR ; cf. 'in medical science, all things, or nearly all things, are uncertain. That knowledge is part of the general experience of mankind': *Thake* v. *Maurice* [1986] QB 644, 686–7, *per* Nourse LJ. And again, at 688: 'of all sciences medicine is one of the least exact'.

[49] Cf. S. McLean, *A Patient's Right to Know* (Aldershot: Dartmouth, 1989), 122.

suitability.[50] In a report on the role of scientific evidence in the courts, the organization Justice described the process in the following terms: '[it] is a preliminary matter for the judge to decide. In theory he should investigate the credentials of the proposed expert to determine whether he has undergone such a course of study or has otherwise acquired sufficient experience to render him qualified as an expert for the purposes of the case in question. In practice, however, this exercise is not undertaken in any detailed or formal way'.[51] In the absence of formal indicia of expertise, judicial reluctance to discount the opinions of medical witnesses confers normative status too easily on outmoded and inferior procedures.

The courts are, of course, engaged in *some* kind of evaluative exercise, even if in practice it often amounts to no more than eliciting whatever suffices to satisfy the judge as to the competence of the defence's expert witness(es). Plainly, also, they can hardly be seen to acknowledge that they are abdicating their decision-making function. Nevertheless, the general thrust of *Bolam*[52] is to allow medical views of acceptable conduct to determine the propriety of what the doctor has done. Cases concerned with diagnosis and treatment consequently revolve almost exclusively around issues of medical technique. They hinge on whether or not the doctor has acted in a manner which is considered technically acceptable within the profession. They are not concerned with respect for the patient or for any rights of the patient beyond the right to technical proficiency.[53] It is important to appreciate how much decisional discretion this affords doctors in practice. It means that, over the whole range of clinical care—the choice of particular diagnostic techniques, particular medical procedures, particular drugs and drug dosages—the practitioner's conduct can be judged by reference to its acceptability within the medical community as *one* possible way of dealing with the condition in

---

[50] Most bodies that keep lists have generally been unwilling to advise on suitability: see Justice, *Science and the Administration of Justice* (London: Justice, 1991), 43, though some, such as the British Academy of Experts, APIL and AVMA, increasingly provide advice on the kind of expert to use: *Lawyer*, 12 Oct. 1993.   [51] Justice, n. 50, 6.

[52] And to a large extent of cases such as *Hills* v. *Potter* and *Sidaway*, despite protestations about not abdicating the court's duty to decide.

[53] Cf. J. Montgomery, 'Medicine, Accountability, and Professionalism' (1989) 16 *Journal of Law and Society* 319.

question, with minimal regard to the differential characteristics and possible preferences of patients.

In theory, insisting that 'reasonable' rather than 'ordinary' conduct is at stake has the virtue of making it more likely that the court will consider what kind of approach is appropriate in the circumstances for the particular patient, as distinct from merely endorsing what doctors have commonly considered to be an adequate way of dealing with the particular condition. If practical consequences are to flow from acknowledging that *Bolam* is about the reasonableness of medical norms rather than the existence of medical practices, much depends on judges genuinely believing in themselves as the ultimate arbiters of medical liability, entitled to question those norms. As a first step they would need to resist the impulse to equate practice and expertise, of which the tendency to use the terms 'reasonable' and 'ordinary' as synonyms is itself symptomatic.[54]

A 'Right' to Reasonable Care?

In trying to determine the reasonableness of a medical norm in particular circumstances, we might, both intuitively and for sound ethical, political, and therapeutic reasons, think it natural to give some consideration to the patient's standpoint. If we were to do this, it might also seem natural to consider what rights the patient should have in regard to proposed treatment. Today, such an approach would appear especially relevant on facts such as those of *Bolam*, which involved the administration of ECT without relaxant drugs or manual restraint and without informing the patient about the attendant risk of fractures. Since disclosure, as well as technical proficiency, was in issue, serious attention to what the patient was entitled to be told might seem to be have been called for. But the judge's direction in *Bolam* did not address the plaintiff's situation from a rights perspective, and disclosure was clearly seen as secondary. At the outset, McNair J said that, 'the only question is really a question of professional skill'.[55] After summarizing the differing views of medical witnesses on giving a

---

[54] Cf. 'I respectfully think that some of the cases in England have concentrated rather too heavily on the practice of the medical profession': *F* v. *R* (1982) 33 SASR 189, 201, *per* Bollen J.   [55] *Bolam*, n. 32 above, 586.

warning before administering ECT, he simply asked the jury to consider whether the defendants 'were falling below a proper standard of competent professional opinion on this question'. His own none-too-subtle hint that they were not[56] was followed by the words, 'I now pass to what I venture to believe is the *real* point which you have to consider ' (emphasis added). His approach to the issue of disclosure centred on what constituted acceptable professional practice as a matter of contemporary medical mores, rather than on what constitutes proper respect for the patient's rights. Put another way, communication of risks was not seen at the time as relevant to patient welfare.

From a legal, as well as historical, perspective it is easy to understand why. The case law on medical negligence concerned the quality of care and level of skill shown by doctors as craftsmen and members of a 'learned profession'. The central focus in liability for medical negligence is, by definition, the doctor. The central issue is whether the doctor has fallen below required professional standards in what Lord Diplock was later to describe as 'the exercise of his healing functions',[57] a matter routinely determined on the basis of expert medical opinion. That being so, the case law has been overwhelmingly concerned with alleged technical deficiencies of doctors in their efforts to promote the welfare of their patients. A small minority of cases raise more overtly value-laden questions about disclosure of risks and alternative procedures, which have a more conspicuous bearing on patients' rights. But these cases also demonstrate that most English judges, either unreservedly or with minimal qualification, regard the standard of care required of the doctor as indivisible. Disclosure practices are adjudged as if they, too, were an aspect of medical professionalism that should be measured by the profession's own standards. In Lord Diplock's view, for example,[58] the

---

[56] 'Members of the jury, though it is a matter entirely for you, you may well think that when dealing with a mentally sick man and having a strong belief that his only hope of cure is E.C.T. treatment, the doctor cannot be criticised if he does not stress the dangers, which he believes to be minimal, which are involved in that treatment': ibid. 590. Interestingly, the All ER version of the judgment contains the expression '*submission to* electro-convulsive therapy', not 'E.C.T. treatment': [1957] 2 All ER 118, 124. Emphasis added.

[57] *Sidaway*, n. 37 above, 893.

[58] Endorsed in *Gold* v. *Haringey Health Authority* [1988] QB 481 and *Blyth* v. *Bloomsbury Health Authority* [1993] 4 Med LR 151 (case decided 1987).

Bolam test laid down 'a principle of English law that is comprehensive and applicable to every aspect of the duty of care owed by a doctor to his patient'. The scope of the duty to warn, he said, was 'as much an exercise of professional skill and judgement as any other part of the doctor's comprehensive duty of care to the individual patient.[59]

It is as if judges are saying that the values which underlie all medical decision-making inhere in medicine itself, making it easier to argue that it is for doctors alone to establish what needs to be disclosed and whether or not disclosure has been adequate.[60] But treating disclosure as merely one facet of a comprehensive, unitary duty governed by customary standards[61] can serve to disguise or obscure its distinctive nature as an issue which transcends ordinary medical and clinical expertise. Judicial observations favouring the unitary view abound. The various judgements in *Sidaway*, the leading authority on disclosure, are replete with them. Thus the disclosure requirement 'can only be tested by applying the standards of the profession'.[62] It is 'very much a matter for professional judgement'[63] and 'primarily . . . a matter of clinical judgement'.[64] Browne-Wilkinson LJ went as far as to say that:

. . . whether the risk is material and the adequacy of the disclosure will fall to be determined by reference to the accepted practices of the medical profession and not, as in the ordinary case of the professional man, by the court applying its own standards.[65]

It is true that he qualifies this statement by mentioning the need to have regard to 'the circumstances of the particular patient', but he does not elaborate the point by reference to any factors beyond the normal bounds of clinical judgement.

The clear message is that on matters of disclosure we are squarely in the realm of professional duty narrowly conceived. It is therefore of interest that, in *Sidaway*, Lord Scarman's rejection of the *Bolam* test for disclosure derived from an analysis firmly based

---

[59] *Sidaway*, n. 37 above, 895.
[60] See also R. Veatch, *The Patient–Physician Relation* (Bloomington and Indianapolis: Indiana University Press, 1991) 264–7.
[61] Cf. 'part of the overall *clinical* judgement of the doctor': *Sidaway* [1984] 2 WLR 778, 795, *per* Dunn LJ. Emphasis added.   [62] Ibid.
[63] Ibid. 791, *per* Lord Donaldson MR.
[64] *Sidaway* [1985] AC 871, 900, *per* Lord Bridge.
[65] *Sidaway* [1984] 2 WLR 778, 800.

on patients' rights or, more specifically, on 'the patient's right to make his own decision, which *may be seen as* a basic human right protected by the common law'.[66] Thus, 'in a medical negligence case where the issue is as to the advice and information given to the patient as to the treatment proposed, the available options, and the risk, the court is concerned primarily with a patient's right. The doctor's duty arises from his patient's rights.'[67] And again, '*if it be recognized that* a doctor's duty of care extends not only to the health and well-being of his patient but also to a proper respect for his patient's rights, the duty to warn can be seen to be part of the doctor's duty of care'.[68] The tentative locutions reflect the lack of authority for this position. It is submitted that it is an ahistorical, essentially aspirational, view describing a *moral* right which, at least within the category of negligence, never enjoyed legal protection.[69] As we have seen, even in the consent-based case of *Slater* v. *Baker*[70] the justification for requiring disclosure was not a 'basic human right' as such, but the essentially pragmatic desire to help the patient face the procedure, thereby enabling it to be carried out more safely. Rights discourse of the kind proposed by Lord Scarman simply does not square with the conceptual basis of liability for negligence as developed in the case law.

Nowhere is the incongruity more clearly and powerfully spelt out than in the first instance judgment of Woodhouse J in *Smith* v. *Auckland Hospital Board*.[71] The case is commonly cited for the appellate court's views on the extent of the doctor's duty to answer specific questions truthfully.[72] However, perhaps because his decision was overruled on other grounds, Woodhouse J's analysis and conclusions regarding the general nature of medical negligence have gone largely unremarked.[73] The particular issue in the case was the extent of the duty to warn about the risks inherent in

---

[66] [1985] AC 871, 882. Emphasis added.   [67] Ibid. 888.

[68] Ibid. 885. Emphasis added.

[69] Cf. 'Lord Scarman traces [the source of the duty] to the right of the patient in the integrity of his body . . . *In doing so, Lord Scarman confuses two distinct causes of action, trespass and negligence*': D. Cassidy, 'Malpractice—Medical Negligence in Australia' (1992) 66 *Australian Law Journal* 67, 85.

[70] (1767) 95 ER 860.   [71] [1964] NZLR 241.

[72] [1965] NZLR 191.

[73] Though they were not contradicted on appeal and were endorsed in the Canadian decision of *Male* v. *Hopmans*, both at first instance, (1965) 54 DLR (2d) 592, and on appeal, (1967) 64 DLR (2d) 105. See also allusions to the judgment in McLean, *A Patient's Right to Know*, n. 49 above, 91, 93

carrying out an aortogram. Woodhouse J repeatedly condemns the attempt to protect the patient's rights within the framework of negligence as a species of category error, saying at one point, 'I find it difficult to relate these complaints to negligence at all.'[74] 'If', he observes, 'the issue in the case was the maintenance of the individual's right of self-determination, the matter would quickly resolve itself. But it is not. This is a question within the duty of care concept in negligence.'[75] And again, 'while doctors could not unreasonably and deliberately usurp the patient's right to choose for himself, I do not think this leads to any absolute answer to the limits of their duty of care in negligence. Negligence is not concerned with injury to dignity, but to the body or property.'[76] 'The issue in negligence is the duty to take reasonable care to avoid undue risk of injury, and not whether the treatment was unauthorized.'[77] 'It is not . . . personal rights which the duty of care is designed to satisfy or protect; it is the risk of injury'.[78] And most concretely, in considering the significance of the patient's general inquiry about possible risks, 'I do not think that the inquiry made by the plaintiff enlarged the duty of care in negligence at all. If it affected the legal responsibilities of the parties I think it is because of the need for a real consent which is in the area of assault [i.e. battery]; or by putting the contractual duty of the doctor on a higher level than the duty of care in negligence.'[79]

However, as Woodhouse J had observed at the outset, 'the claim is not that an absence of informed consent has given rise to a successful action for assault. Nor is it pleaded that there has been a breach of some implied but stringent contractual undertaking to supply detailed explanations of every step which the doctors propose to take.'[80] Any duty to warn or inform 'must involve the doctor in the same exercise of judgement founded upon the same medical experience and knowledge as he exercises in the field of technique. In this area of his responsibility, therefore, his duty of care should logically be measured by the same standards and upon the same principles.'[81] Relying, *inter alia*, on *Hunter* v. *Hanley* and *Bolam*, he defined these principles as 'the reasonable skill, prudence, and performance of his own kind'.[82] 'any duty to warn

[74] [1964] NZLR 241, 252.
[75] Ibid. 247.
[76] Ibid

[77] Ibid. 250.
[78] Ibid. 254.
[79] Ibid. 252.

[80] Ibid. 242.
[81] Ibid. 247.
[82] Ibid. 248.

cannot be defined absolutely merely because personal rights are involved, and the scope of the duty must be found in the practice of the competent and prudent doctor.'[83] 'The paramount consideration is the welfare of the patient, and . . . the exercise of [the doctor's] discretion in the area of advice must depend on the patient's overall needs'.[84]

CONCLUSION

Judges are not well versed in the intricacies and complexities of medical practice. They have shown themselves singularly reluctant to question the judgement of doctors, especially, though not exclusively, in matters of diagnosis and treatment. Consequently, where there is evidence of compliance with approved methods, in practice doctors have become virtually unassailable. Yet as Lloyd LJ said in *Gold*, 'I can see no possible ground for distinguishing between doctors and any other profession or calling which requires special skill, knowledge or experience.'[85] Medicine is not a uniquely complex activity. Even if it were, there is no reason within the conventional understanding of negligence—essentially as a judgement on reasonableness in the circumstances—to remove the determination of its existence from the court, informed where necessary by expert witnesses. In medicine, as in other spheres, their proper role is to provide evidence which will assist the court in assessing the reasonableness or otherwise of the doctor's conduct. Essentially this consists of explaining the risks and benefits associated with the defendant's conduct so that the court may decide whether or not an adequate standard has been attained. It is not the function of the expert to say what professional practice is, as such, and there is certainly no reason why customary practice should be deemed dispositive.[86]

Thus, in principle, the court has an evaluative role even in respect of diagnosis and treatment, which are not exclusively technical or value-free activities. As regards the scope of the duty to disclose risks, it is even clearer that we are beyond the realms of

[83] [1964] NZLR 248.   [84] Ibid. 250.
[85] [1988] QB 481, 489.
[86] Cf. Silver, 'One Hundred Years of Harmful Error: The Historical Jurisprudence of Medical Malpractice', n. 9 above, 1214–9.

the merely technical. Today, pondering a case with facts similar to *Bolam*, we might be disposed to think in terms of the patient's 'right' to decide whether or not to undergo the treatment. But in the mid-1950s arguments about informed consent were only just beginning to make their appearance in the American case law. In England, the doctor's duty of care and skill was simply not articulated in terms of patients' rights; in *Bolam*, McNair J gave short shrift to the question of warning. When courts in the United Kingdom were subsequently to consider the informed consent doctrine their consistent rejection of it was doubtless much influenced by non-legal considerations,[87] but it was also adequately explained by the inability to accommodate a doctrine based on the right of patient self-determination within a form of action geared to technical medical competence in the pursuit of patient welfare.

In other words, what counts as negligence in respect of non-disclosure is properly construed in terms of the reasonable care and skill to be expected of doctors, as distinct from an examination of whether the doctor has been insufficiently sensitive to the patient's moral autonomy.[88] The orthodox approach was reiterated when the scope of the doctor's duty to warn was considered in the recent Scottish case of *Moyes* v. *Lothian*. Once again, the accent was firmly on patient welfare, with rights occupying a residual role, significant only in so far as deemed relevant to safety: 'recognition by the doctor of the adult patient's right to make decisions about the risks he incurs is essentially an aspect of the duty to take reasonable care for his safety'.[89] And again, 'the paramount expectation is that the doctor will do what is best to care for the patient's health'.[90]

Of course, there have always been policy considerations which help to explain why the liability rules have been more responsive

[87] See R. Schwartz and A. Grubb, 'Why Britain can't Afford Informed Consent' (Aug. 1985) 15 *Hastings Center Report* 19.

[88] Cf. the 'alleged "right of self-determination" . . . is a premise which, however ethically valid, is unknown to negligence theory': D. Manderson, 'Following Doctors' Orders: Informed Consent in Australia' (1988) 62 *Australian Law Journal* 430, 439.

[89] *Moyes* v. *Lothian Health Board* [1990] 1 Med LR 463, 469, *per* Lord Caplan. Cf. '[the doctor] owes a duty to the patient to use due caution in undertaking the treatment': *R.* v. *Bateman*, n. 30 above.

[90] Ibid. Cf. 'their prime responsibility [is] to care for the health of their patients': *Smith* v. *Auckland Hospital Board* [1964] NZLR 241, 251.

to particular conceptions of the public interest than to concern for
the 'rights' of individual patients. Lord Denning openly voiced his
fears that broadening the scope of doctors' liability would have
detrimental social and economic effects on the community,[91] fears
shared to a greater or lesser extent by subsequent appellate
judges, as evidenced by the manner in which they were to reject
the informed consent doctrine. In the current economic climate,
the case for a more expansive conception of medical negligence is
bound to be adversely affected by the retrenchment and reversion
to incrementalism generally in negligence. Despite calls for more
accountability of doctors, the greater the emphasis on cost
containment in medicine, the greater will be the pressure to resist
enlarging the standard of care by requiring more extensive
disclosure of risks or mandatory disclosure of alternative procedures in the name of the 'rights' of the individual patient.

All in all, the enormous influence that was to be exerted by
Bolam, a suspect first instance decision based on a somewhat
confusing jury direction, remains one of the more remarkable
features of medical law. The readiness with which it was construed
to allow medical opinion a decisive voice needs to be seen in the
context of mounting fears in the 1950s that the emergence of the
NHS, legal aid, and vicarious liability of hospital authorities for
negligence was encouraging an undue increase in medical claims.
It is evident that McNair J was acutely aware of such considerations. His parting shot to the jury consisted of extensive, not to say
tendentious, quotation of Lord Denning's 'very wise words' in *Roe*
v. *Minister of Health*, counselling against imposing liability on
hospitals and doctors for everything that happens to go wrong.[92] It
is also of interest that in his address to the Medico-Legal Society
he said, 'I am fully conscious of the fact that the medical world . . .
have been and are profoundly disturbed by the spate of litigation
in [hospital] cases in recent years.'[93]

The analytical framework of negligence is such that any right or
entitlement of patients, whether in regard to diagnosis, treatment,

---

[91] See e.g. *Roe* v. *Minister of Health* [1954] 2 QB 66; *Hatcher* v. *Black*, *The
Times*, 2 July, 1954; *Lim Poh Choo* v. *Camden and Islington Area Health Authority*
[1978] 3 WLR 895.

[92] Ibid. See *Bolam* [1957] 1 WLR 582, 593–4.

[93] McNair J, 'Medical Responsibility in Hospitals' [1957] *Medico-Legal Journal*
129.

or disclosure, can be no greater than what is deemed to be required by the exercise of reasonable care. In the next chapter, we will argue that proper regard for the patient's legitimate interests and expectations is attainable within such a framework, in a manner fully consistent with the case law and legal principle.[94] What needs to be stressed here is that negligence—unlike trespass and contract—is not even *designed* to protect patients' rights, but instead focuses on patient welfare via the objectivized standard of care which it imposes on doctors. The scope of the doctor's duty is not expressed in terms of the patient's rights, except in the weak, implicit sense of 'the right not to be negligently injured', that is, the right to competent performance of the doctor's duty.[95] The unique interpretation of the professional custom standard in medical cases, crystallizing in *Bolam*, is eloquent testimony to the mystique of medicine and the strength of its professionalisation and entrenchment from the late nineteenth century onwards.

[94] The argument gains support from the widespread rejection of the *Bolam* test in Commonwealth jurisdictions, of which the latest major example is the incisive criticism to which it was subjected by the Australian appellate courts in the important recent decision on disclosure of *Rogers* v. *Whitaker*. See 222–4 below.

[95] Cf. 'liability in negligence depends on the duty of care to be observed by the defendant; it does not depend on the "rights" of the plaintiff, other than the plaintiff's right not to be negligently injured': *Sidaway* [1984] 2 WLR 778, 798, *per* Browne-Wilkinson LJ.

6

Collaborative Autonomy

In *Sidaway*, Lord Scarman alone favoured incorporating what he called the 'transatlantic doctrine of informed consent'[1] into English law. He saw the doctrine as embodying the doctor's obligation to satisfy the patient's right to know. In his view, this obligation forms part of the doctor's duty of care derived from the patient's rights—the 'right to be informed of the risks inherent in the treatment which is proposed'[2] so as to be able to exercise the right of 'self-determination'. We have suggested that this rationale is misconceived. However, though a *rights*-based justification of informed consent is problematic within the context of negligence, and though the vocabulary of rights has been misleadingly deployed under the ægis of negligence by jurisdictions that have embraced the doctrine, it remains possible to accommodate a conception of informed consent within negligence as a dimension of the doctor's duty of care. Properly conceived, the doctrine represents both a noble aspiration and a practical aid to doctor–patient relationships which the law should endorse.

The expression 'informed consent' is not clear on the face of it. When we say that a person has been informed about something, we signify merely that he or she has been told about it. To say that someone has made an 'informed' decision, however, suggests a process of deliberation based on understanding. An unfortunate ambiguity of 'informed consent' as a medico-legal concept is the way in which the phrase elides the distinction between the comprehending patient and one who has merely been notified; between the essentially one-way process of imparting information and the kind of dialogue that truly equips the patient to work towards a decision. In fact, the adjectival use of 'informed' more

---

[1] *Sidaway* v. *Board of Governors of the Bethlem Royal Hospital and the Maudsley Hospital* [1985] AC 871, 883.   [2] Ibid. 882.

naturally connotes communication which results in understanding, a sense not borne out by the case law.[3]

Jurisdictions which apply the doctrine have almost without exception focused on the element of disclosure—disclosure of risks, and sometimes of alternative procedures.[4] The law, like many doctors, defines the obligation almost exclusively in terms of information-giving. As Katz has observed, 'judges' sole focus on disclosure, to the exclusion of consent, tends to perpetuate physicians' disengaged monologues'.[5] Often eloquent in their defence of the patient's 'right to information', courts have been much less concerned about the extent to which the decisions patients make exhibit understanding, despite empirical evidence indicating that patients often understand less of the information presented to them than their doctors believe to be the case,[6] and disturbingly little about procedures which they have undergone.[7] Under an informed consent regime, the patient is said to have a 'right' to material information. In much the same way, many legal systems now confer on patients the additional 'right' to see their medical records, *inter alia*, to help them decide about treatment. But neither of these formal rights is capable of eliciting a meaningful consent to treatment from patients who insufficiently

[3] In jurisdictions which subscribe to informed consent, there is no general requirement of patient understanding; rather there is 'a duty to make a reasonable effort to communicate information to the patient': M. Jones, *Medical Negligence* (London: Sweet & Maxwell, 1991), 244. In *Kelly* v. *Hazlett* (1976) 75 DLR (3d) 536, 565, Morden J somewhat ambiguously refers to a 'duty [in negligence] to be reasonably satisfied that the patient is aware of those risks associated with the treatment of which he or she should be aware'. Some Canadian courts are beginning to interpret *Reibl* v. *Hughes* as requiring patient understanding. See G. Robertson, 'Informed Consent Ten Years Later: The Impact of *Reibl* v. *Hughes* (1991) 70 *Canadian Bar Review* 423, 430–1 and n. 33. And see *Reibl* v. *Hughes* (1980) 114 DLR (3d) 1, 34.

[4] Cf. P. Tulley, 'Towards a Wider View of Informed Consent to Medical Treatment' (1992) 8 *Professional Negligence* 74.

[5] J. Katz, 'Informed Consent — A Fairy Tale? Law's Vision' (1977) 39 *University of Pittsburgh Law Review* 137, 147.

[6] See L. Wallace, 'Informed Consent to Elective Surgery: The "Therapeutic" Value?' *Social Science and Medicine* 22 (1986), 29, 31. Cf. T. Wade, 'Patients May Not Recall Disclosure of Risk of Death: Implications for Informed Consent' (1990) 30 *Medicine, Science, and the Law* 259.

[7] e.g. D. Byrne, A. Napier, and A. Cuschieri, 'How Informed is Signed Consent?' *British Medical Journal* 296 (1988), 839. When interviewed between 2 and 5 days after their operations, 27% of patients did not know which organ had been operated on and 44% were unaware of the exact nature of the surgical procedure.

appreciate the nature and implications of their medical condition. The discourse of rights can flatter to deceive. What many patients seek is sufficient understanding to reach an 'informed' decision in the fuller sense of the term; this can seldom be achieved without the kind of dialogue, and the kind of relationship, to which the collaborative model of medical practice alone aspires.

The word 'reach' rather than 'make' is used deliberately here, because it is unusual for serious medical decisions to be taken instantaneously. The medical information which doctors impart is itself often tentative and uncertain. In so far as it depends on the outcome of diagnostic tests and on the natural course of a disease, its revelation may be both gradual and subject to modification. Ideally, then, decisions will reflect a considered view based on an assessment over time of technically available options which takes account of the patient's circumstances and values. In practice, the initiative as to treatment will typically come from the doctor. It is ironic that 'informed consent' should often be portrayed as a powerful symbol of *self*-determination. For not only do many patients who have been informed remain 'uninformed' in the fuller sense of the term, but when, as so often, they 'consent' to treatment in response to 'disengaged monologues', their conduct is tantamount to mere compliance, at best a coming to terms with treatment first proposed by the doctor: 'most questions about consent are formulated by physicians in such a way as to induce the kind of answers physicians want'.[8]

Projecting informed consent as an issue of patients' rights is psychologically hazardous, and doubly so when it is presented as a question of patients' *legal* rights. For one cannot ignore the fact that the doctrine entails an approach to medical practice at odds with traditional medical ethics and training and perceived by many practitioners as a tiresome, time-consuming irrelevance, an intrusive challenge to their judgement and expertise, threatening the very foundations of their professionalism. It is not easy to fashion an effective legal instrument in the face of such sentiments.[9] It would thus be naïve to expect, even in jurisdictions

[8] R. Zussman, *Intensive Care* (Chicago: University of Chicago Press, 1992), 220.
[9] 'As a specifically legal doctrine, informed consent presupposes a model of decision making that has little to do with the realities of medical care. [It] . . . requires of physicians a style of thought (and explanation) radically different from that to which they are accustomed': Ibid. 82.

strongly wedded to the doctrine, that the day-to-day conduct of doctors is greatly affected by its precise legal requirements. Indeed, there is considerable empirical evidence of widespread ignorance or lack of concern among doctors about them.[10]

Resistance from medical practitioners to informed consent cuts deeper than the challenge which it represents to routinized modes of dealing with individual patients, important though that is. It reflects the sensitive territorial debate over the proper ambit of technical medicine, highlighting the tension between doctors, who are prone to convert moral, social, and economic issues into technical ones, and other interested parties and institutions pulling in the opposite direction. As we have seen, doctors' 'technical' judgements are often infused with or coloured by values traditionally considered to be central to the practice of medicine, such as the primacy of preserving life, the principle of beneficence, and commitment to clinical freedom. To a greater or lesser extent, their judgements will also be influenced by changes in the social climate, bureaucratic and financial constraints, and their own personalities and values.[11] These myriad considerations are the more likely to come into play because of the pervasive lack of consensus in medicine, whether as regards what the appropriate treatment is or how it should be provided. As Veatch points out, 'for every single medical case, there are countless choice points where there is more than one plausible way to proceed: different drugs, different dosages, different lengths of stay in the hospital, different health care institutions, different styles of interacting between professional and lay person'.[12] However, the range of choices available in medicine, and the potential influence of both the doctor's values and external pressures on medical practice, strengthen rather than diminish the case for enabling patients to be

[10] See e.g. G. Robertson, 'Informed Consent in Canada: An Empirical Study' (1984) 22 *Osgoode Hall Law Journal* 139.

[11] Cf. R. Veatch, *The Patient–Physician Relation* (Bloomington and Indianapolis: Indiana University Press, 1991), ch. 27, especially 270–1.

[12] Ibid. 270. Cf. Zussman, on decisions to limit treatment: 'the judgement of physicians in these matters is not simply technical. It is also shaped by their own interests and by adaptations to the stresses of medical practice, as well as by apparently high-minded concerns that are at best ambiguously patient centered. Whether physicians report a patient as "terminal" or the possibility of recovery "realistic" does involve technical judgement, but technical judgement shaped by the distinctive values of their occupation': n. 8 above, 221.

more involved in their treatment should they so wish. We now examine the part informed consent as a legal doctrine has played in this respect, as well as the role it might have in the future.

The Development of Informed Consent in the United States

In identifying the origins of informed consent, United States courts almost invariably invoke Judge Cardozo's statement that '[e]very human being of adult years and sound mind has a right to determine what shall be done with his own body; and a surgeon who performs an operation without his patient's consent commits an assault'.[13] Thus formulated the notion is a straightforward appeal to patients' rights, grounded in the ancient common law principle that an unauthorized touching constitutes battery.[14] The rationale of self-determination is explicit.

The actual phrase 'informed consent' first surfaced in *Salgo* v. *Leland Stanford, Jr, University Board of Trustees*.[15] This was one of the first cases to acknowledge that a patient needs adequate information about the nature of proposed treatment, its risks, and feasible alternatives in order to make an intelligent choice about whether or not to undergo it. However, the Court, while drawing on Cardozo's dictum, expressly held that the content of the disclosure was a matter for professional medical judgement. *Salgo*, in its equivocal language, set a pattern which has characterized the informed consent doctrine in the United States ever since. While proclaiming the rhetoric of self-determination and 'patients' rights' it contrived to leave substantial scope in practice for medical paternalism. As Katz has pointed out, this internal contradiction is encapsulated in the following passage: 'in discussing the element of risk a certain amount of *discretion* must be employed consistent with the *full* disclosure of facts necessary to an informed consent'.[16]

As already indicated, in a number of important respects it would be advantageous to plaintiffs, and conceptually more in keeping with a model of patients' rights, if absence of consent to treatment

---

[13] *Schloendorff* v. *Society of New York Hospital*, 211 NY 125, 129–30 (1914).
[14] See e.g. *Cole* v. *Turner* (1704) 6 Mod 149.
[15] 154 Cal App 2d 560 (1957).
[16] Ibid. 578. Emphasis added. See Katz, 'Informed Consent—A Fairy Tale. Law's Vision', n. 5 above, 138.

were analysed as an issue in trespass rather than negligence.[17] When, in the course of the 1960s, it became evident that the negligence approach was to prevail, the prospect of a pronounced shift in the direction of enhanced patient autonomy, if anything, receded. In trespass the issue was relatively straightforward—did the doctor intentionally touch the patient without consent? By contrast, the move to negligence theory focused the court's attention on what doctors ought to disclose in order to discharge their duty of care. It was inevitable that doctors' views on this matter would play a central part. Though the dimension of professional ethics thus introduced could, in principle, be separated from matters of technical judgement, centuries of doctor-centred 'medical ethics' and the readiness of judges to condone the medicalization of moral issues argued otherwise. The negligence model was to guarantee a role for expert medical evidence which was superfluous in trespass.

Ostensibly a drive for greater patient autonomy did begin to take place, within a negligence framework, in the early 1970s. The landmark decision was *Canterbury* v. *Spence*,[18] in which the court declared that 'respect for the patient's right of self-determination on particular therapy demands a standard set by law for physicians rather than one which physicians may or may not impose upon themselves'.[19] The focus was to be on what the doctor knew, or should have known, to be the patient's 'informational needs'. In the same year, courts in two other states adopted *Canterbury*'s reasonable or prudent patient test, requiring doctors to disclose such information as would be deemed material by a reasonable person in the patient's position.[20] The prevailing professional standard was criticized as often difficult to identify and a potential screen for non-disclosure. Subject to the extent that medical judgement was called for, proof of materiality was no longer to require expert testimony.

However, this proviso—'when medical judgement enters the picture . . . prevailing medical practice must be given its just

---

[17] See 96–8 above. Some American jurisdictions, unlike the English courts, occasionally treated failure to disclose a known inherent risk as negating consent for the purposes of battery: e.g. *Gray* v. *Grunnagle*, 223 A. 2d 663 (Pa 1966), and see other cases cited in W. Prosser and R. Keeton, *Torts* (5th edn.) (St Paul, Minn.: West Publishing Company, 1984), 120, n. 67.
[18] 464 F 2d 772 (1972).   [19] Ibid. 784.   [20] Ibid. 787.

due'—greatly undermined the apparent commitment to patient autonomy. For Judge Robinson did not seek to elaborate in a detailed way on the scope of medical decision-making. The readiness of many judges to take a broad view of what comes within the realm of medical expertise would allow considerable room for the therapeutic privilege exception. While there are plainly situations in which disclosure is medically harmful, the privilege is open to abuse. As indicated in the Presidential Commission Report, *Making Health Care Decisions*, 'there is much to suggest that therapeutic privilege has been vastly over-used as an excuse for not informing patients of facts they are entitled to know'.[21]

The rhetoric of self-determination was further belied by the extent to which the test of liability was objectivized. Not only is the criterion for disclosure that of the *reasonable* patient, but in *Canterbury*, and in almost all of the jurisdictions which were to follow it, the test of proximate causation is whether a 'prudent person in the patient's position'[22] would have agreed to the treatment. This approach contrasts with the normal rule in negligence that causation is determined on a subjective basis. It also sits oddly with the Court's premise that 'the patient's right of self-decision shapes the boundaries of the duty to reveal',[23] its concern that 'all risks potentially affecting the decision must be unmasked'[24] and its desire 'to safeguard the patient's interest in achieving *his own* determination on treatment'.[25] An objective test

[21] *Making Health Care Decisions: The Ethical and Legal Implications of Informed Consent in the Patient–Practitioner Relationship* (Washington: President's Commission for the Study of Ethical Problems in Medicine and Biomedical and Behavioral Research, 1982), 1, 96. Cf. 'disguising complex moral judgements as medical judgements' quoted from A. Buchanan, 'Medical Paternalism' *Philosophy and Public Affairs* 7 (1978), 370, 390.

[22] *Canterbury* v. *Spence*, n. 18 above, 791.   [23] Ibid. 786.

[24] Ibid. 787.

[25] Ibid. Emphasis added. See also the conclusion of a joint Australian Law Reform Commission Report, that the medical profession objects to general guidelines on disclosure because 'doctor–patient relationships are so varied that it is not useful to state general rules concerning the information to be given to patients': *Informed Decisions about Medical Procedures* (Melbourne and Sydney: Law Reform Commission of Victoria, Australian Law Reform Commission and New South Wales Law Reform Commission, 1989), 23–4: cited in D. Giesen and J. Hayes, 'The Patient's Right to Know—A Comparative View' (1992) 21 *Anglo-American Law Review* 101, 117. As Giesen and Hayes observe, 'This shows that *outside the court-room* it is often the medical profession which is the first to stress

can be justified by familiar evidential considerations, centring on the often suspect nature of testimony given by injured patients with the benefit of hindsight, but it is still inconsistent with the proclaimed rationale of individual choice. In practice it is also an insurmountable obstacle for many plaintiffs; for the defence will often be able to adduce evidence that fully informed patients have very rarely refused to undergo the procedure in question.

In *Canterbury* and its progeny the main emphasis was on the doctor having to make a sufficient *disclosure* of risks. The significance of whether the patient had absorbed and understood what was disclosed has scarcely been addressed. Though a fully subjective approach might prove unworkable,[26] placing a very heavy burden on the defendant, the *Canterbury* formula does allow for a more subjective analysis than it has generally been accorded in the case law. For the Court indicated that a risk would be material 'when a reasonable person, in what the physician knows or should know to be *the patient's position*, would be likely to attach significance to the risk or cluster of risks in deciding whether or not to forgo the proposed therapy'.[27]

Much then depends on how broadly one construes the phrase 'in the patient's position'. In *Fain* v. *Smith*, for example, the court held that 'the objective standard requires consideration by the factfinder of what a reasonable person with *all* of the characteristics of the plaintiff, including his idiosyncracies and religious beliefs, would have done under the same circumstances'.[28] Such a formulation does not fall far short of the fully subjective approach which, it has been forcefully argued, is dictated both by the

the diversity in patients' characters. The doctor who subscribes to this view cannot argue, without contradiction, in favour of a "reasonable patient" test for disclosure standards.'

[26] Cf. 'ideally, the court should ask itself whether in the particular circumstances the risk was such that this particular patient would think it significant if he was told it existed. I would think that, as a matter of ethics, this is the test of the doctor's duty. The law, however, operates not in Utopia but in the world as it is': *Sidaway* [1985] AC 871, 888, *per* Lord Scarman. By contrast, it will be recalled that in *Gillick* Lord Scarman indicated that a child under 16 is capable of consenting to medical treatment only 'when the child achieves a sufficient understanding and intelligence to enable him or her to understand fully what is proposed': *Gillick* v. *West Norfolk and Wisbech Area Health Authority* [1986] AC 112, 189.

[27] 464 F 2d 772, 787. Emphasis added.

[28] 479 So 2d 1150, 1154–5 (Ala, 1985). Emphasis added. See also *MacPherson* v. *Ellis*, 287 SE 2d 892 (1982) and *Scott* v. *Bradford*, 606 P 2d 554, 559 (1979) for a subjective approach to causation.

rationale of *self*-determination in the case law[29] and by the claims of patient autonomy as an ethical imperative, however irrational the proposed choice may be.[30]

It is, however, easier to insist on the self-determination of patients than to be clear about the state of mind and degree of knowledge which this implies. In its purest form it would entail awareness in a fully comprehending patient of anything which he or she might want to know before reaching a decision. In speaking of the 'comprehending' patient, we are not, it is true, referring to a grasp of technical niceties; appreciation of the health implications of treatment would suffice. But, in the first place, it is impossible to guarantee comprehension. Secondly, however extensive and searching the dialogue, issues which might have been of concern to the particular patient in making an informed choice may go unexplored. Relevant links may not be made, partly because patients cannot always appreciate, nor doctors always divine, everything that might be medically significant in the particular circumstances. Equally there are bound to be limits to the knowledge and understanding that doctors have about the personal situation of their patients. Above all, within the framework of negligence one cannot legitimately demand more of the doctor than the exercise of 'reasonable' care. It would be strange to claim that this obligation is not fulfilled unless the patient has been *made* to understand.

As presently applied, the *Canterbury* formula promises more than it delivers. In so far as doctors adhere to it, they often do so in a largely formal and impersonal manner, achieving little in the way of patient involvement and comprehension. The doctrine has fostered in hospitals a misplaced preoccupation—excessive even from a legal standpoint—with the sheer quantity of information disclosed and the mechanics of obtaining signatures to elaborate and abstruse consent forms.[31] At the same time, many doctors

---

[29] e.g. J. Katz, 'Informed Consent—A Fairy Tale? Law's Vision', n. 5 above, 160–2; A. Capron, 'Informed Consent in Catastrophic Disease Research and Treatment' (1974) 123 *University of Pennsylvania Law Review* 340, 420–1.

[30] See e.g. D. Brock and S. Wartman, 'When Competent Patients Make Irrational Choices', *New England Journal of Medicine* 322 (1990), 1595.

[31] Though purely evidential, in some American states the written consent is only rebuttable by strict proof of fraud or misrepresentation. A survey cited in *Making Health Care Decisions* found that 62% of doctors and 86% of the public believed that a patient's signature constituted consent. See n. 21 above, 108.

have remained more influenced by traditional professional ethics and accepted medical standards than by changes in legal principle of which they may be only dimly aware. They are, as it were, more familiar and comfortable with the therapeutic privilege which largely nullifies the rule than with the rule itself.[32]

In short, informed consent within a framework of objectivized, external standards in negligence, dominated in practice by the opinions of medical experts on the presumptive needs of the 'reasonable patient', has proved largely ineffective as a means of promoting the rights of real individual patients. This was a predictable outcome of key elements in *Canterbury* v. *Spence*: the doctor's duty is to disclose only the risks to which a *reasonable* patient would attach significance; the test of proximate causation is whether the '*prudent* person in the patient's position' would have agreed to treatment, and information may be withheld on grounds of 'therapeutic privilege' if, by reference to a professional judgement standard, disclosure is deemed medically contra-indicated. All this may be defensible; none of it is consistent with self-determination.[33] In the absence of patient comprehension, it is as artificial to speak of autonomy being exercised as it is in the context of trespass to claim that a patient who has not understood the risks can 'consent' to the nature of an operation. The seemingly dramatic shift away from medical paternalism in substituting the test of the 'prudent patient' for that of the 'prudent doctor' was largely illusory.

Furthermore, fears that this 'radical' doctrine would seriously exacerbate the medical malpractice 'crisis' of the mid-1970s helped generate a legislative backlash, the most conspicuous results of which have been widespread reaffirmation, or reintroduction, of the professional practice standard and the requirement of expert

---

[32] Cf. the finding that some two years after the Canadian Supreme Court's judgment on informed consent in *Reibl* v. *Hughes*, 75% of the 1,000 surgeons surveyed were unaware of the decision; of the remaining 25% only 42% said it led them to spend more time discussing risks: G. Robertson, 'Informed Consent in Canada: An Empirical Study' (1984) 22 *Osgoode Hall Law Journal* 139.

[33] Cf. 'there is, in the end, little difference between an objective patient standard and one set solely by reference to medical opinion and practice': M. Brazier, 'Patient Autonomy and Consent to Treatment: The Role of Law?' (1987) 7 *Legal Studies* 169, 187.

evidence.[34] To this day, contrary to popular belief, informed consent on a reasonable patient basis is far from being the legal norm in the United States. Mainly as a result of legislative enactments, there is a wide range of approaches. For example, a few states require only an obligation to inform the patient in general terms about the nature of the treatment; some have imposed significant statutory limitations on disclosure requirements, and a sizeable number apply the reasonable doctor standard.[35] In many jurisdictions expert medical evidence to determine whether the content of disclosure was reasonable is mandatory.

The undue stress placed by many courts on disclosure at the expense of comprehension, and on self-determination rather than on mutual participation as a rationale, served to stifle the growth of a more mature conception of informed consent based on therapeutic alliance. We noted earlier that when the transmission of information becomes too formalized and impersonal it often turns into a substitute for genuine communication. Far from inspiring confidence, it can alienate patients from physicians, so that they come to perceive the procedure itself as a defensive device to ward off potential litigation, perhaps ironically thereby making it more likely. At the same time, the rising cost of health care and the trend towards routinized, often episodic, medical encounters are increasingly invoked by critics to cast doubt on the cost-effectiveness of informed consent and on the feasibility of achieving it in a sufficiently sensitive and individualized manner.[36]

The Canadian Experience

Scepticism about the impact of informed consent as conceived in *Canterbury* is reinforced by Robertson's highly instructive account of how little its Canadian counterpart, *Reibl* v. *Hughes*, has

[34] See W. Wadlington, 'Legal Responses to Patient Injury: A Future Agenda for Research and Reform' (1991) 54(2) *Law and Contemporary Problems* 199.

[35] See D. Meyers, *The Human Body and the Law* (2nd edn.) (Edinburgh: Edinburgh University Press, 1990), ch. 5.

[36] For an illuminating recent analysis of these and other current concerns about informed consent in the USA, see P. Schuck, 'Rethinking Informed Consent' (1994) 103 *Yale Law Journal* 899.

affected either litigation or medical practice.[37] *Reibl* also effectively espoused a test for disclosure based on what a reasonable person in the patient's position would want to be told, coupled with a causation test based on whether a reasonable person in the patient's position would have accepted or declined the treatment if adequately informed. The case was decided in 1980. Assessing its impact ten years on, Robertson concluded that 'informed consent plays only a minor role in malpractice litigation, and . . . the fundamental doctrinal changes . . . far from expanding professional liability, have in fact restricted it'.[38]

In an analysis of 117 Canadian cases decided after *Reibl*, he found that the doctrine was the sole basis of the claim in only thirteen and seemed to be a subsidiary factor in the remainder. A key feature of his findings was that though most courts took an expansive view of the informational needs of the (reasonable) patient, they were generally restrictive on the causation issue, being reluctant to hold that 'reasonable' patients would have rejected recommended treatment had there been adequate disclosure of risks. Thus statistically remote risks, especially if very serious and related to elective procedures, have been deemed sufficiently material to require disclosure, and so have plausible alternative procedures. In a few cases a duty has even been cast on the doctor to ensure that the plaintiff clearly understands the information given.[39] Moreover, the acceptance of informed consent as an appropriate norm of medical practice is underlined by the negative attitude of the courts to the defence of therapeutic privilege, and by a holding that hospitals have a non-delegable duty to see that informed consent is obtained.[40] However, this responsiveness to the patient's 'right to know' is severely undermined by a strong presumption, readily reinforced by expert evidence, that reasonable patients trust their doctor: 'human nature being what it is, people tend to consent to procedures recommended by their doctors'.[41] To approach the issue in this

---

[37] G. Robertson, 'Informed Consent Ten Years Later: The Impact of *Reibl* v. *Hughes*' (1991) 70 *Canadian Bar Review* 423.   [38] Ibid. 426.

[39] *Ciarlariello* v. *Schachter* (1993) 100 DLR (4th) 609. 622–3 *per* Cory J. See also *Kellett* v. *Griesdale*, 26 June 1985, Vancouver Registry No C833053, [1985] BCD Civ 3385–09, transcript; *Schanczl* v. *Singh* [1988] 2 WWR 465, cited in Robertson, n. 37, 431.

[40] *Lachambre* v. *Nair* [1989] 2 WWR 749 (Sask QB).

[41] *Meyer Estate* v. *Rogers* (1991) 78 DLR (4th) 307 (Ont Gen Div).

way hardly accords with the spirit of *Reibl*.[42] It means that, in most cases, 'the claim for non-disclosure of information is almost doomed to fail,'[43] and paternalism reasserts itself.

The English Approach

Sidaway and its Aftermath

In *Sidaway*, a few years after the decision in *Reibl*, the English appellate courts were called upon for the first time to determine the extent of the doctor's duty of disclosure.[44] Mrs Sidaway had been partially paralysed as a result of damage to her spinal column, sustained in the course of an operation to relieve pain in her neck and shoulder. There was no question of any negligence in the performance of the operation. It did however entail a risk of spinal cord damage customarily considered by her surgeon as too slight to disclose. In view of the latter's death prior to the trial, there was little hard evidence as to exactly what had been disclosed. The judge nevertheless found on a balance of probabilities that he had explained the general nature of the operation and had mentioned the risk of damage to the nerve root, but not the danger to the spinal cord.

The expert medical witnesses were understandably reluctant to express the risks involved as precise percentages. In crude terms, however, it seems that the aggregate risk of damage to the nerve root or spinal cord, with consequences 'ranging from the mild to the catastrophic', was between 1 and 2 per cent, while the risk of damage to the spinal cord alone was specified only as being less than 1 per cent. The court accepted that the operation was one of choice, in that it could have been postponed or even refused at the price of continued and possibly increasing pain.

Although he held that Mrs Sidaway would not have consented to the operation had she been more fully informed, the judge found in favour of the defendants, on the basis that the surgeon's

[42] In European civil law jurisdictions where the test of causation is subjective, expert evidence that most patients accept a given form of treatment even after disclosure of the risks is inadmissible. D. Giesen, *International Medical Malpractice Law* (Tübingen: J. C. B. Mohr; Dordrecht: Martinus Nijhoff Publishers, 1988), 350. [43] Robertson, n. 37 above, 435.

[44] [1985] AC 871, [1984] 2 WLR 778 (CA). See H. Teff, 'Consent to Medical Procedures: Paternalism, Self-Determination or Therapeutic Alliance?' (1985) 101 *Law Quarterly Review* 432, from which much of the material on pp. 208–13 and 218–21 is drawn.

conduct would have been accepted as proper by a responsible body of skilled and experienced neuro-surgeons. He held in other words that the 'professional judgement' criterion applied to disclosure.[45] In effect the Court of Appeal took the same view, despite some not very convincing attempts to assert the law's ultimate authority in the matter.[46]

The subsequent endorsement by Lord Scarman of informed consent as expounded in *Canterbury* v. *Spence* has attracted much attention, but his approach differed markedly from that of the other Law Lords. On one level it could be interpreted as a demonstration in the medical context of his outspoken support for the 'right to know' as a democratic principle.[47] Though this is nowhere made explicit, he did, for example, observe that the patient's right to decide 'may be seen as a basic human right'.[48] At the other end of the spectrum, Lord Diplock had no doubts as to the applicability of the *Bolam* test to disclosure, and regarded any attempt to apply different criteria of liability to different aspects of the doctor's overall duty of care as 'neither legally meaningful nor medically practicable'.[49] Both of them saw adequate disclosure as an element in the doctor's duty of care.

Lord Bridge (with whom Lord Keith concurred) expressly rejected the *Canterbury* doctrine as 'quite impractical'[50] and proposed a modification to the *Bolam* test modest enough in its own terms and, it is submitted, almost indistinguishable from *Bolam* in practice. After deciding that the requisite degree of disclosure 'must primarily be a matter of clinical judgement . . .' to be determined 'primarily on the basis of expert medical evidence, applying the *Bolam* test', he suggested that there could be cases where the judge might conclude that non-disclosure was a breach of duty even where expert evidence indicated that it conformed to 'accepted and responsible medical practice'. 'The kind of case that I have in mind', he said, 'would be an operation involving a substantial risk of grave adverse consequences, as, for example, the 10 per cent risk of a stroke from the operation which

[45] Cf. *Chatterton* v. *Gerson* [1981] QB 432 and *Hills* v. *Potter* [1984] 1 WLR 641.
[46] See I. Kennedy, 'The Patient on the Clapham Omnibus' (1984) 47 *Modern Law Review* 454.
[47] Lord Scarman, 'The Right to Know', 1984 Granada Guildhall Lecture. And see *Home Office* v. *Harman* [1983] 1 AC 280, 309.
[48] *Sidaway* [1985] AC 871, 882. [49] Ibid. 893.
[50] Ibid. 899.

DLR (3d) 1 . . . [assuming] the absence of some cogent clinical reason why the patient should not be informed.'[51]

This would indeed be a case where a doctor 'could hardly fail to appreciate the necessity for an appropriate warning'.[52] But in *Reibl* v. *Hughes*, the doctor, as well as being found liable on an informed consent basis by the Supreme Court, was found liable at first instance *on a professional judgement standard*.[53] There will be very few circumstances[54] where non-disclosure of a risk which 'no reasonably prudent medical man' would fail to disclose could satisfy even the *Bolam* requirement of acting 'in accordance with a practice accepted as proper by a *responsible* body of medical men skilled in [the] particular art'.[55]

Given that Lord Bridge does envisage some departure from *Bolam*, its scope on his analysis would partly depend on what qualifies as a 'cogent clinical reason' for not informing the patient. It is unfortunate that the decision does not concern itself with the *medical* benefits associated with disclosure. When Lord Diplock baldly asserted that 'the only effect that mention of risks can have on the patient's mind, if it has any at all, can be in the direction of deterring the patient from undergoing the treatment',[56] he was overlooking its important therapeutic functions, in encouraging realistic expectations, preparing the patient emotionally and facilitating a sense of control, considerations hinted at even in the courts as long ago as 1767 in *Slater* v. *Baker*.[57] We have seen that for many patients, more especially when they are aware in broad terms that their condition is or might be serious, a medical exchange which conveys the sense of the doctor's engagement and honest appraisal is a positive experience which instils greater trust

---

[51] *Sidaway* [1985] AC 900.   [52] Ibid.

[53] '[a] matter essentially of medical judgement, one to be determined by the Court on the basis of expert medical evidence.' And '[t]he duty of the surgeon as defined by accepted general practice in the neurosurgical community': *Reibl* v. *Hughes* (1977) 78 DLR (3d) 35, 43.

[54] See A. Grubb, 'The Emergence and Rise of Medical Law and Ethics' (1987) 50 *Modern Law Review* 241, 253–5.   [55] Emphasis added.

[56] *Sidaway* [1985] AC 871, 895.

[57] 'it is reasonable that a patient should be told what is about to be done to him, that he may take courage and put himself in such a situation as to enable him to undergo the operation'. And see M. Kirby, 'Informed Consent: What does it Mean?' *Journal of Medical Ethics* 9 (1983), 69; P. Devlin, *Samples of Law Making* (Oxford: Oxford University Press, 1962), ch. 5 especially 97–9.

and confidence than vacuous reassurance. It would be salutary if judicial discussion of disclosure requirements were more informed by such findings and less influenced by unsubstantiated, intuitive assertion.

If it is accepted that patient involvement is often intrinsically therapeutic, disclosure can be seen as an integral aspect of professionalism in treatment, as itself a form of *medical* intervention, which may be desirable even when not apparently 'clinically' dictated in a narrower, technical sense. Viewed from this perspective, at least, Lord Diplock's reservations about the medical practicability of dissecting the doctor's duty of care into component parts may be justified. In fact, however, from his standpoint, the characterization of information disclosure as a technical medical concern seems rather to have been a device for restricting the scope of liability. Maintaining that the ambit of disclosure was as much a matter of professional expertise as diagnosis and treatment, so that 'expert medical evidence in this matter should be treated in just the same way', was essentially a way of avoiding what he took to be the dangerous extension of liability inflicted on the United States by the doctrine of informed consent.

Lord Templeman considered that a simple, general explanation of the nature of the operation—which was deemed to have been given—should have made it obvious to Mrs Sidaway that damage in the area of the spinal cord was possible.[58] Her failure to question the surgeon about his recommended treatment, thus entitled him to assume that, on the basis of his explanation, she regarded the risk as sufficiently remote to be ignored.[59] But to attach such significance to a patient's failure to question her surgeon is most unsatisfactory. First it ignores the fact that the average patient would commonly fail to ask relevant questions because of limited medical knowledge. More importantly, it ignores the natural inhibitions felt by most hospital patients in the presence of a surgeon—the psychological and social realities of the surgeon–patient relationship in the hospital setting, as experienced by the bulk of the population. It is revealing in this context that Lord Templeman couched his analysis in contractual terms,

---

[58] *Sidaway* [1985] AC 871, 902.   [59] Ibid. 902–3.

was the subject of the Canadian case of *Reibl* v. *Hughes* (1980) 114 despite the fact that Mrs Sidaway had been treated under the NHS.[60]

Lord Templeman went on to say that 'a doctor ought to draw the attention of a patient to a danger which may be special in kind or magnitude or special to the patient' and, like Lord Bridge, cited *Reibl* v. *Hughes* as an example.[61] Naturally it is often impossible to say in the abstract whether a particular risk is substantial enough to require disclosure. It is of interest however that the medical witnesses in *Sidaway* would all have given some warning of possible nerve root damage. If there is general agreement about the need to disclose a risk no higher than 2 per cent of minor pain and localized numbness, is there not a strong case, at least in an *elective* operation, for revealing a near 1 per cent risk of partial paralysis? The very fact that this might alarm the patient is perhaps stronger evidence of materiality than of grounds for non-disclosure. As for dangers 'special to the patient', their effective identification would often presuppose dialogue and a degree of mutuality in the relationship. Yet in the absence of questioning by the patient, Lord Templeman seems to envisage an essentially one-way process, at times conveying the impression that doctors have an intuitive grasp of their patients' 'best interests'.[62] At all events, there is little in his characterization of the doctor's 'overriding duty to have regard to the best interests of the patient' to indicate any significant departure from *Bolam*.

It is thus possible to formulate the majority holding in *Sidaway* as follows. A doctor will normally discharge the duty of disclosure by acting in accordance with a practice accepted at the time as proper by a body of skilled and experienced medical practitioners. But where there is a substantial risk of grave consequences, which no reasonably prudent doctor would fail to disclose without having a compelling clinical reason, the court may deem its disclosure to be necessary. It is immediately apparent that this formula falls far short of implementing an informed consent doctrine along *Canterbury* lines, which according to Lord Bridge was unworkable

---

[60] *Sidaway* [1985] AC 904. He also somewhat curiously maintained that the doctor's liability originated in contract.   [61] Ibid. 903.

[62] e.g. '[t]he doctor *is* able, with his medical training, with his knowledge of the patient's medical history and with his *objective* position to make a balanced judgement as to whether the operation should be performed or not': ibid. 904. Emphasis added.

and in Lord Diplock's view had a juristic basis 'contrary to English law'.

None the less, *Sidaway* has been hailed by some commentators as a landmark in the vindication of patients' rights, signalling an end to judicial endorsement of medical paternalism. Certainly it is noteworthy for the extent to which it proclaims the importance of the patient as person. In varying degrees, the speeches of all the Law Lords purport—within a negligence framework—to explain the doctor's duty to warn in terms of the patient's right to decide. Lord Scarman, in addition to viewing the doctor's duty of care as embracing 'a proper respect for his patient's rights',[63] spoke of 'the existence of the patient's right to make his own decision, which may be seen as a basic human right protected by the common law',[64] Lord Templeman referred to 'the patient's right of information which will enable the patient to make a balanced judgement',[65] and Lord Bridge said that 'in . . . an operation involving a substantial risk of grave adverse consequences . . . in the absence of some cogent clinical reason why the patient should not be informed, a doctor, recognizing and respecting his patient's right of decision, could hardly fail to appreciate the necessity for an appropriate warning'.[66] A failure to warn in such circumstances 'would effectively exclude the patient's right to decide in the very type of case where it is most important that he should be in a position to exercise that right'.[67] Lord Diplock, too, sensed a rights dimension, albeit somewhat limited in scope, when he ventured the thought that 'the kind of training and experience that a judge will have undergone at the Bar makes it natural for him to say (correctly) it is my right to decide whether any particular thing is done to my body, and I want to be fully informed of any risks'.[68]

That said, *Sidaway* is more significant for what is ultimately the inability of the judges to break loose from the received wisdom of 'doctor knows best'. Though conscious of changes in social attitudes towards medical relationships, several of the judges in both the Court of Appeal and the House of Lords seemed to find it difficult to abandon the assumption that a doctor's training and instinct provide a sure and authoritative guide to the patient's best interests. Many of the sentiments which they expressed suggest a

---

[63] Ibid. 885. [64] Ibid. 882. [65] Ibid. 905.
[66] Ibid. 900. [67] Ibid. 898. [68] Ibid. 895.

belief that communication, when needed at all, is essentially a matter of the doctor telling things to an attentive patient.[69] For professionals perpetually engaged in the sifting and weighing of evidence, judges are noticeably prone to resort to conventional assumptions about medical practice. In *Sidaway* they at times embrace the language of patient autonomy, but their hearts do not really seem to be in it.[70] In this respect there is a parallel with the way doctors, too, may be fully committed to the need for scientific and rational inquiry on technical medical issues, yet remain resistant to empirical findings which point to the preference of many patients for dialogue and the benefits which it has to offer.

The dominant message to emerge from *Sidaway* is not identical with that of *Bolam*, but it is much closer to the *Bolam* end of the spectrum than to a patients' rights model of disclosure. Lord Scarman, speaking *ex cathedra*, subsequently described the majority position[71] as 'that very tentative move away from what some of us had seen as a predominance of power vested in the doctor'.[72] Any belief that a substantial shift had occurred was soon to be dispelled. *Bolam* was strongly reaffirmed in two subsequent Court of Appeal decisions, where, on the facts, the arguments in favour of enhanced disclosure seemed particularly strong. In *Gold*, the plaintiff was described by the judge at first instance as 'a perfectly normal sensible woman with no particular psychiatric

[69] See e.g. n. 62 above, *per* Lord Templeman. Cf. 'matters which the doctor *will* have taken into consideration in determining, in the exercise of his professional skill and judgement, that it is in the patient's interests that he should take the risk involved and undergo the treatment recommended by the doctor'. Emphasis added. Ibid. 891, *per* Lord Diplock, and compounded by his ill-informed, open invitation to doctors *not* to disclose: 'The only effect that mention of risks can have on the patient's mind, if it has any at all, can be in the direction of deterring the patient from undergoing the treatment which in the expert opinion of the doctor it is in the patient's interest to undergo': Ibid. 895. Cf. in the Court of Appeal, Lord Donaldson's reference to determining the patient's 'true interests', Lord Justice Dunn's assumption that most patients 'prefer to put themselves unreservedly in the hands of their doctors', and the view of Browne-Wilkinson LJ that 'in relation to doctors the duty to disclose should be approached on a different basis from that applicable to ordinary professional men' such that 'all questions of disclosure will be decided by reference to the practice of the profession', subject only to account being taken of the patient's particular circumstances.

[70] As we have seen, Lord Scarman tempers his rights-based analysis with a 'reasonable' patient test as regards both disclosure and causation.

[71] i.e. of Lords Bridge, Keith, and Templeman.

[72] 'Consent, Communication and Responsibility', *Journal of the Royal Society of Medicine* 79 (1986), 697.

social or medical problems'[73] who agreed to be sterilized. The failure to tell her that the alternative of male vasectomy carried a smaller risk of reversal[74] was not deemed to be negligent, because of expert evidence that at the time (1979) some (responsible) gynæcologists would not have provided this information. Despite Schiemann J's persuasive rejection of *Bolam* on the ground that there was no 'cogent clinical reason' for non-disclosure in this non-therapeutic context, all three members of the Court of Appeal adopted the most uncompromising position to emerge from *Sidaway*, as embodied in Lord Diplock's judgment.[75] Their approach was very much at odds with Lord Donaldson's observation that, 'what the patient needs to have placed fairly before him or her are the alternatives'.[76] In *Blyth*, too, the Court of Appeal rejected the lower court's refusal to be bound by the *Bolam* test, even though the plaintiff, a trained nurse, had apparently asked for a considerable amount of information and advice. According to Kerr LJ, 'the question of what a patient should be told in answer to a general enquiry cannot be divorced from the *Bolam* test, any more than when no such enquiry is made'.[77]

Inferring from Lord Templeman's speech in *Sidaway* that 'the *Bolam* test is all-pervasive in this context', Kerr LJ continued:

Indeed I am not convinced that the Bolam test is irrelevant even in relation to the question of what answers are properly to be given to specific enquiries, or that Lord Diplock or Lord Bridge intended to hold otherwise. It seems to me that there may always be grey areas, with differences of opinion, as to what are the proper answers to be given to any enquiry, even a specific one, in the particular circumstances of any case.[78]

Lord Bridge did say in *Sidaway* that when questioned specifically about risks, 'the doctor's duty must . . . be to answer both

---

[73] *Gold* v. *Haringey Health Authority* [1987] 1 FLR 125, 140.
[74] 12 times less risky.
[75] *Gold* v. *Haringey Health Authority* [1988] QB 481.
[76] *Sidaway* [1984] 2 WLR 778, 792.
[77] *Blyth* v. *Bloomsbury Health Authority* [1993] 4 Med LR 151, 157. Cf. 'the amount of information to be given must depend upon the circumstances, and as a general proposition it is governed by what is called the Bolam test': Ibid. 160 (case decided 1987).
[78] Ibid. 157. Cf. 'this duty is subject to the exercise of clinical judgement as to the terms in which the information is given and the extent to which, in the patient's interests, information should be withheld': *Lee* v. *South West Thames Regional Health Authority* [1985] 1 WLR 845, 850, *per* Lord Donaldson MR (obiter).

truthfully and as fully as the questioner requires'.[79] However, like all the comments in the case about how to respond to inquiries, this was only obiter. Lord Diplock rather vaguely observed that, 'no doubt . . . the doctor would tell him whatever it was the patient wanted to know'.[80] But, at the outset of his speech, he made it clear that the *'clinical* judgement' which a neuro-surgeon would have to exercise in response to questions (emphasis added) is subject to the 'paramount duty of care' to 'exercise his skill and judgement in endeavouring to heal'.[81]

The treatment in English law of the doctor's duty in regard to specific questions encapsulates, perhaps more. than any other issue, the lack of nexus between the patients' rights model and orthodox negligence theory. In general, the right to have a straight answer to a straight question about one's health is morally compelling.[82] But we ought not to find the approach taken in *Blyth* surprising; rather it is almost a necessary consequence of legal categorization, that is, of inquiring whether the doctor has acted 'negligently' in this aspect of attending to patients. Under the *Bolam* test, the enquiring patient is no more entitled to an honest answer than is the non-enquiring patient entitled to information beyond what the test entails.[83] Within a negligence framework, patients are not entitled to information as such. That said, because doctors know that most, if not all, patients are concerned about the risks of treatment, determining whether or not non-disclosure is negligent should not depend simply on whether the concerns of patients have been articulated, or on their precise locutions and the degree of specificity in their questions.[84]

---

[79] [1985] AC 871, 898.   [80] Ibid. 895.   [81] Ibid. 891.

[82] Cf. 'this decision [*Blyth*] may seem surprising in the light of the dicta in *Sidaway*, and may leave patients wondering just what they have to do in order to obtain full and truthful information': Jones, *Medical Negligence*, n. 3 above, 249. And see J. Montgomery, 'Power/Knowledge/Consent: Medical Decisionmaking' (1988) 51 *Modern Law Review* 245, 248.

[83] Cf. 'there may be circumstances in which reasonable care for the patient may justify or even require an evasive or less than fully candid answer even to a direct request': *F* v. *R* (1983) 33 SASR 189, 192, *per* King CJ. See also *Rogers* v. *Whitaker* (1992) 67 ALJR 47, 50. On the other hand, a deliberate lie or deliberate evasiveness about risks will sometimes negate consent for the purposes of an action in battery: see Jones, *Medical Negligence*, 214–15.

[84] See especially *Rogers* v. *Whitaker* (1992) 67 ALJR 47, 53: 'the opinion that the respondent should have been told of the dangers of sympathetic ophthalmia only if she had been sufficiently learned to ask the precise question seems curious'.

If further evidence of the resilience of *Bolam* were needed, Lord Caplan's judgment in the Scottish case of *Moyes* v. *Lothian* supplies it in abundance:

In my view the *Sidaway* case in no way alters the pre-existing view of the law that the appropriate tests to apply in medical negligence cases are to be found in *Hunter* v. *Hanley* and *Bolam*. Indeed the majority of the court in *Sidaway* confirmed specifically that the *Bolam* test applies not only to cases of treatment and diagnosis but to cases where advice is not tendered.[85]

Significantly, he added that he could see:

nothing in the majority view in *Sidaway* which suggests that the extent and quality of warning to be given by a doctor to his patient should not *in the last resort* be governed by medical criteria. The risks inherent in a particular operation or procedure, the manner in which the operation may affect or damage a particular patient, the medical need for the operation and the ability of the patient to absorb information about his situation without adding damage to his health, are all matters where the doctor, with his own clinical experience and the benefit of the experience of other practitioners, is best able to form a judgement as to what the patient can safely be told in the exercise of medical care.[86]

This reassertion of almost unalloyed medical paternalism was endorsed not long afterwards in another Scottish decision.[87] In 1988, Kennedy concluded that 'the message of *Sidaway* is clear . . . Medical paternalism has had its day.'[88] The general direction of recent case law would suggest that this was a premature conclusion. As Lord Scarman himself said a little while after the decision in *Sidaway*, the speeches of Lord Bridge (Lord Keith concurring) and Lord Templeman 'were perhaps truer to the spirit of English law than I was'.[89]

---

[85] [1990] 1 Med LR 463, 469.

[86] Ibid. Emphasis added.

[87] *Gordon* v. *Wilson* 1992 SLT 849, 852: 'In my opinion nothing in the speech of Lord Bridge was intended to qualify the *Bolam* test. That was the view taken by Lord Caplan in *Moyes* and I respectfully agree with his comments.' Cf. *King* v. *King* (CA), 9 April 1987, Lexis transcript, where Croom-Johnson J refers to the Bolam test as having been 'adopted' in *Sidaway*.

[88] I. Kennedy, *Treat Me Right* (Oxford: Oxford University Press, 1988), 210.

[89] 'Consent, Communication and Responsibility', *Journal of the Royal Society of Medicine*, n. 72 above, 697.

A 'Fiduciary' Duty to Disclose?

From the perspective of enhanced medical relationships, *Sidaway* was a disappointing decision. The majority essentially reaffirmed the paternalism of *Bolam*; while Lord Scarman forced a diluted patients' rights formula into a negligence framework. The former approach minimizes the collaborative potential of the medical exchange; the latter, in emphasizing rights, could also impede it. The one line of argument advanced on behalf of the plaintiff which, at first sight, captures the spirit of therapeutic alliance predictably failed. This was the claim that the surgeon, in advising Mrs Sidaway, was a 'quasi-trustee'[90] and as such had a duty to disclose all material facts to the patient by virtue of their 'fiduciary' relationship.

In so far as it was expressed as a claim for equitable relief, drawing on notions of fiduciary duty and the presumption of undue influence,[91] the argument was not legally compelling. It is one thing to set aside an excessive medical account,[92] as in the case of, say, any unconscionable financial transaction. Equally, one could envisage a doctor who has benefited financially from prescribing a new drug, or by referring a patient to a particular institution, being held to account for failing to declare an interest. In 1990, the California Supreme Court recognized a cause of action for breach of fiduciary duty when a doctor failed to disclose pre-existing research and commercial interests in a patient's cells prior to performing certain medical procedures,[93] even if it did reject his three billion dollar damages claim, largely on the basis that he had not suffered an infringement of property rights.[94] By

---

[90] *Sidaway* [1985] AC 871, 874, *arguendo*. Cf. *Hedley Byrne & Co. Ltd* v. *Heller & Partners* [1965] AC 465, 485–6. *per* Lord Reid.

[91] See *Nocton* v. *Lord Ashburton* [1914] AC 932.

[92] *Billage* v. *Southee* (1852) 9 Hare 534.

[93] 'A physician who is seeking a patient's consent for a medical procedure must, in order to satisfy his fiduciary duty to obtain the patient's informed consent, disclose personal interests unrelated to the patient's health, whether research or economic, that may affect his medical judgement': *Moore* v. *Regents of the University of California*, 793 P 2d 479, 485 (1990).

[94] See S. Perley, 'From Control over one's Body to Control over one's Body Parts: Extending the Doctrine of Informed Consent' (1992) 67 *New York University Law Review* 335, arguing that the right to self-determination involves more than a narrow interest in bodily integrity and should cover broader dignitary interests in one's body and body parts, and hence a right to control what happens to excised tissues and cells, i.e. wholly independent of any possible technical property right.

extrapolation, and more controversially, perhaps there is scope for fiduciary analysis where doctors, anxious about jeopardizing their future employment, allow their clinical judgement to be unduly influenced by the budgetary priorities of the hospital manager. But it is quite different to assert that the doctrine of fiduciary relationships routinely requires informed consent to medical treatment. Unsurprisingly, the Court of Appeal in *Sidaway* restated the orthodox position, confining the obligation of full disclosure to situations involving the disposition of property, typically where the defendant has abused a position of trust in order to make a personal profit.[95]

It is true that in *Canterbury* v. *Spence* the court referred to the 'fiducial qualities' of the doctor–patient relationship, describing the patient's reliance on the doctor for information about risks as a 'trust of the kind which has traditionally exacted obligations beyond those associated with arm's-length transactions'.[96] But the authority cited in the case to this effect concerned non-disclosure of medical records to a deceased man's son as a form of concealed fraud in a dispute over limitation of actions.[97] As in several other American cases which refer to the relationship between doctor and patient as a 'fiduciary' one,[98] it was the interest in being able to bring suit which was the nub of the issue, not a general entitlement to information about treatment. References to a fiduciary relationship in leading Canadian decisions on the scope of the disclosure requirement are equally unavailing. At most one finds an expectation of honesty on the part of the surgeon, coupled with some loose extrapolation from *Nocton* v. *Ashburton* of the very kind which was summarily dismissed in *Sidaway*.[99] In *Kenny* v.

---

[95] *Sidaway* [1984] 2 WLR 778, 793–4, *per* Dunn LJ and 796–7, *per* Browne-Wilkinson LJ. Cf. *Sidaway* [1985] AC 871, 884, *per* Lord Scarman.

[96] 464 F 2d 772, 782 (1972), *per* Robinson J. Cf. *Truman* v. *Thomas*, 611 P 2d 902 (1980), where the court recognized a duty of informed refusal of medical care, on the basis that the doctor had a fiduciary duty to disclose the risks of declining therapy; and see *Moore*, n. 93 above.

[97] *Emmett* v. *Eastern Dispensary and Casualty Hospital*, 396 F 2d 931, 935 (1967).

[98] e.g. *Sheets* v. *Burman*, 322 F 2d 277, 279–80 (5th Cir, 1963); *Guy* v. *Schuldt*, 236 Ind 101, 138 NE 2d 891, 895 (1956); *Perrin* v. *Rodriguez* 155 So 555, 556–7 (La App, 1934).

[99] e.g. *Hopp* v. *Lepp* (1986) 112 DLR (3rd) 67, 75–7; *Reibl* v. *Hughes* (1980) 114 DLR (3rd) 1, 7.

Lockwood, a Canadian case which examined this issue at length, Fisher JA put the matter as follows:

There can be no doubt that a medical man, placed in a position of trust and confidence towards his patient, in connection with a patient's property, requires from the medical man the same degree of good faith and conduct which the law requires shall subsist between trustee and *cestui que trust*, or a solicitor and client, and any other relations of the same character. But that principle does not in my opinion apply to a properly qualified physician or surgeon who has exercised ordinary care and skill towards a patient who has consulted him in connection with any bodily ailment.

It is quite conceivable that one surgeon might point out both sides of the question and give the patient the opportunity of electing, while another surgeon, equally careful and skilful, would not think it advisable to point out all the possibilities and probabilities and the serious consequences incidental to an operation, and to hold that if a physician or surgeon did not do so was a breach of duty would, in my opinion, be imposing upon them an unwarranted responsibility not justified by any decided authority that I have been able to find.[100]

Precedent apart, the fiduciary duty analysis does have a superficial appeal. Doctors, as professionals entrusted with our health, are seen and see themselves as having 'fiduciary' obligations regarding our welfare. This 'very special' relationship[101] can be characterized as 'fiduciary' because of its confidential nature and the doctor's superior expertise and potential for exercising disproportionate control over someone in a state of dependency. In particular, there is the natural urge to argue that if such a doctrine can be invoked in respect of property interests it should, by the close of the twentieth century, cover bodily integrity. Had not Blackstone identified malpractice as a wrong because 'it breaks the trust which the party placed in his physician'?[102] In *Norberg* v. *Wynrib*,[103] the Canadian Supreme Court found a doctor who traded prescriptions for sex liable in battery, on the basis that consent was negated by the equitable doctrine of unconscionable transactions. This doctrine had previously been confined to setting aside unconscionable contracts, in order to

---

[100] [1932] 1 DLR 507, 528.   [101] *Sidaway* [1985] AC 871, 884.
[102] *Commentaries* (19th edn.) (London: Sweet & Maxwell and Stevens & Sons, 1836), 3, 122.   [103] (1992) 92 DLR (4th) 449.

redress inequality of bargaining power and unfairness; it had not been thought of as negating consent. Though the majority did not expressly refer to fiduciary duty, McLachlin J did see it as the basis of the liability.[104]

Yet the appeal remains superficial. Certainly it would be difficult to justify extending fiduciary analysis along such lines in the quest for a therapeutic alliance. Ironically, its deployment could have a negative effect in this respect. To insist that the fiduciary element in medical relationships renders consent invalid for want of full or extensive disclosure would logically, but inappropriately, breathe new life into the trespass action,[105] by requiring more than that the patient be 'informed in broad terms of the nature of the procedure which is intended'.[106] At the same time, the fiduciary concept can assist therapeutic alliance only if it does entail extensive disclosure and communication. However, the medical relationship is distinguishable from other relationships treated in equity as of a fiduciary nature by the extent to which good faith permits non-disclosure. Honesty and good faith on the part of the doctor are compatible with a large measure of paternalism. To concentrate on fiduciary obligation in equity is to risk being distracted both from the paucity of precedent and the inadequacy of the concept in characterizing the relevant duty.[107] For what is primarily at stake in this 'very special' relationship is a duty rooted in the doctor's obligation of reasonable care and skill in attending to the health and well-being of the patient.

---

[104] 'I do not find that the doctrines of tort or contract capture the essential nature of the wrong done . . . Only the principles applicable to fiduciary relationships and their breach encompass it in its totality': ibid. 484, *per* McLachlin J. In her view, trust, not self-interest, was at the core of the fiduciary relationship (485–9), and fiduciary obligations were capable of protecting not only narrow legal and economic interests, but also fundamental human and personal ones (499). Cf. *McInerney* v. *MacDonald* (1992) 93 DLR 415, where the Supreme Court of Canada upheld a patient's claim for access to records that her current doctor had received from previous ones. The doctor–patient relationship was described as a fiduciary one based on trust and confidence, such that the defendant held the records in trust for the benefit of the plaintiff, whose [equitable] 'beneficial interest' entitled her to access: see further, R. Tjiong, 'Are Physicians Fiduciaries?' (1993) 67 *Australian Law Journal* 436.

[105] See ch. 4 above. Cf. *Sidaway* [1984] 2 WLR 778, 797, *per* Browne-Wilkinson LJ.   [106] *Chatterton* v. *Gerson* [1981] QB 432, 443.

[107] See P. Finn, 'Good Faith and Non-Disclosure' in Finn (ed.), *Essays on Torts* (Sydney: Law Book Company, 1989) ch. 7 especially at 164–6.

Rogers v. *Whitaker*

Sidaway itself, and even more so the subsequent decisions on disclosure, represent a reassertion of professional autonomy at the very time that professionals, both in medicine and elsewhere, are being subjected to more and more external scrutiny. It runs counter to the temper of the times that the standards that any professional group adheres to or professes should be taken on trust. *Bolam* is ripe for reappraisal and in any such process the recent decision by the High Court of Australia in *Rogers* v. *Whitaker*[108] could prove to be a turning point. The patient in the case, who was almost blind in one eye, was advised by her surgeon that he could operate on it to remove scar tissue and improve her sight. She 'incessantly questioned' him about possible complications. She also expressed concern about the danger of unintended or accidental interference with her 'good' eye, though without specifically asking whether it could be adversely affected by the operation. There was normally only a 1 in 14,000 chance of this happening (sympathetic ophthalmia), though the risk was 'slightly greater' if, as in her case, the eye to be operated on had previously suffered a penetrating injury. The surgeon made no reference to the risk. In the event, though the operation was conducted with appropriate care and skill, the patient did develop sympathetic ophthalmia and within a year or so became virtually blind. Despite the extreme remoteness of the risk; the fact that she had not asked about it in terms, and the submission of expert evidence to the effect that some reputable practitioners would not have mentioned it unless explicitly asked,[109] it was held that the failure to warn constituted a breach of the duty of care.

The Court endorsed the concept of the 'single comprehensive duty' of due care but, as to its discharge, saw the issue of disclosure as involving considerations different from those applicable to matters of diagnosis and treatment. It was a question 'of a different order'.[110] Interestingly, as well as repudiating the *Bolam* test outright as regards disclosure, the Court expressed distinct reservations about its applicability to diagnosis and treatment:

---

[108] [1992] ALJR 47 (High Court);[1992] 3 Med LR 331 (SC of NSW (CA).
[109] All would have done so if asked.   [110] [1992] ALJR 47, 52.

In Australia . . . [the] standard is not determined solely or even primarily by reference to the practice followed or supported by a responsible body of opinion in the relevant profession or trade. Even in the sphere of diagnosis and treatment, the heartland of the skilled medical practitioner the *Bolam* principle has not always been applied. Further, and more importantly, particularly in the field of non-disclosure of risk and the provision of advice and information, the *Bolam* principle has been discarded and, instead, the courts have adopted the principle that . . . it is for the courts to adjudicate on what is the appropriate standard of care.[111]

Gaudron J (in a concurring opinion) was especially forthright:

. . . even in the area of diagnosis and treatment there is, in my view, no legal basis for limiting liability in terms of the rule known as 'the *Bolam* test'.[112] . . . even in cases of that kind, the nature of particular risks and their foreseeability are not matters exclusively within the province of medical knowledge or expertise. Indeed . . . they are often matters of simple commonsense.[113]

As regards disclosure, she went as far as to say that normally 'there is simply no occasion to consider the practice or practices of medical practitioners in determining what information should be supplied', since this will depend on the 'needs, concerns, and circumstances of the patient'.[114]

The Court held that (subject to therapeutic privilege) a doctor has a duty to warn of material risks on a reasonable patient basis; that is, where 'a reasonable person in the patient's position, if warned of the risk, would be likely to attach significance to it (or if the medical practitioner is or should reasonably be aware that the particular patient, if warned of the risk, would be likely to attach significance to it)'.[115] In effect, the Court was saying that the *Canterbury* test was applicable whether or not questions had been asked. It noted that it 'would be reasonable for a person with one good eye to be concerned about the possibility of injury to it from a procedure which was elective',[116] and that the patient had in fact indicated concern, albeit of a general nature, to that effect. In addition, though this was not in issue before the High Court, in the

---

[111] Ibid. Joint judgment of Mason, Brennan, Dawson, Toohey and McHugh JJ, 50–1, citing *Albrighton v Royal Prince Alfred Hospital* [1980] 2 NSWLR 542, 562–3; *F* v. *R* (1983) 33 SASR 189, 196, 200, 202, 205; *Battersby* v. *Tottman* (1985) 37 SASR 524, 527, 534, 539–40; *E* v. *Australian Red Cross* (1991) 27 FCR 310, 357–60.
[112] Ibid. 54.   [113] Ibid.   [114] Ibid.
[115] Ibid. 52.   [116] Ibid. 53.

courts below the test for causation was held to be subjective,[117] making for a lighter burden of proof than patients must discharge in Canada and many United States jurisdictions.

The view, clearly expressed in the appeal to the Australian High Court, that the facts of the case exposed the limitations of the *Bolam* test, had been equally evident in the Supreme Court of New South Wales. There much emphasis was laid on what a *reasonable* medical practitioner should have done.[118] In the words of Mahoney JA, 'the reasonable person whose response is the test in law of these matters . . . would, I think, have expected that the response of her medical practitioner to her persistent enquiries would be to warn her of a complication apt to send her blind'.[119] 'As a matter of common sense', said Handley JA, 'a patient . . . who was interested in complications affecting her bad eye would be even more interested in complications affecting her good eye.' And again, 'this is a simple case which is not governed, and which ought not to be governed by the *Bolam* test'.[120]

NEGLIGENCE AS THE APPROPRIATE CATEGORY

Courts in a number of United States jurisdictions, in Canada, and Australia[121] have so defined the standard of care required of a doctor as to entail disclosure of risks (and of alternative procedures) to which a reasonable patient would be likely to attach significance in deciding whether or not to undergo the proposed treatment. We have seen that in much of the case law, the underlying rationale

[117] *Rogers* v. *Whitaker* [1992] 3 Med LR 331, 340–1. Cf. *F* v. *R* (1983) 33 SASR 189. And see D. Chalmers and R. Schwartz, '*Rogers* v. *Whitaker* and Informed Consent in Australia' (1993) 1 *Medical Law Review* 139, 154–6.

[118] As a specific instance of the general principle in negligence: see *Wyong Shire Council* v. *Shirt* (1980) 146 CLR 40.

[119] [1992] 3 Med LR 331, 335. 'the surgery was elective and not provoked by a significant need. The complication involved, sympathetic ophthalmia, was apt to be catastrophic: she could become blind' (334). 'That was the kind of complication which was peculiarly likely to influence her judgment whether to undergo the procedures' (335). Cf. 'there was no therapeutic reason for not disclosing it', *per* Handley JA (339). Cf. Schiemann J in *Gold* v. *Haringey Health Authority* [1987] 1 FLR 125.   [120] Ibid.

[121] As well as in several civil law jurisdictions. See D. Giesen, 'Vindicating the Patient's Rights: A Comparative Perspective' (1993) 9 *Journal of Contemporary Health Law and Policy* 273, 292–306.

has been expressed in terms of the patient's right to self-determination.[122] *Rogers* v. *Whitaker* derives much of its inspiration from this body of case law. The High Court noted that, as regards disclosure, Australia has adopted the principle that it is for the courts to adjudicate on the standard of care, 'after giving weight to "the paramount consideration that a person is entitled to make his own decisions about his life" '.[123] However, it is instructive that the High Court itself was later at pains to disavow the rationale of self-determination in respect of the duty to disclose:

In this context, nothing is to be gained by reiterating the expressions used in American authorities, such as 'the patient's right of self-determination' . . . [an expression] which is, perhaps, suitable to cases where the issue is whether a person has agreed to the general surgical procedure or treatment, but is of little assistance in the balancing process that is involved in the determination of whether there has been a breach of the duty of disclosure. Likewise the phrase 'informed consent' is apt to mislead as it suggests a test of the validity of a patient's consent. Moreover, consent is relevant to actions framed in trespass, not in negligence.[124]

Plainly the court was unhappy with the tension between patient self-determination and negligence, especially given its acceptance that 'material' disclosure should be confined to what the 'reasonable person in the patient's position' would want to know.

Meanwhile, English law retains its paternalistic reasonable doctor test, maintaining that it is the doctor's duty which is in issue and that judgement of how much disclosure this duty demands is essentially a matter for medical professional expertise. It is common ground among paternalists and advocates of a more collaborative approach that what the doctor tells the patient and how they interact are aspects of the treatment which affect the

---

[122] e.g. Robinson J, 'it is the prerogative of the patient, not the physician, to determine for himself the direction in which his interests seem to lie': *Canterbury* v. *Spence*, 464 F 2d 772, 781 (1972). Cf. 'what is under consideration here is the patient's right to know what risks are involved in undergoing or foregoing certain surgery or other treatment': *Reibl* v. *Hughes* (1980) 114 DLR (3d), 1, 13, *per* Laskin CJC; 'the right of every human being to make decisions which affect his own life and welfare and to determine the risks which he is willing to undertake': *F* v. *R* (1983) 33 SASR 189, 192, *per* King CJ.

[123] i.e. citing King CJ's comment in *F* v. *R*, n. 122, 193.

[124] [1992] 67 ALJR 47, 52.

patient's condition. Modern medical thinking suggests that, in general, enhanced disclosure and communication are beneficial elements in the healing process, which should at least genuinely be on offer. In his judgment in *Sidaway*, Lord Diplock described the *Bolam* test as 'laying down a principle of English law that is comprehensive and applicable to every aspect of the duty of care owed by a doctor to his patient *in the exercise of his healing functions* as respects that patient'.[125] We have argued that in so far as the absence of disclosure and communication connotes inadequate medical 'treatment', it should, in the name of patient welfare, be seen as a derogation from the standard of care required by the law of negligence, the only realistic category for resolving the overwhelming majority of disputes concerned with medical injury.[126]

Whatever the difficulties of analysing the duty to disclose as a negligence issue,[127] it is evident that even in English law *some* degree of non-disclosure is negligent, namely non-disclosure of those risks which, under the *Bolam* test, all responsible doctors would divulge. The difficulty with this formula is its lack of any substantive content. It merely asserts that there is an irreducible minimum standard of responsible medical conduct. The *Bolam* test as it currently operates remains an obstacle to judicial endorsement of the therapeutic alliance model.[128] Defendants can still often find '*a* responsible body of medical opinion' which considers minimal dialogue and disclosure consistent with 'proper practice.' Is there no way round this apparent impasse?

It is submitted that there is, and that it can be derived from *Sidaway*. The value of the *Bolam* test, in the words of Lord Diplock, 'is that it brings up to date and re-expresses in the light of

[125] *Sidaway* [1985] AC 871, 893–4. Emphasis added. Interestingly, in the extract from Lord Diplock's speech which Lloyd LJ quotes in *Gold* v. *Haringey AHA* [1988] QB 481, 487, when applying the *Bolam* test to the provision of non-therapeutic contraceptive advice, the above passage is not included.

[126] Cf. when Lord Donaldson suggested that doctors owe their patients a 'duty of candid disclosure', he said that it was 'but one aspect of the general duty of care, arising out of the patient–medical practitioner or hospital authority relationship and gives rise to rights both in contract and in tort': *Naylor* v. *Preston AHA* [1987] 1 WLR 958, 967.

[127] *Smith* v. *Auckland Hospital Board* [1964] NZLR 241, see ch. 5 above; cf. *Sidaway* [1985] AC 871, 894, *per* Lord Diplock.

[128] See M. Brazier, 'Patient Autonomy and Consent to Treatment: The Role of Law?', n. 33 above, 189–91.

modern conditions in which the art of medicine is now practised an ancient rule of common law'.[129] Medical practices, as he indicates, 'are likely to alter with advances in medical knowledge'. Among those advances is a substantial body of research findings to the effect that better-informed patients typically benefit both psychologically and clinically. In *Sidaway*, the House of Lords clearly endorsed Lord Donaldson's view that ultimately the courts, and not medical witnesses, are the arbiters of liability for negligence.[130] He had been at pains to modify the *Bolam* test in the context of disclosure by the 'important caveat' that the doctor must act 'in accordance with a practice *rightly* accepted as proper'.[131] To indicate what he considered the law would recognize as constituting a 'rightly' accepted or 'proper' medical practice, he expressed the doctor's general duty as follows:

to take such action by way of giving or withholding information as is reasonable in all the circumstances of which the doctor knows or ought to know, including the patient's true wishes, with a view to placing the patient in a position to make a rational choice whether or not to accept the doctor's recommendation.[132]

In similar vein, Browne-Wilkinson LJ proffered a modification of *Bolam* in asserting that a doctor's 'omission to disclose risks could not be justified solely by reference to a practice of the profession which does not rely on the circumstances of the particular patient'.[133] Lord Templeman stated that 'a doctor ought to draw the attention of a patient to a danger which may be . . . special to the patient'.[134] It is not easy to see how an adequate attempt to assess the patient's 'true wishes', the 'circumstances of the particular patient' or dangers 'special to the patient' can be made except within the framework of a genuinely collaborative approach. In the words of Browne-Wilkinson LJ, 'the law should establish that there is a prima facie duty to inform'.[135] It is submitted that a modern fault-based conception of medical negligence should, and can, incorporate an expectation of dialogue and disclosure before decision-making as a norm of good

---

[129] *Sidaway* [1985] AC 871, 892.
[130] Ibid. 900, *per* Lord Bridge.
[131] *Sidaway* [1984] 2 WLR 778, 792.
[132] Ibid. 791.
[133] Ibid. 800.
[134] *Sidaway* [1985] AC 871, 903.
[135] *Sidaway* [1984] 2 WLR 778, 801.

medical practice, subject only to waiver and a narrowly-defined doctrine of therapeutic privilege to withhold information detrimental to health. In English law, though there is no specific defence of 'therapeutic privilege' as such, it is implicit in the doctor's right to exercise clinical judgement about whether or not to disclose. Just as therapeutic privilege makes little sense except by reference to the anticipated reactions of the *particular* patient, so, too, 'material' disclosure must have regard to the particular patient. The doctor must do what is reasonable *in the circumstances*, and, as was recognized in *Rogers* v. *Whitaker*, the characteristics of the particular patient are a key facet of them.

It is no doubt a natural impulse to see the patient's interest in disclosure as rooted in rights, but if, as Lord Scarman grants, it can only be adequately protected within the framework of negligence, it is more natural to think of it as a welfare interest embodied in and helping to shape the standard of care expected of the responsible doctor. English medical law lost its way by identifying that standard so strongly with customary practice as to dispense with the focus on the particular patient which, properly understood, reasonableness in the circumstances entails. In *Rogers* v. *Whitaker*, it was said that:

even if a court were satisfied that a reasonable person in the patient's position would be unlikely to attach significance to a particular risk, the fact that the patient asked questions revealing concern about the risk would make the doctor aware that *this patient* did in fact attach significance to the risk. Subject to the therapeutic privilege, the question would therefore require a truthful answer.[136]

The focus here on the particular patient is to be welcomed, but it would be unfortunate if the scope of the doctor's obligations were too narrowly defined by reference to whether or not the patient has asked questions. As a minimum, reasonable care entails the doctor being amenable to dialogue with a view to eliciting the true wishes of the particular patient. By definition, this involves a subjective element. It is wholly consonant with the orthodox understanding of reasonable care in negligence to maintain that doctors have an obligation to involve their patients. Such an obligation can scarcely be considered less obviously a part of their professional role than some of the moral functions which the

[136] [1992] 67 ALJR 50.

courts have been content to define as within their remit. It is both perfectly intelligible and consistent with general negligence principles to say that the doctor's duty is to make such disclosure as is reasonable in the circumstances, that is, given what has emerged in the context of an appropriately collaborative relationship. It is *more* consistent with the historical development of malpractice liability to measure the doctor's duty of *care* by the standard of ordinary reasonableness in the circumstances than by professional custom. If, as we have maintained, it is medically desirable for doctors to be open to the pursuit of therapeutic alliance, the standard *of* reasonable care is also a standard *for* reasonable care.

7

Providing Reasonable Care

The healing relationship in which doctors and patients are ideally involved has to take account of what doctors can in practice deliver, given the internal constraints and external pressures to which they are subject. If one thing is clear about medical treatment, it is that we would prefer to receive it from doctors than from bioethicists, health economists, or lawyers. The effectiveness of any proposed change in the way medical relationships are conceived, whether legally mandated or promulgated by official bodies within the profession, is heavily dependent on the co-operation of individual practitioners. This is far more likely to be forthcoming if they are genuinely persuaded that proposals can be justified in therapeutic terms. One does not have to be as protective of doctors as Lord Denning was to recognize that the quality of medical care will suffer if those engaged in the highly practical activity of providing it have no faith in what they are doing; if they are required to modify tried and tested routines in ways which they think of as unhelpful to patients and, perhaps, as constituting an implicit challenge to their professionalism and the core values of their calling.

We have argued that the collaborative approach is distinctive in seeking to deepen medical relationships by encouraging genuine participation for those patients who seek it. By contrast, paternalism, increasingly unacceptable to patients, and self-determination, resented by many doctors, dilute the very concept of relationship. Naturally, though all patients have an interest in knowing how their lives will be affected by the outcome of treatment, many have no wish to make decisions about what form it should take. Beyond what is minimally required, there is no justification for insisting that they engage in dialogue with the doctor or have information foisted on them. No doubt it is easier to assert this in the abstract than it often is for a doctor to gauge matters in a delicate clinical situation. But the crucial point is that, in any given case, the doctor should not simply *presume* how much the patient wants or needs to know. In medical practice, neither the unquestioned certitudes of paternalism nor the implacable, often harsh, logic of self-determination should be seen as the beginning and end of wisdom. It is too easy to gloss over 'the reality and sadness of illness.'[1] Patients demonstrate their maturity by acknowledging the dependent state as a factor in the process of working towards optimum decisions, rather than by denying or wholly succumbing to it; doctors demonstrate theirs by being receptive to patients who want to be involved.

Recharacterizing the legal obligations of doctors along the lines proposed in the previous chapter could, in the long term, have considerable symbolic force as an authoritative statement of how society wants its doctors to behave. Essentially what is proposed is a model of 'collaborative autonomy'. Though such a model, in common with outright self-determination, is at variance with the medical profession's traditional ethic, it has the instrumental virtue of being eminently defensible in therapeutic terms. The importance of this characteristic of a collaborative approach cannot be overestimated. Realism dictates that whatever modifications are envisaged in doctor–patient relationships, doctors will continue to play a crucial role in the disclosure and exchange of information, continuing to exercise immense influence over decision-making as well as treatment.

It would be odd if members of a profession charged with providing medical care were not trained to do their utmost to preserve or promote the health of their patients as conventionally understood in medical terms.[2] Their predominant focus is understandably on achieving results rather than on the process of decision-making. It can therefore be difficult for doctors to embrace decisions likely to produce outcomes which they see as contrary to the interests of their patients' health, and in that sense inimical to their own ethical obligation to care for their patients. 'Relinquishing belief in the rightness of one practice or standard and replacing it with something that may be almost the opposite is hard for anyone. It is especially hard for professionals, for they

---

[1] T. Duffy, 'Agamemnon's Fate and the Medical Profession' (1987) 9 *Western New England Law Review* 21, 28.
[2] Cf. B. Dickens, 'Patients' Interests and Clients' Wishes: Physicians and Lawyers in Discord,' *Law, Medicine and Health Care* 15 (1987), 110.

invest themselves generously and intensely in their actions. To change those actions they have to change themselves.'[3]

Though the profession has begun the difficult task of rethinking its ethical remit to accommodate more active patient participation, in the hospital context particularly, resistance to such modification persists. In a recent investigation of general surgery, for example, Meredith found that the surgeons whom he interviewed 'were not enthusiastic at the prospect of devoting more time to discussing surgical alternatives, risks, and complications, and outlook indicators for their patients' benefit'.[4] Citing a familiar litany of justifications—patients not taking in what was said, being incapable of assessing alternatives and tending to overestimate risks—'some surgeons were pessimistic about increasingly serving the "patient consumer" being modelled by the "Patient's Charter" '.[5] As Meredith points out, 'differences between the patients' descriptions of their frustrations over participation, and the surgeons' judgements of the merits of exposing patients to decision-making criteria indicated a conflict of two forms of discourse'.[6] Consultations tended to be so dominated by the 'clinical-diagnostic discourse' of the doctor as to inhibit participation and virtually preclude the 'practical discourse' of patients about how what was being proposed would affect their lives.

In occupations where both individual judgement and group loyalty are highly valued, external regulation is apt to carry less weight than training and socialization.[7] These influences are particularly strong for low visibility activities, of which the medical exchange is a classic instance. We have seen how central professional norms have been throughout the history of medical practice and how comparatively limited has been the impact of imperfectly understood and often resented legal constraints. Altering the ethos of the profession—including, in the hospital context, the culture of the ward[8]—to meet patients' legitimate

[3] C. Williamson, *Whose Standards?* (Buckingham: Open University Press, 1992), 132.

[4] P. Meredith, 'Patient Participation in Decision-making and Consent to Treatment: The Case of General Surgery', *Sociology of Health and Illness* 15 (1993), 315, 330.   [5] Ibid. 331.   [6] Ibid.

[7] R. Reiner, *The Politics of the Police* (2nd edn) (Hemel Hempstead: Harvester Wheatsheaf Books, 1992), ch. 3.

[8] See A. Arluke, 'Roundsmanship', *Social Science and Medicine* 14 (1980), 297.

expectations of involvement, requires change from within that is difficult to accomplish in the face of some of the pressures from without.[9]

In the marketized NHS, the focus on cost controls and competition, the growing dominance of hospital administrators and fundholding practices, and the pervasiveness of block contracts, thinly disguised by the ersatz service orientation of Charterism, subtly and not so subtly alter perceptions of medical relationships, eroding the spirit of co-operation within the NHS. They constitute as much of a barrier to therapeutic alliance as to paternalism. At the same time, growth in the elderly population[10] and improved technological capacity to treat patients mean that the demand for health care is set to continue rising, leaving no reason to anticipate any let-up in the pressures on medical personnel. The current generation of hospital doctors, struggling to get through long waiting lists, will not easily be convinced by counter-intuitive, if supportable, findings that non-directive, open-ended consultations are not unduly time-consuming. When throughput is a major performance indicator, talk of deepening medical relationships may appear unreal.

Yet now more than ever the virtues of collaboration and communication in doctor–patient relationships are being advocated by the GMC and the BMA, and on occasion described as representative of present practice. If the goal of therapeutic alliance is to be furthered for those who seek it, medical education, broadly conceived, must be the key instrument. As well as demonstrating a commitment to enhanced standards of technical expertise and safety in medical procedures, by such means as continuing education and medical audit, the profession needs to ensure that steps are taken to instil the values of partnership and collaboration which are being officially promulgated. To make this a reality, the GMC will have to take a stronger stand on education

---

[9] Cf. D. Mechanic, 'Social Research in Health and the American Sociopolitical Context: The Changing Fortunes of Medical Sociology', *Social Science and Medicine* 36 (1993), 95, pointing to a 'debasement of co-operative values' in the face of a dominant 'economizing perspective'.

[10] 'In 1992 the NHS spent more than £1,000 a head on the over-75s, compared with less than £250 each on the under-65s. The health budget, now £37 billion, is rising fast . . . it has no obvious ceiling': *The Economist*, 29 May 1993.

and training. As Myerscough points out,[11] 'there is evidence that the process of undergraduate medical education may, in some instances, inhibit rather than promote the development of interviewing skills . . . If a student is "imprinted" with a conceptual framework of function and disease based solely on the physical sciences, he may acquire a view of patients as disordered machines before he even begins to learn to talk to them as people . . . early and continuing contact with patients is important in promoting the facility for good communication.'

The beginnings of a policy in some medical schools of attachments for *pre*-clinical students to families where they can see the impact of illness on patients and their families in the home setting is one imaginative and concrete development,[12] which could help inform discussion in courses on medical ethics and sociology. So, too, the evidence that interviewing skills can be significantly improved by being taught suggests that medical students would benefit from greater exposure to the kind of video and role play techniques already more commonly used in courses for professions allied to medicine, such as nursing, pharmacy, and social work.

Medical education broadly conceived also embraces leading by example, not only by the surgeon's approach to the ward round but also by the GMC setting the cultural tone of the profession. Detailed assessment of the Council's complaints procedures and other grievance mechanisms within the NHS is beyond the scope of this book, but brief reference to this contentious area is needed if only to highlight the extent of concern that such processes are not conducted in a constructive spirit,[13] not least because even

---

[11] *Talking with Patients* (2nd edn.) (Oxford: Oxford University Press, 1992), 181–2.

[12] e.g. the scheme recently introduced by the University of Birmingham: 'Students see the patient in the community over 12 months. It exposes them to a range of experiences in learning how health problems affect the patient, their carers and the health services. It enables them to think about why a patient becomes ill; they have to take into account non-medical factors such as unemployment, housing, the environment': *Times Higher Education Supplement*, 15 Jan. 1993, 9.

[13] In 1992 alone there were at least 5 reports recommending reform of existing procedures: Association of Community Health Councils for England and Wales and Action for Victims of Medical Accidents, *A Health Standards Inspectorate* (London: ACHCEW/AVMA, 1992); Consumers' Association, *NHS Complaints Procedures* (London: Consumers' Association, 1992); National Association of

non-litigious investigation of medical complaints suffers from the pervasiveness of the *Bolam* approach:

This principle is paramount throughout all the accountability procedures. Not only at law,[14] but in any circumstance in which medical practitioners might be called to account, the profession has insisted that their peers should make the judgements . . . In the GMC itself, although lay persons have been present at disciplinary hearings since 1926, the decision is determined by the medical members, albeit informed by a lay input. Professional self-regulation is clearly implicit in every form of medical accountability.[15]

The GMC recently produced a consultation paper proposing additional powers of self-regulation under which incompetent doctors who exhibit 'seriously deficient performance' over a period of time would have to undergo retraining or face dismissal.[16] If implemented, these proposals could help compensate for the current lack of machinery to deal with situations where care has been inadequate without amounting to 'serious professional misconduct', but there is also concern that this elusive concept has

Health Authorities and Trusts Complaints Working Party, *Suggested future NHS Complaints arrangements* (London: NAHAT, 1992); General Medical Services Committee Complaints Review Working Party, *Draft Report* (London: GMSC, 1992); General Medical Council, *Proposals for New Performance Procedures* (London: GMC, 1992). See F. Winkler, 'Complaints by Patients', *British Medical Journal* 306 (1993), 472. See further, Department of Health, *Being Heard: The Report of a Review Committee on NHS Complaint Procedures* (London: Department of Health, 1994).

[14] Detailed examination of compensation mechanisms is beyond the scope of this book, but it is convenient to note here that our adversarial mode of court resolution for medical negligence claims is virtually programmed to accentuate any hostility, concern, or distress felt by patients. Instituting a less confrontational approach to such disputes could help normalize personal relationships between patient and doctor. At a time when much thought is being given generally to the benefits for all participants (including the state) of procedures aimed at the consensual resolution of disputes (through alternative dispute resolution, arbitration, mediation, reform of complaints procedures, etc.), it should be emphasized that conceiving of dispute resolution as a *healing* process is especially appropriate in the case of injured patients.

[15] M. Stacey, 'Medical Accountability: A Background Paper' in A. Grubb (ed.) *Challenges in Medical Care* (Chichester: John Wiley & Sons, 1992), 109, 122. Cf. J. Robinson, *A Patient Voice at the GMC* (London: Health Rights, 1988).

[16] General Medical Council, *Proposals for New Performance Procedures* (London: General Medical Council, 1992). See also, L. Donaldson, 'Doctors with Problems in an NHS Workforce', *British Medical Journal* 308 (1994), 1277.

been too narrowly interpreted as applied to complaints of professional incompetence.[17]

We have contended that the law could, and should, assert principles that facilitate therapeutic alliance; in particular, that it should require of doctors fuller disclosure, or greater readiness to disclose, than is presently deemed necessary within the law of negligence. However, the law cannot ensure effective communication in practice and legal actions based on claims of inadequate disclosure are relatively rare and difficult to establish. The difficulty is not greatly reduced where causation is determined on a subjective basis, because of judicial scepticism about self-serving testimony. Apart, then, from producing what we have argued is a more coherent formal account of liability in negligence, would anything be achieved?

There is little doubt that medical behaviour can be influenced by legal decisions, even if doctors are rarely well-informed as to their content. Most doctors will not be familiar with the niceties of *Sidaway* and the restrictive way in which it has subsequently been interpreted. As we have seen, some governmental and professional guidance refers to the need for extensive disclosure and informed consent as if they were already legal requirements.[18] Ironically, then, the very misperceptions which many doctors entertain about the law may themselves have a contribution to make to more open doctor–patient relationships. Whatever *Sidaway* actually decided, its intimation that the courts can have the final say has not gone unnoticed in the profession,[19] and Lord Scarman's powerful plea for more disclosure has undoubted symbolic importance, and added impact because he so unequivocally identified the issue as rooted in the patient's right of decision.

However, it is plainly unsatisfactory that, uniquely in the

---

[17] See Medical Act 1983, s. 36(1), and R. Palmer, 'Accountability and Discipline' in C. Dyer (ed.), *Doctors, Patients and the Law* (Oxford: Blackwell Scientific Publications, 1992) 180, 191. Of the GMC's two distinct disciplinary procedures—for health and conduct—conduct procedures, i.e. complaints about disregard of professional responsibilities to patients, now form the largest single category considered by the Council. In 1991–2, 1,300 complaints were received: 24 reached the health procedures committee and 34 the conduct committee.

[18] e.g. the Patient's Charter and the BMA's *Medical Ethics Today* (London: British Medical Association, 1993).

[19] See e.g. Lord Caplan's observation in the Scottish case of *Moyes* v. *Lothian Health Board* [1990] 1 Med LR 463, 471, commenting on increasing disclosure of the risks of angiography, ch. 1, no. 249 above.

medical sphere, English appellate courts are still prepared to regard as virtually dispositive evidence of what may be generally thought inferior professional practice. It is possible that the introduction of medical audit,[20] aimed at developing good practice guidelines and improving quality assurance, will encourage them to question whether the *Bolam* test is sufficiently demanding.[21] But the prospects of achieving a medical consensus on recommended treatment for the majority of conditions appears slim,[22] and, in any event, medical audit has little to offer as regards those cases which turn on the scope of the duty to disclose risks. It remains open to the House of Lords to break loose from *Bolam* and revive the historically more accurate principle that the doctor's duty is to be measured by the ordinary rule of reasonableness in all the circumstances, taking due account, *inter alia*, of the individual patient's informational requirements. By so doing, it would restore legal coherence and enhance the prospect of cases being more appropriately resolved, especially, though not exclusively, as far as questions of disclosure are concerned. But beyond this, it would be performing a major act of symbolic affirmation, in providing a legal stamp of approval for a more patient-centred ethic.

Stripped of its rhetoric, the decision in *Sidaway* suggests that medical paternalism remains in essence unexceptionable. That said, Lord Bridge did acknowledge that patients are entitled to an '*informed* choice'.[23] Any contribution which the law can make to patients being genuinely informed will be the more effective if the legal formulation of the doctor's duty is seen to be shaped by an understanding of the therapeutic aims of enhanced communication. By contrast, the rights-justification which Lord Scarman saw as the key to liability for non-disclosure is liable to be an impediment to doctors discharging their professional 'duty of

[20] Incorporated into consultants' contracts and GPs' terms of service in 1991, as a facet of the recent NHS reforms.

[21] The desirability of having practice guidelines to which doctors should adhere in the particular context of PVS was specifically referred to by Lord Goff and Lord Browne-Wilkinson in *Airedale NHS Trust* v. *Bland* [1993] AC 789, 870–1 and 885, respectively.

[22] See R. Smith, 'Where is the Wisdom . . . ?' *British Medical Journal* 303 (1991), 798–9, reporting Eddy's finding that only about 15% of medical interventions are supported by solid scientific evidence.

[23] [1985] AC 871, 900. Emphasis added.

caring', as well as being a conceptually deficient basis for determining the standard of care owed in negligence.

In *Sidaway*, it will be recalled, the plaintiff referred to her neurosurgeon as a man of 'very, very few words.' In the Annual Reports of the Health Service Commissioner which have been produced since 1974 detailing complaints of hospital maladministration, inadequate communication is a persistent and prominent theme.[24] Offering patients dialogue has more therapeutic value than offering them consent forms. So, too, the right to see the medical records, in the name of a right to be informed, is of questionable value if there is no opportunity to discuss them. There is much to be said for tackling the issue of medical relationships more as one of practical health care and patient welfare and less as an exercise in abstract rights. Important as the autonomy of patients is, to view it exclusively as an end in itself is to ignore the psychological realities of medical relationships. Those realities can be reconciled with proper regard for patients, by recognizing the value of their active contribution to decision-making in a process aimed at enhancing both their health and autonomy.[25]

The law alone cannot effect a substantial change in the routine behaviour of doctors, but it can have some symbolic impact on their perception of what is appropriate in relationships with patients. As Somerville has said, law, like medicine, can be viewed as having as its ultimate goal the relief of suffering.[26] Doctors have to be convinced that the end result of any legally mandated requirements is compatible with the fundamental

[24] See e.g. Health Service Commissioner for England, for Scotland, and for Wales, *Annual Report for 1993–4*. And see C. Vincent, M. Young and A. Phillips, 'Why Do People Sue Doctors? A Study of Patients and Relatives Taking Legal Action', *Lancet* 343 (1994), 1609.

[25] See J. Murphy, 'Beyond Autonomy: Judicial Restraint and the Legal Limits Necessary to Uphold the Hippocratic Tradition and Preserve the Ethical Integrity of the Medical Profession' (1993) 9 *Journal of Contemporary Health Law and Policy* 451, 461, observing that the 'conceptual momentum of autonomy has been so potent that there now exists what Dr Pellegrino calls a "tendency to absolutize autonomy . . ." ' so that it is 'misconstrued and elevated as a right, not merely a claim, of the patient'. E. Pellegrino, 'The Relationship of Autonomy and Integrity in Medical Ethics' *Bulletin of the Pan American Health Organization* 24 (1990), 361. See also D. Callahan, 'Autonomy: A Moral Good, Not a Moral Obsession' (October 1984), 14 *Hastings Center Report* 40.

[26] M. Somerville, 'Pain and Suffering at Interfaces of Medicine and Law' (1986) 36 *University of Toronto Law Journal* 286, 310–17.

ethical underpinnings of their vocation. In the process of developing a more mature conception of doctor–patient relationships, a collaborative approach rooted in patient welfare is best calculated to promote due respect for patients and serve their interests, at the same time as engaging the attention, respect, and ultimately co-operation of the medical profession. Tort law can play a part in this process by proclaiming appropriate standards for medical practice as social norms.

Bibliography

ALLAN, T., 'Constitutional Rights and Common Law' (1991) 11 Oxford Journal of Legal Studies 453.

ALLEN, I., Any Room at the Top?: A Study of Doctors and Their Careers (London: Policy Studies Institute, 1988).

ARLUKE, A., 'Roundsmanship', Social Science and Medicine 14 (1980), 297.

ARMSTRONG, D., 'What do Patients Want?' British Medical Journal 303 (1991), 261.

Association of Community Health Councils for England and Wales and Action for Victims of Medical Accidents, A Health Standards Inspectorate (London: ACHCEW/AVMA, 1992).

ATIYAH, P., 'Medical Malpractice and the Contract/Tort Boundary' (1986) 49(2) Law and Contemporary Problems 287.

Audit Commission, What Seems to be the Matter: Communication between Hospitals and Patients (London: HMSO, 1993).

Australian Law Reform Commission, Informed Decisions about Medical Procedures (Melbourne and Sydney: Law Reform Commission of Victoria, Australian Law Reform Commission, and New South Wales Law Reform Commission, 1989).

AVMA, 10th Anniversary Report (London: AVMA, 1992).

BARRON, A. and SCOTT, C., 'The Citizen's Charter Programme' (1992) 55 Modern Law Review 526.

BARTLETT, A., 'The Preparation of Experts' Reports', Counsel, October 1993, 21; November/December 1993, 23.

BEAUCHAMP T., 'The Promise of the Beneficence Model for Medical Ethics' (1990) 6 Journal of Contemporary Health Law and Policy 145.

BECK E., LONSDALE, S., NEWMAN, S., and PATTERSON, D. (eds.), In the Best of Health? (London: Chapman & Hall, 1992).

BEECHAM, L., 'Royal Colleges Criticise Fundholding Distortions,' British Medical Journal 307 (1993), 1092.

BELL, A., 'The Doctor and the Supply of Goods and Services Act 1982' (1984) 4 Legal Studies 175.

BENNET, G., The Wound and the Doctor (London: Secker & Warburg, 1987).

BENNETT, A. (ed.), Communication between Doctors and Patients (London: Oxford University Press, 1976).

BERLANT, J., Profession and Monopoly: A Study of Medicine in the United

States and Great Britain (Berkeley: University of California Press, 1975).

—— 'Medical Ethics and Professional Monopoly', *Annals of the American Academy of Political and Social Science* 437 (1978), 49.

BETTLE, J., 'Suing Hospitals Direct: Whose Tort was it Anyhow?' (1987) 137 *New Law Journal* 573.

BLACKBURN, R. and TAYLOR, J. (eds.), *Human Rights for the 1990s* (London: Mansell, 1991).

BLACKSTONE, Sir W., *Commentaries on the Laws of England* (19th edn.) (London: Sweet & Maxwell, 1836).

BLAU, J., 'Time to let the Patient Speak', *British Medical Journal* 298 (1989), 39.

BLAY, S., 'Onus of Proof of Consent in an Action for Trespass to the Person' (1987) 61 *Australian Law Journal* 25.

BOON, N., 'New Deal for Old Hearts', *British Medical Journal* 303 (1991), 70.

BOVBJERG, R. and HAVIGHURST, C. (eds.), 'Medical Malpractice: Can the Private Sector Find Relief?' (1986) 49(2) *Law and Contemporary Problems*.

—— and METZLOFF, T., (eds.), 'Medical Malpractice: Lessons for Reform' (1991) 54 (1 & 2) *Law and Contemporary Problems*.

BRAHAMS, D., 'Unwanted Hysterectomies', *Lancet* 342 (1993), 361.

BRAZIER, M., 'Patient Autonomy and Consent to Treatment: The Role of Law?' (1987) 7 *Legal Studies* 169.

—— 'NHS Indemnity: The Implications for Medical Litigation' (1990) 6 *Professional Negligence* 88.

—— *Medicine, Patients and the Law* (2nd edn.) (Harmondsworth: Penguin Books, 1992).

—— and LOBJOIT, M. (eds.), *Protecting the Vulnerable* (London: Routledge, 1991).

BREARLEY, S., 'Medical Manpower' T. Richards (ed.), *Medicine in Europe* (London: British Medical Journal, 1992) 45.

BRENNAN, C., 'The Right to Die' (1993) *New Law Journal* 1041.

BRENNAN, T., *Just Doctoring: Medical Ethics in the Liberal State* (Berkeley: University of California Press, 1991).

BREWIN, T., 'How Much Ethics is Needed to Make a Good Doctor?' *Lancet* 341 (1993), 161.

British Medical Association, *Report of the Working Party on No Fault Compensation for Medical Injury* (London: British Medical Association, 1987 and 1991).

—— *Statement on Advance Directives* (London: BMA, 1992).

—— *Complementary Medicine: New Approaches to Good Practice* (Oxford: Oxford University Press, 1993).

—— *Medical Ethics Today* (London: BMJ Publishing Group, 1993).

BRITTEN, N., 'Hospital Consultants' views of their patients' (1991) 13 *Sociology of Health and Illness* 83.

BROCK, D., and WARTMAN, S., 'When Competent Patients make Irrational Choices', *New England Journal of Medicine* 322 (1990), 1595.

BUCHANAN, A., 'Medical Paternalism' *Philosophy and Public Affairs* 7 (1978), 370.

BUCKLEY, R., *The Modern Law of Negligence* (London: Butterworths, 1988).

BUNKER, J., 'Can Professionalism Survive in the Marketplace?', *British Medical Journal* 308 (1994), 1179.

BURLING, S., LUMKY, J., McCARTHY, L., MYTTON, J., NOLAN, J., SISSON, P., WILLIAMS, P., and WRIGHT, L. 'Review of the Teaching of Medical Ethics in London Medical Schools', *Journal of Medical Ethics* 16 (1990), 206.

BYRNE, D., NAPIER, A., and CUSCHIERI, A., 'How Informed is Signed Consent?' *British Medical Journal* 296 (1988), 839.

BYRNE, P. (ed.), *Medicine in Contemporary Society* (London: King Edward's Hospital Fund for London, 1987).

California Medical Association, *Medical Insurance Feasibility Study* (San Francisco: Sutter Publications, 1977).

CALLAHAN, D., 'Autonomy: A Moral Good, Not a Moral Obsession' (October 1984) 14 *Hastings Center Report* 40.

CALNAN, M., CANT, S., and GABE, J., *Going Private: Why People Pay for their Health Care* (Buckingham: Open University Press, 1993).

CAMPLING, E., DEVLIN, H., HOYLE, R., and LUNN, J., *The Report of the National Confidential Enquiry into Perioperative Deaths 1991/92* (London: National Confidential Enquiry into Perioperative Deaths, 1993).

CANE, P., and STAPLETON, J. (eds.), *Essays for Patrick Atiyah* (Oxford: Oxford University Press, 1991).

CANT, S., and CALNAN, M., 'Using Private Health Insurance. A Study of Lay Decisions to Seek Professional Medical Help' *Sociology of Health and Illness* 14 (1992), 39.

CAPOTORTI, F., EHLERMANN, C., FRÖWEIN, J., JACOBS, F., JOLIET, R., KOOPMANS, T. and KOVAR, R. (eds.), *Du Droit International au Droit de l'Intégration: Liber Amicorum Pierre Pescatore* (Baden-Baden: Nomos, 1987).

CAPRON, A., 'Informed Consent in Catastrophic Disease Research and Treatment' (1974) 123 *University of Pennsylvania Law Review* 340.

CAPSTICK, J. and EDWARDS, P., 'Trends in Obstetric Malpractice Claims', *Lancet* 336 (1990), 931.

CARLEN, P., *Magistrates' Justice* (London: Martin Robertson, 1976).

CARSON, D., 'The Sexuality of People with Learning Difficulties' [1989] *Journal of Social Welfare Law* 355.

CASSELL, E., *Talking with Patients* (Cambridge, Mass.: MIT Press, 1985).

CASSIDY, D., 'Malpractice—Medical Negligence in Australia' (1992) 66 *Australian Law Journal* 67.

Central Statistical Office, *Social Trends* (London: HMSO, 1994).

CHALMERS, D., and SCHWARTZ, R., '*Rogers* v. *Whitaker* and Informed Consent in Australia' (1993) 1 *Medical Law Review* 139.

CHAPMAN, C., *Physicians, Law and Ethics* (New York: New York University Press, 1984).

CHILDRESS, J., 'Metaphors and Models of Medical Relationships' (1982) 8 *Social Responsibility* 47.

COLLIER, J., 'Conflicts between Pharmaceutical Company Largesse and Patients' Rights' (1992) 60 *Medico-Legal Journal* 243.

Comment 'Ambulance Chasers in the UK', *Solicitors Journal*, 10 September 1993.

Consumers' Association, *NHS Complaints Procedures* (London: Consumers' Association, 1992).

COSMAN, M., 'Medieval Medical Malpractice: The Dicta and the Dockets', *Bulletin of the New York Academy of Medicine* 49 (1973), 22.

COTTERRELL, R., 'Professional Autonomy and the Construction of Professional Knowledge: Sociology in the Professional Practice of Law and Medicine' (Paper to British Sociological Association Annual Conference, University of Durham, 1980).

CRISP, R., 'Medical Negligence, Assault, Informed Consent, and Autonomy' (1990) 17 *Journal of Law and Society* 77.

CURRAN, W., 'The Confusion of Titles in the Medicolegal Field: an Historical Analysis and a Proposal for Reform' (1975) 15 *Medicine, Science, and the Law* 270.

DANZON, P., *Medical Malpractice: Theory, Evidence, and Public Policy* (Cambridge, Mass.: Harvard University Press, 1985).

DELAMOTHE, T., 'The Citizen's Charter and the NHS', *British Medical Journal* 303 (1991), 203.

DELL, S., *Murder into Manslaughter* (Oxford: Oxford University Press, 1984).

Department of Health, *Working for Patients* (London: HMSO, 1989).

—— *The Patient's Charter* (London: HMSO, 1991).

—— *Arbitration for Medical Negligence in the National Health Service* (London: Department of Health, 1991).

—— *Being Heard: The Report of a Review Committee on NHS Complaints Procedures* (London: Department of Health, 1994).

Department of Health and Social Security, *Patients First* (London: HMSO, 1979).

—— *The NHS Management Inquiry DA (83) 38* (London: DHSS, 1983).

DE VILLE, K., *Medical Malpractice in Nineteenth Century America: Origins and Legacy* (New York: New York University Press, 1990).

DEVLIN, P., *Samples of Law Making* (Oxford: Oxford University Press, 1962).

DEWEES, D., TREBILCOCK, M. and COYTE, P., 'The Medical Malpractice Crisis: A Comparative Empirical Perspective' (1991) 54(1) *Law and Contemporary Problems* 217.

DICKENS, B., 'Patients' Interests and Clients' Wishes: Physicians and Lawyers in Discord', *Law, Medicine and Health Care* 15 (1987), 110.

—— 'The Effects of Legal Liability on Physicians' Services' (1991) 41 *University of Toronto Law Journal* 168.

DINGWALL, R. (ed.), *Socio-Legal Aspects of Medical Practice* (London: Royal College of Physicians of London, 1989).

—— FENN, P., and QUAM, L., *Medical Negligence* (Oxford: Centre for Socio-Legal Studies, 1991).

—— RAFFERTY, A., and WEBSTER, C., *An Introduction to the Social History of Nursing* (London: Routledge, 1988).

DONALDSON, L., 'Doctors with Problems in an NHS Workforce', *British Medical Journal*, 308 (1994), 1277.

DOWNIE, R., and CHARLTON, B., *The Making of a Doctor* (Oxford: Oxford University Press, 1992).

DUFFY, T., 'Agamemnon's Fate and the Medical Profession' (1987) 9 *Western New England Law Review* 21.

DYER, C., 'Manslaughter Convictions for Making Mistakes', *British Medical Journal* 303 (1991), 1218.

—— (ed.), *Doctors, Patients and the Law* (Oxford: Blackwell Scientific Publications, 1992).

EDDY, J., *Professional Negligence* (London: Stevens & Sons, 1955).

EDELSTEIN, L., *Ancient Medicine: Selected Papers of Ludwig Edelstein* (Baltimore: Johns Hopkins University Press, 1967).

EDWARDS, L., The Right to Consent and the Right to Refuse: More Problems with Minors and Medical Consent' (1993) *Juridical Review* 52.

EEKELAAR, J., 'The Emergence of Children's Rights' (1986) 6 *Oxford Journal of Legal Studies* 161.

EISENBERG, L., and KLEINMAN, A. (eds.), *The Relevance of Social Science for Medicine* (London: Reidel, 1981).

ENNIS, M., and VINCENT, C., 'Obstetric Accidents: A Review of 64 Cases' *British Medical Journal* 300 (1990), 1365.

—— CLARK, A., and GRUDZINSKAS, J., 'Change in Obstetric Practice in Response to Fear of Litigation in the British Isles' *Lancet* 338 (1991), 616.

EPSTEIN, R., 'Medical Malpractice: The Case for Contract' (1976) 76 *American Bar Foundation Research Journal* 87.

—— 'Market and Regulatory Approaches to Medical Malpractice: The

Virginia Obstetrical No-Fault Statute' (1988) 74 *Virginia Law Review* 1451.

ERNST, E., 'Complementary Medicine: Scrutinising the Alternatives', *Lancet* 341 (1993), 1626.

FADEN, R., and BEAUCHAMP, T., *A History of Informed Consent* (New York: Oxford University Press, 1986).

—— BECKER, C., and LEWIS, C., 'Disclosure of Information to Patients in Medical Care' *Medical Care* 19 (1981), 718.

FALLOWFIELD, L., 'Giving sad and bad news', *The Lancet* 341 (1993), 476.

FAULDER, C., *Whose Body Is It: The Troubling Issue of Informed Consent* (London: Virago Press, 1985).

FEINBERG, J., *The Moral Limits of the Criminal Law: Harm to Self* (Oxford: Oxford University Press, 1986).

—— 'In Defence of Moral Rights' (1992) 12 *Oxford Journal of Legal Studies* 149.

FELDMAN, D., 'Public Law Values in the House of Lords' (1990) 106 *Law Quarterly Review* 246.

—— *Civil Liberties and Human Rights in England and Wales* (Oxford: Clarendon Press, 1993).

FIFOOT, C., *History and Sources of the Common Law: Tort and Contract* (London: Stevens & Sons, 1949).

FINN, P. (ed.), *Essays on Torts* (Sydney: Law Book Co, 1989).

FIRTH-COZENS, J., 'Stress in Medical Undergraduates and House Officers' *British Journal of Hospital Medicine* 41 (1989), 161.

FITZPATRICK, R., HINTON, J., NEWMAN, S., SCAMBLER, G., and THOMPSON, J. *The Experience of Illness* (London: Tavistock Publications, 1984).

FLEMING, J., 'Developments in the English Law of Medical Liability' (1959) 12 *Vanderbilt Law Review* 633.

—— *The Law of Torts* (8th edn.) (Sydney: The Law Book Company, 1992).

FLETCHER, J., 'The Evolution of the Ethics of Informed Consent' *Progress in Clinical and Biological Research* 128 (1983), 187.

FLETCHER, N. 'The Nurses, Midwives and Health Visitors Act 1992' (1992) 8 *Professional Negligence* 94.

FOX, N., *The Social Meaning of Surgery* (Buckingham: Open University Press, 1992).

FRASER, A., 'Do Patients Want to be Informed?' (1984) 52 *British Heart Journal*, 468.

FREDERIKSON, L., 'Designing a Doctor: Do They have the "Strong Silent Type" in mind' (paper presented to the British Psychological Society, London: 18 Dec. 1991).

FREEMAN, M. (ed.), *Medicine, Ethics and Law* (London: Stevens and Sons, 1988).

FREIDSON, E., *Profession of Medicine* (New York: Dodd Mead, 1970).

—— *Professional Dominance* (New York: Atherton, 1970).

—— *Medical Work in America* (New Haven: Yale University Press, 1989).

FRENCH, R., and WEAR, A. (eds.), *British Medicine in an Age of Reform* (London: Routledge, 1991).

GABE, J., CALNAN, M., and BURY, M. (eds.), *Sociology of the Health Service* (London: Routledge, 1991).

GALANTER, M., 'Law Abounding: Legalisation around the North Atlantic' (1992) 55 *Modern Law Review* 1.

GARFIELD, J., 'Ethico-Legal Aspects of High-Risk Neurosurgery', *Journal of the Medical Defence Union* 8 (1992), 76.

General Medical Council, *Professional Conduct and Discipline: Fitness to Practise* (London: GMC, 1991).

—— *Undergraduate Medical Education. The Need for Change* (London: GMC, 1991).

—— *Proposals for New Performance Procedures* (London: GMC, 1992).

—— *Tomorrow's Doctors* (London: GMC, 1994).

GENERAL MEDICAL SERVICES COMMITTEE COMPLAINTS REVIEW WORKING PARTY, *Draft Report* (London: GMSC, 1992).

GIESEN, D., *International Medical Malpractice Law* (Tübingen: J. C. B. Mohr; Dordrecht: Martinus Nijhoff Publishers, 1988).

—— 'Vindicating the Patient's Rights: A Comparative Perspective' (1993) 9 *Journal of Contemporary Health Law and Policy* 273.

—— and HAYES, J., 'The Patient's Right to Know—A Comparative View' (1992) 21 *Anglo-American Law Review* 101.

GINSBURG, W., KAHN, S., THORNHILL, M., and GAMBARDELLA, S., 'Contractual Revisions to Medical Malpractice Liability' (1986) 49(2) *Law and Contemporary Problems* 253.

GLENDON, M., *Rights Talk: The Impoverishment of Political Discourse* (New York: Free Press, 1991).

GOODPASTER, G., 'On the Theory of American Adversary Criminal Trial' (1987) 78 *Journal of Criminal Law and Criminology* 118.

GORDON, R., and BARLOW, C., 'Competence and the Right to Die' [1993] *New Law Journal* 1719.

GRUBB, A., 'The Emergence and Rise of Medical Law and Ethics' (1987) 50 *Modern Law Review* 241.

—— and PEARL, D., *Blood Testing, AIDS and DNA Profiling* (Bristol: Family Law, 1990).

—— (ed.), *Challenges in Medical Care* (Chichester: John Wiley & Sons, 1992).

—— (ed.), *Choices and Decisions in Health Care* (Chichester: John Wiley & Sons, 1993).

GRUNDER, T., 'On the Readability of Surgical Consent Forms', *New England Journal of Medicine* 302 (1980), 900.

HAM, C., DINGWALL, R., FENN, P., and HARRIS, D. *Medical Negligence: Compensation and Accountability* (London: King's Fund Institute, 1988).

HARPER, G., 'Breaking Taboos and Steadying the Self in Medical School', *Lancet* 342 (1993), 913.

HARRIS, J., 'The Price of Failure' *Health Service Journal* (14 Apr. 1994), 9.

HARRIS, N., 'Medical Negligence Litigation: The Need for Reform' (1992) 60 *Medico-Legal Journal* 205.

Harvard Medical Practice Study Group, *Patients, Doctors and Lawyers: Medical Injury, Malpractice Litigation, and Patient Compensation in New York* (Cambridge, Mass.: Harvard University, 1990).

HAVARD, J., 'Privilege' (1987) 55 *Medico-Legal Journal* 206.

—— ' "No Fault" Compensation for Medical Accidents' (1992) 32 *Medicine, Science, and the Law* 187.

HAVIGHURST, C., 'Altering the Applicable Standard of Care' (1986) 49(2) *Law and Contemporary Problems* 265.

—— 'Private Reform of Tort-Law Dogma: Market Opportunities and Legal Obstacles' (1986) 49(2) *Law and Contemporary Problems* 143.

HAWKINS, C., *Mishap or Malpractice* (Oxford: Basil Blackwell, 1985).

HAWKINS, C., and PATTERSON, I., 'Medicolegal Audit in the West Midlands Region: Analysis of 100 Cases', *British Medical Journal* 295 (1987), 1533.

Health Service Commissioner for England, for Scotland and for Wales, Annual Report for 1993–94 (London: HMSO, 1994).

HEWSON, B., 'When "No" means "Yes" ' *Law Society Gazette*, 9 Dec. 1992, 2.

HOLDSWORTH, Sir W., *A History of English Law* (3rd edn.) (London: Methuen, 1923).

HOLLAND, T., *Jurisprudence* (13th edn.) (Oxford: Oxford University Press, 1924).

HOLMES, O., *The Common Law* (Boston: Little Brown, 1881).

HOPE, R., 'The Birth of Medical Law' (1991) 11 *Oxford Journal of Legal Studies* 247.

House of Lords Select Committee, *Medical Ethics* (London: HMSO, 1994).

HUGHES, D., 'The Reorganisation of the National Health Service: The Rhetoric and Reality of the Internal Market' (1991) 54 *Modern Law Review* 88.

Human Fertilisation and Embryology Authority, *Donated Ovarian Tissue in Embryo Research and Assisted Conception* (London: HFEA, 1994).

ILLICH, I., *Medical Nemesis: The Expropriation of Health* (London: Calder & Boyars, 1975).

INGLEFINGER, F., 'Arrogance' *New England Journal of Medicine* 303 (1980), 1507.

Institute of Medical Ethics, *Report of a Working Party on the Teaching of Medical Ethics* (The 'Pond Report') (London: IME Publications, 1987).

Institute of Population Studies, *Sexual Health and Family Planning Services in General Practice* (London: Family Planning Association, 1993).

JONES, J., 'Telling the Right Patient', *British Medical Journal* 283 (1981), 291.

JACKSON, R., and POWELL, J., *Professional Negligence* (3rd edn.) (London: Sweet & Maxwell, 1992).

JACOB, J., *The Fabric of English Civil Justice* (London: Stevens, 1987).

JACOB, J. and DAVIES, J. (eds.), *Encyclopedia of Health Services and Medical Law* (London: Sweet & Maxwell, 1987).

JENNETT, B., 'The Persistent Vegetative State: Medical, Ethical and Legal Issues', in Grubb (ed.), *Choices and Decisions in Health Care*, 139.

JONES, C., *Expert Witnesses* (Oxford: Clarendon Press, 1993).

JONES, M., *Medical Negligence* (London: Sweet & Maxwell, 1991).

JONES, M., and MORRIS, A., 'Defensive Medicine: Myths and Facts', *Journal of the Medical Defence Union* 5 (1989), 40.

JONES, W. (trans.), *Hippocrates*, 4 vols. (Cambridge, Mass.: Harvard University Press, 1923–31).

JOWELL, J., and LESTER, A., 'Beyond *Wednesbury*: Substantive Principles of Judicial Review' [1987] *Public Law* 369.

JUSTICE, *Science and the Administration of Justice* (London: Justice, 1991).

KATZ, J., 'Informed Consent—A Fairy Tale? Law's Vision' (1977) 39 *University of Pittsburgh Law Review* 137.

—— *The Silent World of Doctor and Patient* (New York: The Free Press, 1984).

KEELEY, D., 'The Fundholding Debate: Should Practices Reconsider the Decision not to Fundhold?' *British Medical Journal* 306 (1993), 697.

KENNEDY, I., *The Unmasking of Medicine* (London: Allen & Unwin, 1981).

—— 'The Patient on the Clapham Omnibus' (1984) 47 *Modern Law Review* 454.

—— *Treat Me Right* (Oxford: Oxford University Press, 1988).

—— 'Patients, Doctors and Human Rights' in Blackburn, R., and Taylor, J. (eds.), *Human Rights for the 1990s* (London, Mansell, 1991).

KEOWN, J., *Abortion, Doctors and the Law* (Cambridge: Cambridge University Press, 1988).

—— 'The Ashes of AIDS and the Phoenix of Informed Consent' (1989) 52 *Modern Law Review* 790.

KERRIGAN, D., THEVASAGAYAM, R., WOODS, T., MCWELCH, I., THOMAS, W., SHORTHOUSE, A., AND DENNISON, A. 'Who's Afraid of Informed Consent?' *British Medical Journal* 306 (1993), 298.

KING, M., *The Framework of Criminal Justice* (London: Croom Helm, 1981).

King's College Centre of Medical Law and Ethics, *Advance Directives and AIDS* (London: KCCMLE, 1992).

KIRALFY, A., *A Source Book of English Law* (London: Sweet & Maxwell, 1957).

KIRBY, M., 'Informed Consent: What Does it Mean?' *Journal of Medical Ethics* 9 (1983), 69.

—— The Hon Justice, 'Legal Problems: Human Genome Project' (1993) 67 *Australian Law Journal* 894.

KLEIN, R., *The Politics of the National Health Service* (2nd edn.) (London: Longman, 1989).

KNIGHT, B., and McKIM THOMPSON, I., 'The Teaching of Legal Medicine in British Medical Schools', *Medical Education* 20 (1986), 246.

KORGAONKAR, G., and TRIBE, D., 'Medical Manslaughter' (1992) 136 *Solicitors Journal* 105.

LAMONT, L., 'Why Patients don't Sue Doctors', *Journal of the Medical Defence Union* 9 (1993), 39.

LANGLEY, G., QC, HOCHHAUSER, A., and GRIFFITHS, M., *AIDS: Medico-Legal Advice* (London: Medical Defence Union, 1988).

LARSON, M., *The Rise of Professionalism* (Berkeley: University of California Press, 1977).

LAUFER, S., 'Aggrieved Patients Who Claim They were Not Told' (1990) 20 *University of Western Australia Law Review* 489.

LAVERY, R., 'What is the Patient's Charter?' (1992) 60 *Medico-Legal Journal* 201.

Law Commission, *Mentally Incapacitated Adults and Decision-Making: An Overview* (London: HMSO, 1991), Consultation Paper No. 119.

—— *Mentally Incapacitated Adults and Decision-Making: A New Jurisdiction* (London: HMSO, 1993), Consultation Paper No. 128.

—— *Mentally Incapacitated Adults and Decision-Making: Medical Treatment and Research* (London: HMSO, 1993), Consultation Paper No. 129.

LAWS, JUSTICE, 'Is the High Court the Guardian of Fundamental Constitutional Rights?' [1993] *Public Law* 59.

LEE, R., 'Vaccine Damage: Adjudicating Scientific Dispute' in *Product Liability, Insurance and the Pharmaceutical Industry: an Anglo-American Comparison*, ed. Howells, G. (Manchester: Manchester University Press, 1991).

—— 'Confidentiality and Medical Records' in Dyer, C. (ed.), *Doctors, Patients and the Law* (Oxford: Blackwell Scientific Publications, 1992).

—— 'Doctors as Allocators—the Bald Facts' in McVeigh, S., and Wheeler, S. (eds.), *Law, Health and Medical Regulation* (Aldershot: Dartmouth, 1992).

Legal Aid Board, *Annual Report* (1991–92) (London: HMSO, 1992), 53.

—— *Annual Report* (1993–94) (London: HMSO, 1994), 68.

LINDEN, A., 'Custom in Negligence Law' (1968) 11 *Canadian Bar Journal* 151.

LONGLEY, D., *Public Law and Health Service Accountability* (Buckingham: Open University Press, 1993).

LORBER, J., 'Ethical Problems in the Management of Myelomeningocele and Hydrocephalus' *Journal of the Royal College of Physicians* 10 (1975), 47.

LOWE, N., and JUSS, S., 'Medical Treatment—Pragmatism and the Search for Principle' (1993) 56 *Modern Law Review* 865.

LOWRY, S., 'What's Wrong with Medical Education in Britain?' *British Medical Journal* 305 (1992), 1277.

—— 'Student Selection', *British Medical Journal* 305 (1992), 1352.

—— 'A Model for British Medical Education', *British Medical Journal* 307 (1993), 1021.

—— *Medical Education* (London: BMJ Publishing Group, 1993).

MAGUIRE, P., 'Can Communication Skills be Taught?' *British Journal of Hospital Medicine* 43 (1990), 215.

MANDERSON, D., 'Following Doctors' Orders: Informed Consent in Australia' (1988) 62 *Australian Law Journal* 430.

MARKESINIS, B., 'Litigation-Mania in England, Germany and the USA: Are We So Very Different?' (1990) 49 *Cambridge Law Journal* 233.

MARTEAU, T., HUMPHREY, C., MATOON, G., KIDD, J., LLOYD, H., and HORDER, J., 'Factors Influencing the Communication Skills of First Year Clinical Medical Students' *Medical Education* 25 (1991), 127.

MASEIDE, P., 'Possibly Abusive, Often Benign, and Always Necessary. On Power and Domination in Medical Practice' 13 (1991) *Sociology of Health and Illness* 545.

MASON, J., 'Master of the Balancers; Non-Voluntary Therapy under the Mantle of Lord Donaldson' [1993] *Juridical Review* 115.

MASSON, J., 'Re W: Appealing From the Golden Cage' (1993) 5 *Journal of Child Law* 37.

McCALL SMITH, A., 'Ending Life' in Dyer (ed.), *Doctors, Patients and the Law* (Oxford: Blackwell Scientific Publications, 1992).

MACKENZIE STUART, Lord, 'Recent Developments in English Administrative Law—The Impact of Europe' *Du Droit International au Droit de l'Integration: Liber Amicorum Pierre Pescatore*, Capotorti, F., Ehlenmann, C., Fröwein, J., Jacobs, F., Joliet, R., Koopmans, T., and Kovar, R. (eds.), (Baden-Baden: Nomos, 1987), 411.

McINTOSH, D., 'When the Only Winners are the Lawyers', *The Times*, 6 Apr. 1993.

McKEOWN, T., *The Role of Medicine: Dream, Mirage or Nemesis* (London: Nuffield Provincial Hospitals Trust, 1976).

McLEAN, S., *A Patient's Right to Know* (Alderhot, Dartmouth, 1989).

McNAIR, The Hon. Mr. Justice, 'Medical Responsibility in Hospitals' [1957] *Medico-Legal Journal* 129.

McVEIGH, S., and WHEELER S. (eds.) *Law, Health and Medical Regulation* (Aldershot: Dartmouth, 1992).

MECHANIC, D., 'Social Research in Health and the American Socio-political Context: The Changing Fortunes of Medical Sociology', *Social Science and Medicine* 36 (1993), 95.

Medical Defence Union Annual Report, 1947–8 (London: Medical Defence Union, 1948).

MEISEL, A., and ROTH, L., 'What We Do and Do Not Know about Informed Consent' *Journal of the American Medical Association* 246 (1981), 2473.

MEREDITH, P., 'Patient Participation in Decision-Making and Consent to Treatment: The Case of General Surgery', *Sociology of Health and Illness* 15 (1993) 315.

MEYERS, D., *The Human Body and the Law* (2nd edn.) (Edinburgh: Edinburgh University Press, 1990).

MILLER, F., 'Competition Law and Anticompetitive Professional Behaviour Affecting Health Care' (1992) 55 *Modern Law Review* 453.

—— 'Informed Consent in English and American Law' (1992) 18 *American Journal of Law and Medicine* 37.

—— 'Malpractice Liability and Physician Autonomy', *Lancet* 342 (1993), 973.

Monopolies and Mergers Commission, *Services of Medical Practitioners: A Report on the Supply of the Services of Registered Medical Practitioners in Relation to Restrictions on Advertising* (London: HMSO, 1989), Cm 582.

—— *Private Medical Services* (London: HMSO, 1994), Cm 2452.

MONTGOMERY, J., 'Suing Hospitals Direct: What Tort?' (1987) 137 *New Law Journal* 703.

—— 'Power/Knowledge/Consent: Medical Decisionmaking' (1988) 51 *Modern Law Review* 245.

—— 'Medicine, Accountability, and Professionalism' (1989) 16 *Journal of Law and Society* 319.

—— 'Consent to Health Care for Children' (1993) 5 *Journal of Child Law* 117.

MONTROSE, J., 'Is Negligence an Ethical or a Sociological Concept?' (1958) 21 *Modern Law Review* 259.

MORAN, M., and WOOD, B., *States, Regulation and the Medical Profession* (Buckingham: Open University Press, 1993).

MORRIS, J., GODDARD, M., and ROGER, D., 'The Benefits of Providing Information to Patients' (York: Centre for Health Economics, 1989).

MOUNTEER, L., 'Cutting Costs Using Computerised Litigation Support Technology,' (1991) 2(3) *Computers and Law* (NS) 22.

MURPHY, J., 'Beyond Autonomy: Judicial Restraint and the Legal Limits Necessary to Uphold the Hippocratic Tradition and Preserve the Ethical Integrity of the Medical Profession' (1993) 9 *Journal of Contemporary Health Law and Policy* 451.

MYERSCOUGH, P., *Talking with Patients* (2nd edn.) (Oxford: Oxford University Press, 1992).

NATHAN, LORD, *Medical Negligence* (London: Butterworths, 1957).

National Association of Health Authorities and Trusts Complaints Working Party, *Suggested Future NHS Complaints Arrangements* (London: NAHAT, 1992).

—— *Reinventing Healthcare* (Birmingham, NAHAT, 1993).

NAVARRO, V., 'Work, Ideology and Science: The Case of Medicine', *Social Science and Medicine* 14 (1980), 191.

NEWDICK, C., 'Rights to NHS Resources after the 1990 Act' (1993) 1 *Medical Law Review* 53.

NHS Management Executive, *A Guide to Consent for Examination or Treatment*, HC (90) (22) (London: Department of Health, 1990).

—— *Junior Doctors: The New Deal* (London: Department of Health, 1991).

Nuffield Council on Bioethics, *Genetic Screening: Ethical Issues* (London: Nuffield Council on Bioethics, 1993).

OPCS, *General Household Survey 1987* (London: HMSO, 1989).

ORMROD LJ, 'A Lawyer Looks at Medical Ethics' [1977] *Medico-Legal Journal* 18.

OZAR, D., 'Patients' Autonomy: Three Models of the Professional–Lay Relationship in Medicine' (1984) 5 *Theoretical Medicine* 61.

PARKINSON, P., 'The Gillick Case—Just What Has It Decided' (1986) 16 *Family Law* 11.

PARTLETT, D., *Professional Negligence* (Sydney: Law Book Company, 1985).

Patients Association, *Health Address Book* (London: Patients Association, 1992).

PATRICK, D., and SCAMBLER, G. (eds.), *Sociology as Applied to Medicine* (2nd edn.) (London: Bailliere Tindall, 1986).

PEABODY, F., The Care of the Patient', *Journal of the American Medical Association* 88 (1927), 877.

PEARL, D., and GRUBB, A., *Blood Testing, Aids and DNA Profiling* (Bristol: Family Law, 1990).

PELLEGRINO, E., 'The Relationship of Autonomy and Integrity in Medical Ethics' (1990) 24 *Bulletin of the Pan American Health Organization* 361.

—— and THOMASMA, D., *A Philosophical Basis of Medical Practice* (New York: Oxford University Press, 1981).

PERLEY, S., 'From Control over one's Body to Control over one's Body Parts: Extending the Doctrine of Informed Consent' (1992) 67 *New York University Law Review* 335.

POULSEN, J., 'Junior Doctors and the EC Draft Directive on Working Hours' *British Medical Journal* 307 (1993), 1158.

POWERS, M., and HARRIS, N., *Medical Negligence* (London: Butterworths, 1990).

President's Commission for the Study of Ethical Problems in Medicine, *Making Health Care Decisions: The Ethical and Legal Implications of Informed Consent in the Patient–Practitioner Relationship* (Washington: President's Commission for the Study of Ethical Problems in Medicine and Biomedical and Behavioral Research, 1982).

PROSSER, W., *Selected Topics on the Law of Torts* (Ann Arbor: University of Michigan, 1953).

RAMSEY, P., *The Patient as Person* (New Haven: Yale University Press, 1970).

REINER, R., *The Politics of the Police* (2nd edn.) (Hemel Hempstead: Harvester Wheatsheaf Books, 1992).

RELMAN, A., 'Self-Referral—What's at Stake?' *New England Journal of Medicine* 327 (1992), 1522.

RICHARDS, T. (ed.), *Medicine in Europe* (London: British Medical Journal, 1992).

ROBERTS, J., 'Graduate Medical Education is a Brutal Enterprise in Britain', *British Medical Journal* 302 (1991), 225.

ROBERTSON, G., 'Informed Consent in Canada: An Empirical Study' (1984) 22 *Osgoode Hall Law Journal* 139.

—— 'Informed Consent Ten Years Later: The Impact of *Reibl* v. *Hughes*' (1991) 70 *Canadian Bar Review* 423.

ROBINSON, G., 'Rethinking the Allocation of Medical Malpractice Risks between Patients and Providers' (1986) 49(2) *Law and Contemporary Problems* 173.

ROBINSON, J., *A Patient Voice at the GMC: A Lay Member's View of the General Medical Council* (London: Health Rights, 1988).

ROBINSON, R., and LE GRAND, J., *Evaluating the NHS Reforms* (London: King's Fund Institute, 1994).

ROSENBERG, L., 'Medicine under Siege', *Law and Medicine in Confrontation: A Deans' Dialogue*, Yale Law School Program in Civil Liability: Working Paper No. 45 (1986).

Royal College of Physicians, *Compensation for Adverse Consequences of Medical Intervention* (London: Royal College of Physicians, 1990).

Royal College of Surgeons of England and College of Anaesthetists, *Pain after Surgery* (London: RCSE/CoA, 1990).

Royal Commission on Civil Liability and Compensation for Personal Injury (London: HMSO, 1978), Cmnd 7054.

RUSH, B., *The Selected Writings of Benjamin Rush*, ed. D. Runes (New York: Philosophical Library, 1947).

SACKS, O., *A Leg to Stand On* (London: Pan Books, 1986).

SADE, R., 'Medical Care as a Right: A Refutation', *New England Journal of Medicine* 285 (1971), 1288.

SALVAGE, J., 'The Theory and Practice of the New Nursing', *Nursing Times* 86(4) (1990), 42.

SANDERSON, W., and RAYNER, E., *An Introduction to the Law and Tradition of Medical Practice* (London: H. K. Lewis & Co., 1926).

SANDOR, A., 'The History of Professional Liability Suits in the United States', *Journal of the American Medical Association* 163 (1957), 459.

SAUNDERS, P., and HARRIS, C., 'Privatisation and the Consumer' *Sociology* 24 (1990), 57.

SCARMAN, LORD, 'Consent, Communication and Responsibility', *Journal of the Royal Society of Medicine* 79 (1986), 697.

SCHUCK, P., 'Rethinking Informed Consent' (1994) 103 *Yale Law Journal* 899.

SCHWARTZ, R., and GRUBB, A., 'Why Britain Can't Afford Informed Consent', 15 *Hastings Center Report*, Aug. 1985, 19.

SHAW, J., 'Regulating Sexuality' in McVeigh and Wheeler (eds.), *Law, Health and Medical Regulation* (Aldershot: Dartmouth, 1992).

SILVER, G., 'Discordant Priorities', *Lancet*, (1987), 1195.

—— 'A Threat to Medicine's Professional Mandate', *Lancet* 2 (1988), 787.

SILVER, T., 'One Hundred Years of Harmful Error: The Historical Jurisprudence of Medical Malpractice' [1992] *Wisconsin Law Review* 1193.

SIMANOWICZ, A., 'Agencies' in Powers and Harris, *Medical Negligence* (London: Butterworths, 1990).

SIMPSON, M., BUCKMAN, R., STEWART, M., MAGUIRE, P., LIPKIN, M., NOVAK, D., and TILL, J., 'Doctor–Patient Communication: The Toronto Consensus Statement', *British Medical Journal* 303 (1991), 1385.

SKEGG, P., *Law, Ethics, and Medicine* (Oxford: Clarendon Press, 1984).

SMITH, R., 'Profile of the GMC: Discipline II: The Preliminary Screener—A Powerful Gatekeeper', *British Medical Journal* 298 (1989), 1632.

—— 'The Epidemiology of Malpractice', *British Medical Journal* 301 (1990), 621.

—— 'Where is the Wisdom . . . ?' *British Medical Journal* 303 (1991), 798.

SMITH, R. and WYNNE, B. (eds.), *Expert Evidence: Interpreting Science in the Law* (London: Routledge, 1989).

SOMERVILLE, M., *Consent to Medical Care* (Ottawa: Law Reform Commission of Canada, 1980).

—— 'Structuring the Issues in Informed Consent' (1981) 26 *McGill Law Journal* 740.

—— 'Pain and Suffering at Interfaces of Medicine and Law' (1986) 36 *University of Toronto Law Journal* 286.

SPENCER, J., 'The Neutral Expert: An Implausible Bogey' [1991] *Criminal Law Review* 106.

STACEY, M., *The Sociology of Health and Healing* (London: Unwin Hyman, 1988).

STARR, P., *The Social Transformation of American Medicine* (New York: Basic Books, 1982).

STERN, K., 'Advance Directives' (1994) 2 *Medical Law Review* 57.

STOCKING, B., 'Patient's Charter', *British Medical Journal* 303 (1991), 1148.

STONE, A., 'The Ethical Boundaries of Forensic Psychiatry', *Bulletin of the American Academy of Psychiatry and the Law* 12 (1984), 209.

STREET, T., *The Foundations of Legal Liability* (Northport, NY: Thompson, 1906).

STRULL, D., LO, B., and CHARLES, G. 'Do Patients Want to Participate in Medical Decision Making?' *Journal of the American Medical Association* 252 (1984), 2990.

SULMASY, D., 'What's So Special about Medicine?' *Theoretical Medicine* 14 (1993), 27.

Supreme Court Procedure Committee, *Guide for Use in Group Actions* (London: Supreme Court Procedure Committee, 1991).

TAN, K., 'Failure of Medical Advice: Trespass or Negligence' (1987) 7 *Legal Studies* 149.

TEFF, H., 'Liability for Negligently Inflicted Nervous Shock' (1983) 99 *Law Quarterly Review* 100.

—— 'Consent to Medical Procedures: Paternalism, Self-Determination or Therapeutic Alliance?' (1985) 101 *Law Quarterly Review* 432.

—— 'Liability for Psychiatric Illness after Hillsborough' (1992) 12 *Oxford Journal of Legal Studies* 440.

THOMPSON, I., 'Fundamental Ethical Principles in Health Care', *British Medical Journal* 295 (1987), 1461.

TJIONG, R., 'Are Physicians Fiduciaries?' (1993) 67 *Australian Law Journal* 436.

TRIBE, D., and KORGAONKAR, G., 'The Impact of Litigation on Patient Care: An Enquiry into Defensive Medical Practice' [1991] *Professional Negligence* 2.

TUCKETT, D., BOULTON, M., OLSON, C., and WILLIAMS, A. *Meetings between Experts: An Approach to Sharing Ideas in Medical Consultations* (London: Tavistock, 1986).

TULLEY, P., 'Towards a Wider View of Informed Consent to Medical Treatment' (1992) 8 *Professional Negligence* 74.

United States Department of Health, Education and Welfare, *Secretary's Commission on Medical Malpractice* (Washington DC: Department of Health, Education and Welfare, 1972).

VEATCH, R., *A Theory of Medical Ethics* (New York: Basic Books, 1981).

—— 'Autonomy's Temporary Triumph' (1984) 14 *Hastings Center Report* 38.

—— *The Patient–Physician Relation* (Bloomington and Indianapolis: Indiana University Press, 1991).

VINCENT, C., ENNIS, M., and AUDLEY, R. (eds.) *Medical Accidents* (Oxford: Oxford University Press, 1993).

——,YOUNG, M., and PHILLIPS, A.,'Why Do People Sue Doctors? A Study of Patients and Relatives Taking Legal Action', *Lancet* 343 (1994), 1609.

WADDINGTON, I., *The Medical Profession in the Industrial Revolution* (Dublin: Gill and Macmillan, 1984).

WADE, T., 'Patients May Not Recall Disclosure of Risk of Death: Implications for Informed Consent' (1990) 30 *Medicine, Science, and the Law* 259.

WADLINGTON, W., 'Legal Responses to Patient Injury: A Future Agenda for Research and Reform' (1991) 54(2) *Law and Contemporary Problems* 199.

—— and WARREN WOOD, J., III, 'Two "No-Fault" Compensation Schemes for Birth Defects in the United States' (1991) 7 *Professional Negligence* 40.

WAITZKIN, H., 'Doctor–Patient Communication', *Journal of the American Medical Association* 252 (1984), 2441.

WALLACE, L., 'Informed Consent to Elective Surgery: The "Therapeutic" Value?' (1986) 22 *Social Science and Medicine* 29.

WATKINS, S., *Medicine and Labour: The Politics of a Profession* (London: Lawrence and Wishart, 1987).

WEILER, P., *Medical Malpractice on Trial* (Cambridge, Mass.: Harvard University Press, 1991).

WELLS, C., 'Patients, Consent and Criminal Law' (1994) *Journal of Social Welfare and Family Law* 65.

WHARTON, R., and LEWITH, G., 'Complementary Medicine and the General Practitioner', *British Medical Journal* 292 (1986), 1498.

WHIPPY, W., 'A Hospital's Personal and Non-Delegable Duty to Care for Its Patients—Novel Doctrine or Vicarious Liability Disguised?' (1989) 63 *Australian Law Journal* 182.

WHITEHEAD, M., 'Who Cares about Equity in the NHS?', *British Medical Journal* 308 (1994), 1284.

WILLIAMS, G., *Textbook of Criminal Law* (2nd edn.) (London: Sweet & Maxwell, 1983).

—— 'Misadventures of Manslaughter' (1993) 143 *New Law Journal* 1413.

WILLIAMSON, C., *Whose Standards?* (Buckingham: Open University Press, 1992).

WILLIAMSON, V., 'Patients First—Reality or Rhetoric?' *Social Policy and Administration* 22 (1988), 245.

WILSON, P., 'Testing the Boundaries of Consent' (1994) 144 *New Law Journal* 574.

WINKLER, F., 'Complaints by Patients', *British Medical Journal* 306 (1993), 472.

WOOD, C. (ed.), *The Influence of Litigation on Medical Practice* (London: Academic Press, 1977).

WRIGHT, M., 'Medical Treatment: The Right to Refuse' (1993) *Journal of Social Welfare and Family Law* 204.

ZACHARY, R., 'Life with Spina Bifida', *British Medical Journal* 2 (1977), 1460.

ZEPOS, P., and CHRISTODOULOU, P., 'Professional Liability' in *Torts*, xi. *International Encyclopedia of Comparative Law* (Tübingen: J. C. B. Mohr (Paul Siebeck), 1978).

ZUSSMAN, R., *Intensive Care* (Chicago: University of Chicago Press, 1992).

Subject Index

Note: Where there are multiple location references and one reference is major relative to the others, that reference is shown in bold.